Deleuze and Performance

Deleuze Connections

'It is not the elements or the sets which define the multiplicity. What defines it is the AND, as something which has its place between the elements or between the sets. AND, AND, AND – stammering.'

Gilles Deleuze and Claire Parnet, *Dialogues*

General Editor
Ian Buchanan

Editorial Advisory Board
Keith Ansell-Pearson
Rosi Braidotti
Claire Colebrook
Tom Conley
Gregg Lambert
Adrian Parr
Paul Patton
Patricia Pisters

Deleuze and Performance

Edited by Laura Cull

Edinburgh University Press

© in this edition Edinburgh University Press, 2009
© in the individual contributions is retained by the authors

Edinburgh University Press Ltd
22 George Square, Edinburgh

www.euppublishing.com

Reprinted 2011

Typeset in 10.5/13 Sabon
by Servis Filmsetting Ltd, Stockport, Cheshire, and
printed and bound in Great Britain by
CPI Antony Rowe, Chippenham and Eastbourne

A CIP record for this book is available from the British Library

ISBN 978 0 7486 3503 0 (hardback)
ISBN 978 0 7486 3504 7 (paperback)

The right of the contributors
to be identified as authors of this work
has been asserted in accordance with
the Copyright, Designs and Patents Act 1988.

Contents

Act II Confronting Deleuze and Live Performance

Interval

Act III A Digital Deleuze: Performance and New Media

Introduction

Laura Cull

Was performance important to Deleuze? Is Deleuze important to performance – to its practical, as well as theoretical, research? What value might research in Performance Studies have for Deleuze Studies and vice versa? Such are the kind of questions this introduction, and indeed this volume as a whole, aims to address. Further, we might ask, what are the implications of Deleuze's ontological prioritisation of difference, process or becoming for a field in which many continue to privilege the notion of performance as representation, as anchored by its imitation of an identity: 'the world', 'the play', 'the self'? Correlatively, can philosophy follow Deleuze in overcoming the anti-theatrical tradition embedded in its history, perhaps even reconsidering what it means to think in the light of the embodied insights of performance's practitioners?

Given his unorthodox readings of Kafka, animated accounts of Bacon, encyclopaedic knowledge of cinema and diligent attention to music – from Boulez to Cage – one can only imagine Deleuze to have been an extraordinary audience member at a performance, a view the Italian actor and director Carmelo Bene affirmed when he described Deleuze as 'a lucid connoisseur of theatre' (Bene 2002: 1166; see Chiesa, Chapter 4, below). And yet, beyond his engagement with Bene, which will be a focus of this introduction, we have relatively little to go on – at least on first inspection. If theatre and performance were genuinely of interest to Deleuze, why did he (and Guattari) not write more about it, particularly given their direct contact with contemporary practitioners during the flourishing of performance in the 1960s and '70s? Although the arts are frequently privileged in Deleuze's philosophy as sites of fundamental encounter, he seems to have had a complex, even troubled, relation to performance.

For instance, we cannot ignore Deleuze's occasional denigration of theatre in relation to his apparently favoured art of the cinema. In

L'Abécédaire for instance, as Charles Stivale has reported, Deleuze remarks that theatre tends not to provide opportunities for 'encounters', though 'with certain exceptions (like Bob Wilson, Carmelo Bene)'.[1] Likewise in *Cinema 2*, Deleuze argues that film can capture '"conversation for itself", the ebb and flow of a loosely associative, open-ended discourse of rudimentary sociability' (Bogue 2003b: 194), in a manner that eludes theatre. The stage has no equivalent of the camera-eye, Deleuze suggests, with its capacity to reveal inhuman viewpoints, to deterritorialise the eye and the ear of the spectator.

Previously, of course, the notion of theatricality had also appeared less than favourably in *Anti-Oedipus*, as a figure for the psychoanalytic determination of desire. Schizoanalysis, in contrast, sees the unconscious as a factory. But in this latter case, it is only really a specifically *representational* theatre – in which becomings are interpreted as mere stand-ins for the Oedipal characters of mommy, daddy, me – that comes under fire. As the chapters to follow will demonstrate, Deleuze was no anti-theatricalist. On the contrary, and on closer inspection, Deleuze's thought not only adopts the language of performance, but intervenes critically in the field with the production of a new vision of performance as a vital philosophical and political force. As Martin Puchner concludes: 'Clearly, the theatre, here, is not simply a metaphor or a communicative device, but lies at the heart of Deleuze's project, determining its terms, constructions, and arguments' (Puchner 2002a: 524).

What is Performance (Studies)?

'Performance' was chosen as the conjunctive term for this collection in order to indicate a broad engagement with the performing arts, beyond any single genre such as theatre or dance. That is, although historically 'theatre' and 'performance' have been used by some as opposing terms, here 'performance' becomes the umbrella term that incorporates theatre as a sub-category.[2] But while the collection is inclusive from this perspective, it is exclusive from another, given that many Performance Studies scholars, following Richard Schechner, approach performance as

> a 'broad spectrum' or 'continuum' of human actions ranging from ritual, play . . . the enactment of social, professional, gender, race, and class roles, and onto healing (from shamanism to surgery), the media, and the internet. (Schechner 2006: 2)

This approach includes the performing arts, but is by no means limited to them.

As Marvin Carlson has written, 'performance' is 'an essentially contested concept', being perpetually redefined not only by Performance Studies but within a host of other fields – particularly as part of what has been described as the performative turn in the social sciences (Carlson 1996: 5). For some, performance is always a self-conscious activity: performing is '"showing doing" . . . pointing to, underlining, and displaying doing' (Schechner 2006: 28). Others emphasise the idea of performances as 'restored behaviours' – products of preparation and rehearsal, that may be conscious or otherwise. For Schechner – one of the key figures involved in engendering Performance Studies as a discipline[3] – it is the specific historical and cultural context of an event or action, rather than anything intrinsic to it, that determines it as performance, or as not. As such, there is a case for classifying ancient Greek tragedies, for instance, as 'ritual' rather than 'performance'. But if, for Schechner, there are contextual limits to what '*is*' performance, he also goes on to argue that there is 'no finality to performance studies' and that 'anything and everything can be studied "*as*" performance' (28–9, 38–9). Thus, although Andrew Murphie's essay on VJing in this volume points towards this broad-spectrum definition of performance, and Stephen Zepke's essay on Allan Kaprow problematises the distinction between (performance in) 'art' and (in) 'life', it remains outwith the scope of this collection to demonstrate the full breadth of examples that Performance Studies examines through the lens of performance. Indeed, since there can be no totalising representation of what is, by definition, an open field, the focus of this collection will be on performance as it takes place in the arts.

To say that Performance Studies is essentially open is not to say that the discipline lacks focal subjects, key questions, or a specific analytical approach. Regarding the latter, what is of particular relevance to the intersection with Deleuze is Schechner's claim that whatever Performance Studies analyses 'is regarded as practices, events, and behaviours, not as "objects" or "things"' (2). Arguably, as I have already implied, this is more an aspirational than a descriptive remark, but it nevertheless suggests an initial sympathy between Deleuzians and Performance Studies scholars: a shared concern to shift the focus from thinking in terms of discrete objects and subjects, towards a concern with processes, relations and happenings (Schechner 2006: 1–2). Or rather, both affirm the movement and 'liveness' immanent to even the most apparently stable phenomena. All the more surprising then, perhaps, that the field has been slow to appreciate the potential value of Deleuze's thought for performance analysis. From its inception, Performance Studies imported theory from a host of other disciplines, including philosophy, to address its key questions of 'presence, liveness, agency, embodiment, and event' (3).[4] But while Derrida and deconstruction were taken up and explored rigorously from the mid 1980s onwards, Deleuze remains strangely neglected.[5]

Equally, despite the increasing vibrancy of the field of Deleuze Studies in general, it is striking that *Superpositions* (1978) – the short book that combines an essay by Deleuze on theatre and a script by Carmelo Bene – is one of the few of Deleuze's texts to remain unpublished in English in its original form.[6] And, apart from important discussions of Deleuze's contribution – entitled 'One Less Manifesto' – by Mohammed Kowsar (1986) and Ronald Bogue (2003a), Deleuzians have rarely cited this work. Nor, on the whole, have they addressed the importance of theatrical and dramatic concepts for his ontology.[7] In this introduction, I want to use 'One Less Manifesto' as the lynchpin for an overview of Deleuze's engagement with performance and performativity. As we shall see, this essay engages with concepts and debates that are critical not only to Performance Studies, but to Deleuze's philosophical project as a whole: the relation between presence and representation; bodies and language; and, perhaps most importantly, the notion of movement, or variation, as ontological and political process. As such, the aim here is to establish the essay in its broader context by noting areas of continuity and connection with some of Deleuze's better known works: *Nietzsche and Philosophy*, *Difference and Repetition*, *The Logic of Sense*, *Kafka* and *A Thousand Plateaus*.

'One Less Manifesto': Deleuze's Philosophy of Performance

'One Less Manifesto' is *the* critical text for all those interested in Deleuze and performance – not only because it is 'about' theatre, but because it indicates how Deleuze's ontology might alter how we think about performance. 'One Less Manifesto' matters not just because of what is said in the essay itself, but because of how it points to the potential importance of all of Deleuze's philosophy for Performance Studies. First published in Italian in 1978, *Superpositions* was the result of a collaboration between Deleuze and the Italian actor, writer, filmmaker and director Carmelo Bene.[8] Bene's contribution to the collaborative work was the script for his production, *Richard III: or, The Horrible Night of a Man of War*. As Ronald Bogue has discussed, it seems that Deleuze had already been reflecting on Shakespeare's *Richard III* before he saw Bene's production. For instance, as his discussion of the play in *Dialogues* (1977) shows, he was particularly interested in the idea of Richard as a figure of treachery or betrayal, as one who betrays the State (Bogue 2003a: 117).

'One Less Manifesto' is nothing less than a call to arms for theatre practitioners and audiences alike. It is the articulation of an ethico-aesthetic problem, and the laying out of an imperative yet experimental theatrical programme that constitutes one potential course of action in retaliation. The problem is representation. The programme: to construct a theatre that escapes representation and creates the conditions for presence as the encounter with what Deleuze calls 'continuous variation'.[9] But how can theatre 'break free of this situation of conflictual, official, and institutionalized representation?', Deleuze asks. 'How do we account for the underground workings of *a free and present variation* that slips through the nets of slavery and eludes the entire situation?' (Deleuze 1997: 253). In response, Deleuze's essay draws on Bene's example to articulate a tripartite methodology for creating a theatre of 'non-representative force': '(1) deducting the stable elements, (2) placing everything in perpetual variation, (3) then transposing everything in minor (this is the role of the company in responding to the notion of the "smallest" interval)' (246).

In other words, Deleuze suggests, before a performance can affirm the virtual dimension of the present, practitioners need to perform a critical operation: the removal from theatre of what he calls 'the elements of Power'. This is an operation on the *form* of theatre as much as its contents: not only a subtraction of representations *of* power (kings and rulers) but the subtraction of representation *as* power. For Deleuze, representation means the assumption and imposition of stasis upon that which perpetually differs from itself. Following in the tradition of philosophically minded performance theory from Artaud to Grotowski, Deleuze suggests that theatre might be a vehicle or machine that puts us in contact with the real. Deleuze's concept of *theatrical* presence, as a non-representational relation between audience and event, suggests one context in which we might apprehend *ontological* presence as becoming – the perpetual variation or difference-in-itself that, for Deleuze, constitutes the real. In all his philosophy, Deleuze wants to think difference other than in terms of the negation of sameness. As Todd May explains:

> What Deleuze wants is not a derivative difference, but difference in itself, a difference that he believes is the source not only of the derivative difference but of the sameness on the basis of which derivative difference is derived. (May 2003: 144)

Given this call to break with representation, Deleuze's essay can also be situated in the wider context of the long-standing debates concerned with the relation between presence and representation in Performance Studies. Indeed, as I explore in my own research, it can be productively read alongside Derrida's better-known essay on Artaud's Theatre of Cruelty, and used to counter Derrida's contention that 'Presence, in order to be presence and self-presence, has always already begun to represent itself, has always already been penetrated' (Derrida 1978: 249). In contrast, Deleuze allows us to rethink notions of theatrical presence as differentiated not by representation, but by variation or movement. In Bene's theatre, this self-differing of the performance partly takes the form of 'badly behaved' costumes and props that fall off, fall over, or otherwise impede any attempt by the audience to interpret the performance as singular image.

To Have Done With Representation

Deleuze had already evoked the notion of a theatre without representation in *Difference and Repetition*, a profoundly performative text in which Deleuze employs drama – as discourse, as concept, as narrative – to a variety of different ends. For example, as Timothy S. Murphy has discussed, Deleuze reinterprets the central characters of 'the classically Freudian texts of Oedipus and Hamlet' (Murphy 1992: 109) as passing through three stages of relations between self, event and act that correspond to what he calls 'the three-stage structure of repetition', or 'the three syntheses of time'. Neither Oedipus nor Hamlet are tragedies in Aristotle's sense, Deleuze insists, because 'they stage the unmaking of the subject' in the event (Deleuze 1994: 89–92). Deleuze also conceives the history of philosophy in theatrical terms, lining up a cast of characters from the idiot and the pedant of the dogmatic tradition, to the Underground Man (like Artaud), forever faced with the difficulty of thinking (147). In each case, the personification of a mode of thought is, Murphy suggests, 'not intended as a phenomenology, but as a stage direction' (Murphy 1992: 110).[10]

In *Difference and Repetition*, Deleuze locates the origins of the theatre without representation in a theatrical tradition within philosophy, exemplified by Nietzsche and Kierkegaard, who

> want to put metaphysics in motion . . . to make it act, and make it carry out immediate acts . . . It is a question of producing within the work a movement capable of affecting the mind outside all representation . . . of inventing vibrations, rotations, whirlings, gravitations, dances or leaps which directly touch the mind. (Deleuze 1994: 8)

In reconstructing philosophy as immediate act, both thinkers 'invent an incredible equivalent of theatre within philosophy' (8). And as such, Deleuze states, they not only found a new philosophy, but a 'theatre of the future': '*a pure staging without author, without actors and without subjects* . . . There are indeed actors and subjects, but these are larvae, since they alone are capable of sustaining the lines, the slippages and the rotations' (219). In becoming-larval, the authors, actors and audience allow the theatre to manifest itself as a non-representational movement that forces thought. In this sense, Deleuze joins Nietzsche and Kierkegaard as 'men of the theatre', because he too dedicated himself (as a director might) to 'the highest theatrical problem' of how to create 'a movement which would directly touch the soul' (9).

Like Artaud's theatre of cruelty before it, Deleuze's theatre without representation will continue to be branded as 'impossible' by some, or as 'at odds with the actual practices of the theatre as we know it' (Puchner 2002a: 525). And indeed, Deleuze himself acknowledges that no productions of this 'theatre of the future' actually emerged in Nietzsche and Kierkegaard's own time. But this is precisely why Deleuze's essay on Bene is so important: because it brings the notion of a theatre without representation away from the 'futurist performativity' of the manifesto and into actual practice (Puchner 2002b: 452). And yet at the same time it is important to contextualise this essay in order to remember that what Deleuze is essentially presenting us with is an ontology of performance that applies to all performance – including the most apparently representational.

In *A Thousand Plateaus*, this affirmation of a more fundamental movement that comes before representation is also articulated in terms of a primacy of 'affect' or 'becoming' over imitation – a discourse that might be productively employed to rethink theories of acting in Performance Studies. Imitation is not the only way to conceive of how different beings or species might approach one another. 'We fall into a false alternative', Deleuze and Guattari argue, 'if we say that you either imitate or you are'. Becoming-animal, for instance, is not about pretending to be an animal, but equally 'it is clear that the human being does not "really" become an animal any more than the animal "really" becomes something else' (Deleuze and Guattari 1988: 238). Rather, becomings constitute attempts to come into contact with the speeds and affects of a different kind of body, to break with a discrete self and to uproot the organs from the functions assigned to them by this 'molar' identity. As May suggests, actual becomings (animal, molecular, imperceptible) are affirmations of the ontology of becoming: 'they call us back to the becoming of difference as the fundamental non-ground of specific identities' (May 2003: 149).

In the same way, perhaps, we understand nothing about the relation between performers and roles if we continue to subscribe to the paradigm of mimesis. Listen to the practitioners, Deleuze and Guattari suggest. Listen to Robert de Niro when he talks about walking 'like' a crab – not as a metaphor, but as metamorphosis. Listen to the masochist (not the analyst) who uses the apparatus of the bit, bridle and 'the boots of the woman-master' to construct a becoming-horse assemblage, that 'represents nothing' (and no-one) (Deleuze and Guattari 1988: 274, 260).[11] Indeed, amongst this proliferation of becomings-woman, -animal, -imperceptible, these transformative acts, they also cite 'the performances of Lolito, an eater of bottles, earthenware, porcelains, iron, and even bicycles', who 'makes his jaw enter into composition with the iron in such a way that he himself becomes the jaw of a molecular dog'.[12]

The Deleuzian concept of affect or becoming also holds great promise for the analysis of how performance impacts upon an audience, offering an alternative to the over-emphasis on interpretation and the construction of meaning that derives from Performance Studies' embrace of semiotics, critical theory and psychoanalysis. As Barbara Kennedy suggests in this volume, each of these discourses prioritised 'ideological and political foci to the detriment of affectivity and art'. 'Where was the body and feeling in such debates?' she asks; 'Why did none of this theory explain the vital, visceral and electric pulsations of my "autonomic" response to the arts?' While Kennedy's essay positions Deleuze as the palliative to such imbalance, Anthony Uhlmann's piece emphasises the distinction between affect and emotion. Both make clear that an affective approach to audience reception is about focusing not on 'personal feeling' but on affect as becoming: 'the effectuation of a power of the pack that throws the self into upheaval and makes it reel' (Deleuze and Guattari 1988: 240).

Towards a Minor Theatre: The Performativity of Language

Above all though, 'One Less Manifesto' is concerned with the continuous variation of language, a focus that establishes this essay's relationship to Deleuze and Guattari's wider project concerning 'minor literature', but also to Deleuze's concern with the performativity of language. Performativity is not just a central concept in Performance Studies, but a recurring theme in Deleuze's thought, coming to the fore both in Deleuze's discussion of what he calls Nietzsche's 'method of dramatisation' in *Nietzsche and Philosophy*, and in the critique of language as merely 'informational and communicational' in *A Thousand Plateaus*. In the former, Deleuze argues that Nietzsche interprets the meaning of statements by dramatising them as symptomatic of a speaker's resentful or affirmative mode of living. Speech, Deleuze suggests, must be treated as a 'real activity' – as a doing, rather than as representation – and words understood as an expression of a 'will'. This is particularly important with regard to the statement of 'truths' which, Deleuze insists, ought not to be dissociated from the wanting that drives them.

In many ways, this work prefigures the context of May '68, during which time students perceived the complicity of the university with state power, in its production of truth claims that reflected the status quo under a mask of neutrality. But if the state and its organs can use 'the acts internal to speech' – what Deleuze and Guattari call the 'order word' – to issue normative judgements or to impose a hierarchy, then the transformative power of speech acts can also be recuperated by revolutionary politics and, as we shall see, by revolutionary theatre. The order word has 'two tones', they say in *A Thousand Plateaus*: it can operate as a 'flight' as well as a 'little death sentence' (Deleuze and Guattari 1988: 107–8). As Denis Hollier recounts, this is exactly what happened when students (and workers) took the floor, insisting on making their unauthorised voices heard: 'They broke contracts, refusing to answer in exams, calling their professors by their first names, and so on. Once the forms were no longer respected, the relations of power became apparent' (Hollier 1998: 1037).

It is this 'doubleness' of the order word that accounts for the possibility of the 'major' and 'minor' as 'two different treatments of language' (Deleuze and Guattari 1988: 106–7). Deleuze argues that minor usages of language allow us to apprehend 'language's most inherent, creative property'; they affirm a fundamental variability at the heart of language by placing it in 'continuous variation' (Deleuze 1997: 245). Whereas the structuralist distinction between *langue* and *parole* suggests that there is an underlying set of rules or constants, in relation to which specific enunciations are understood to be deviations from a norm, Deleuze argues that any given language ought to be understood as 'a multiplicity of semantic worlds' in which all possible differences of meaning are virtually present (Bogue 1989: 147).

In 'One Less Manifesto', Deleuze suggests that Bene's *Richard III* affirms this immanent variability of language, giving the example of Lady Anne's differential repetition of the phrase 'You disgust me!'. There is no fixed meaning to this enunciation, Deleuze argues:

> It is hardly the same [enunciation] . . . when uttered by a woman at war, a child facing a toad, or a young girl feeling a pity that is already consenting and loving . . . Lady Anne will have to move through all these variables. She will have to stand erect like a woman warrior, regress to a childlike state, and return as a young girl – as quickly as possible on a line of . . . [perpetual] variation. (Deleuze 1997: 246)

In this performance of a minor usage of language, the actress playing Lady Anne transmits an enunciation through 'all the variables that could affect it in the shortest amount of time' (245), allowing the audience to encounter the multiplicity of potential affects internal to any one phrase.

Deleuze also argues that the power of language to perpetually differ is presented by Bene's musical treatment of language, in the performance of stutterings and stammerings that deform words, and of shouts and whispers at the limits of audibility. Regarding this second example, Deleuze is clear that although minor usage does not submit to conventional or constant relations of form and meaning, neither is it simply a reduction of language to gibberish or meaningless noise. Rather, Deleuze argues, new meanings emerge when language is no longer 'spoken perfectly and soberly' (247); as in the case of Artaud's glossolalia, asignifying sounds open out to the possibility of new thoughts. As Ronald Bogue explains: 'Rather than obliterate the relationship between expression and content, a minor usage reverses the conventional relationship between dominant forms of content and dominated forms of expression' (Bogue 1989: 119). Equally, whereas the dialogue of representational theatre is complicit with the maintenance of social order by conventionalised linguistic exchange, Bene rejects conventional theatrical dialogue in favour of the construction of an assemblage of overlapping recorded and live voices in a complex score.

In this way, 'One Less Manifesto' suggests that to address the minority is not only to become a foreigner in one's own language in *writing*, it is also to make language stutter through performance. Indeed, Bogue contends that:

> What becomes especially clear in *Superpositions* . . . is that Deleuze's concept of a minor usage of language necessarily extends well beyond that of a writer's manipulation of words on a page, and that *the performance of language provides Deleuze with the fullest instance of a minor style.* (Bogue 2003a: 141)

It is important that Deleuze chose Bene as an example, partly to preemptively dispel any assumptions that the theatre without representation is somehow 'anti-literary', or 'anti-textual' (as Puchner describes the theatre of cruelty). However, in this sense, we might be justified in holding almost the opposite set of doubts that Puchner seems to have about Deleuze's theatricalism. For Puchner, Deleuze is interested in theatre because it is a live performing art involving the 'precarious form of presence that characterizes live human bodies on a stage' (Puchner 2002: 526). In contrast, it could be noted that Deleuze's main choice of examples – Bene, Kleist, Beckett – all privilege the role of writing and

From left to right: Hopi Lebel, Jean-Jacques Lebel, Félix Guattari, Gilles Deleuze, Fanny Deleuze, Paris 1990. Photograph by Sacha Goldman. Courtesy of Jean-Jacques Lebel Archives. ADAGP.

language in the creation of theatre. Equally, despite his reputation as the arch-enemy of the script, it seems that the work of Artaud's that Deleuze and Guattari most admire is the radio play, *To have done with the judgement of god*, that is essentially a performance of Artaud's poetry. As such, we might say that Deleuze concentrates on the performance of language at the expense of analysing how the usage of other theatrical elements – from light to movement – might effect a becoming-minor.[13]

In noting Deleuze's focus on the use of language in theatre, I am not suggesting that Deleuze is a thinker of a dis-embodied or de-materialised theatre, echoing Peter Hallward's recent critique (which follows that of Alain Badiou). It is only to say that there is more work to be done to articulate the different forms that a Deleuzian performance might take. In 'One Less Manifesto', Deleuze does provide a list of practitioners whose work he would consider as other examples, other manifestations of this theatre without representation ('Artaud, Bob Wilson, Grotowski, the Living Theatre. . .') (Deleuze 1997: 241). Such a list not only makes clear Deleuze's awareness of historical and recent theatre, but emphasises the idea that this minor theatre has no prescribed form or definitive methodology. In fact, given the ontological claims Deleuze makes for his philosophy of difference, any brand of theatre or performance whatever could serve as an example of presence as perpetual variation. One kind may allow that difference to flourish while another attempts to suppress it, but all theatres – no matter how stratified by theatrical conventions – have this perpetual variation, this life-line running through them.

Performance as Political Practice: The Missing Example of Jean-Jacques Lebel

Theatre and performance were fully enveloped in both the destructive and creative energies of the events of May '68 that were to form the socio-political context for Deleuze and Guattari's collaboration. Mass demonstrations borrowed forms and practices from performance traditions – in, for instance, burning effigies of de Gaulle and the French riot police amidst 'funny, theatrical rituals' (Lebel 1969: 113). But more fundamentally, the question of who gets to define what is real and what is not, what is 'realistic' and what is 'impossible', was clearly a fundamental one for the protesters during the events of May '68. Likewise, many of the theatre practitioners of that period came to see performance as a profoundly political act in which realities alternative to the one proposed by the state could not only be staged, but *lived*, as they undid the conventional distinctions between audience and performance, acting and not-acting, the fictional and the real. The cultural industry, along with its institutions and power elites, became targets of the wider critique of capitalism. The state-sponsored Odéon Theatre was occupied. Such institutions were seen to create artificial barriers between art and life, politics and performance, theatrical action and activism. As such, and as the Committee for Revolutionary Action (CAR) declared, the occupation of 'the ex-theatre of France' was, itself, a theatrical and political act.

Perhaps the strangest absence of all then, with regard to the relative lack of detailed discussion by Deleuze of examples from the performing arts, is that of the French artist-poet and activist, Jean-Jacques Lebel. As Kristine Stiles (1998) explains, Lebel first met Deleuze between 1955 and 1956, and Deleuze and Guattari attended Lebel's Happenings in the 1960s. Lebel took both of them on a trip to America in 1975,[14] travelled back to the States with Guattari on a number of other occasions in the 1970s and '80s, and attended countless seminars and lectures by Deleuze in both Vincennes and Saint Denis.[15] In the aftermath of '68, Lebel was part of a group of around forty Vincennes students, almost none of whom had any theatrical experience, but who saw street theatre 'as a means to provoke encounters and discussions among people who usually shut themselves off from each other . . . as a means of breaking down the Berlin Wall in people's heads and helping them out of their state of passive acceptance' (Lebel 1969: 115). They were by no means interested in theatre or art *per se*, but in performance as an instrument of anti-capitalist sabotage, and as a communication tool to engage those who had somehow 'missed' May, but might still be compelled to act by exposure to its enduring call for economic and social revolution.[16]

One resultant street performance by Lebel's group was made up of simple 'frame-by-frame' scenes involving 'four archetypal characters': 'The Third World Peasant (the immediate victim of imperialism), The Guerrillero (the peasant turned revolutionary), The Ugly White Man (Nixon, the Ruler, the Wall Street King), The Army Officer (General Motors, the capitalist cop).' But since they were working on the noisy stage of the street or subway, the group replaced dialogue with phrases written on cardboard which were either held up or yelled out during the performance. The drama itself only lasted 'about two minutes', but was frequently followed by impromptu discussions with the assembled audience, which often lasted 'more than an hour' (117). From Lebel's account of these 'post-show discussions', we can see that it was less a case of street theatre operating as a consciousness-raising mechanism, than of it serving as a hub for the exchange of ideas among those who were already fired up by the idea of another revolution – one in which the students and workers would not allow themselves to be betrayed by the Communist Party, nor lured out of occupation and back to work.

Might Lebel's directly political performance serve as a better example of minor theatre than Carmelo Bene's? As Lorenzo Chiesa suggests in this volume, it could be argued that Deleuze employs Bene for his own political ends in a manner that looks untenable in relation to Bene's own remarks on the relation between theatre and politics. Likewise, Mark Fortier has insisted that Bene's political attitude 'flies in the face of Deleuze', who positions the minor theatre within his wider notion of a revolutionary micropolitics. This is not least because, unlike the historical avant-garde (whom Bene calls the '*crétins de l'extrême-gauche*'), 'Bene does not believe in or work towards a future or goal. As he sees it, theatre can precipitate a crisis, but only for a moment.' If Bene's theatre is political at all, Fortier contends, 'its political function is solely in its total refusal to accept life in any foreseeable society' (Fortier 1996: 6–7).

Interviews with Lebel also provide a vital, albeit anecdotal resource for helping scholars to understand Deleuze and Guattari's relation to the contemporary art going on around them, particularly performance. For instance, in one interview Lebel recalls an occasion when he took Guattari to a show by Wolf Vostell: 'He did not like it. I did my best, but it took years to get him to "come over" to performance art.' Indeed, Lebel goes as far as to say that Guattari's 'tastes were not experimental in art', despite the affirmation of experimentation as value in *Anti-Oedipus*. However, notwithstanding this initial hesitancy, Guattari 'made the jump into actual performance', Lebel reports, when he participated in a collective piece by Lebel at the 1979 poetry-performance festival, *Polyphonix* (Stiles 1998: n.p.).[17]

But what about Deleuze? Based on interviews and correspondence with Lebel from over two decades, Stiles' article insists that the Deleuze–Lebel relationship was not characterised by a one-way flow of influence: Lebel claims to have introduced Deleuze to Burroughs' 'cut-up method', to Ginsburg, to Happenings and to mescaline. His

> simultaneously contemplative and intuitively immediate approach to life and work inspired the philosopher and psychiatrist who repeatedly extolled such qualities in *L'Anti-Oedipe*, *Mille Plateaux*, and elsewhere when they celebrated artists' abilities to unseat history, tradition, institutions, and theory itself in just such condensed and yet creative acts. (Stiles 1998: n.p.)

As such, Stiles convincingly asserts the value of rethinking 'the role that artists like Lebel have played in informing theory' and criticises Deleuze and Guattari, despite the role-call of names in their indices, for failing to acknowledge such informants. In this regard, Lebel is not the only missing example. That is, it seems odd that although Deleuze and Guattari culled the notion of 'assemblage' in part from visual art practice in order to develop their theorisation of the rhizome, they 'never mentioned the living artists who invented and developed assemblage' (Stiles 1998: n.p.): artists like Allan Kaprow (discussed by Stephen Zepke in this volume), who met Lebel in the early '60s, after which they became life-long friends.[18]

Curtain Up: Introducing the Essays

Given Deleuze's neglect by Performance Studies, I am particularly honoured that the 'Prologue' to this collection is a new essay by Herbert Blau – among the first in the field to address the value of Deleuzian ideas for performance. Blau's essay gathers us up in its vital momentum, carrying the reader through the theatrical aspects of Deleuze's oeuvre, via string theory and particle physics, all the while plugging connections with a proliferation of practitioners: from Brecht, Dada and Futurism, to the Living Theatre and Blau's own KRAKEN group. Blau persistently interrogates the implications of Deleuze's work for performance. Is Deleuzian performance

Gilles Deleuze on the beach at Big Sur, in California, 1975. Photograph by Jean Jacques-Lebel (no.5 in a series of 5 images). Courtesy of Jean-Jacques Lebel Archives. ADAGP.

'the autoerotic on automatic in runaway machines'; a children's theatre without mommy and daddy; or a kind of performative void, like Cage's 'notorious performance of 4'33' of silence'? Or is it that, for Deleuze, the whole world is a stage with 'all of us performing to the rhizomatics of theatricality on the thousand plateaus'? This opening chapter prepares us for what is to come, not least because Artaud, too, is given a central role for his invocation of the cosmological as 'the forgotten domain of theatre'.

The chapters in this volume are grouped into three different acts, interrupted by two intervals: Act I focuses on those practitioners about whom Deleuze wrote the most (Artaud, Kleist and Beckett, and Bene), Act II on live performance, and Act III on new media and digital practices in performance. Of course, these distinctions have a degree of arbitrariness to them, given the interdisciplinary nature of most performance and the necessary reprisal of key ideas from Deleuze's writing on specific theatrical practices in the different contexts of each chapter. But although there are several other ways in which these essays could be productively configured, I hope the version of the script I have composed here makes its own kind of sense.

There is a 'ubiquitous Artaudianism' in Deleuze and Guattari, Edward Scheer argues, particularly in their development of the concept of the body without organs (or BwO) – the Deleuzian idea, he suggests, 'which resonates most powerfully as a concept for and of performance'. In his chapter, Scheer gives a detailed account of *To have done with the judgement of god* – the radio play from which Deleuze and Guattari borrow the notion of the BwO – contending that this work, and indeed Artaud's oeuvre as a whole, should not be interpreted as merely symptomatic of schizophrenic experience. Rather, Scheer argues, Artaud is '*performing* the schizophrenic production of reality'; Artaud actively develops a glossolalia beyond everyday language in order to destratify the bodies of his listeners. In the next chapter, Anthony Uhlmann positions Beckett, as well as Kleist and Edward Gordon-Craig, within what he calls a 'minor tradition of acting'. Uhlmann employs Kleist's short story 'On the Marionette Theatre' (1810) and Deleuze's *Expressionism in Philosophy: Spinoza* (1968) to frame this minor tradition as one that aims to create a theatre which 'moves away from the inner world of an actor in favour of developing affects which express an external composite world'. He contends that Deleuze's work on Spinoza and Leibniz – in which 'expression' is conceived as the mutual implication, rather than opposition, of an inside and outside – allows us to appreciate the stakes of a particular form of expression: the staging of a Beckett performance.

Moving into a more critical position in relation to Deleuze, Lorenzo Chiesa argues that 'One Less Manifesto' conceives the theatre of continuous variation, and specifically Carmelo Bene's theatre, as one that is 'initiated and sustained by subtraction' – a position that diverges, so Chiesa suggests, from the emphasis on repetition in the notion of an anti-representational theatre put forward in *Difference and Repetition*. At the heart of Chiesa's critique is the question of the compatibility of Deleuze's 'vitalist concept of subtraction', particularly in so far as he equates it with an erotic politics, with Bene's own concept of the subtractive, which Chiesa calls 'subtraction towards *extinction*'.

At this point we arrive at the first Interval, during which we take an excursion through the Black Forest, with Daniel Watt and Julian Wolfreys, to explore the notion of territory in both Deleuze and Heidegger. Does the 'oppressed, bastard, lower, anarchical, nomadic, and irremediably minor race' which Deleuze invokes 'ever find a place to "dwell"'?, Watt asks; does this race and its minor theatre even want a dwelling place, or is there political potential within the body without organs 'which offers a resistance to the homely conception of "dwelling"'? Drawing from *Kafka* and *Essays Critical and Clinical*, Watt provides a valuable contextualisation of this future theatre in the Deleuzo-Guattarian project of 'minor literature' as a whole. But, like Blau and Chiesa, he also expresses doubts about Deleuze's chosen paths and proposes other routes, particularly questioning the practicality of the schizo-stroll and the BwO. Finally, the interval closes with a perhaps even more doubting response, from Wolfreys, invoking the event of death as the only proper future, an inauthenticity haunting deterritorialisation and, therefore, the minor theatre, and yet, also, a home where 'one might dwell, and yet not be territorialized'.

In Act II, we move away from Deleuze's own choices of exemplary practices and into new territory, starting with Allan Kaprow – the artist who coined the term 'Happening' – and then addressing a series of contemporary live practices. Stephen Zepke's chapter argues that Kaprow makes a shift akin to Deleuze's move from 'expressionism' to 'constructivism' between *The Logic of Sense* and *Anti-Oedipus*, in so far as Kaprow's early Happenings dramatise or express the 'virtual score', whereas the later Happenings produce or construct the score in the event. However, having addressed the politics of Kaprow's practice in this period by way of Deleuze's concept of counter-actualisation, Zepke ultimately breaks with Kaprow, seeing his later Activities as offering 'a process of self-reflective meditation on everyday actions and experiences that does not construct new counter-actualisations, but simply promises a mystical transcendence of life'. Contra Kaprow's Zen-influenced concept of 'performing life', Zepke affirms the alternative of Adrian Piper's practice as one that creates performance events 'capable of catalysing new social territories in and as life'. This is followed by a chapter written by myself and Matthew Goulish emphasising Deleuze's Bergsonism and the notion of multiplicity with respect to 'latitude' and 'longitude', and the relation between the spatial and the temporal in performance. Against narratives of disappearance, or correlative (over-)emphases on virtuality, this double-chapter insists upon the complexity of the ordinary and the thickness of the present.

Maaike Bleeker's essay proposes that 'the theatre as cultural practice may illuminate what it means, or could mean, to "find one's bearings in thought"', an argument she explores specifically in relation to a contemporary performance by Ivana Müller and to the tripartite characterisation of thought – as concept, function and affect – in *What is Philosophy?* Such performance does not simply represent thought, Bleeker argues, but constitutes a participatory practice of thinking. Anna Hickey-Moody employs the Deleuzian concepts of 'becoming' and 'affect' to interpret the integrated dance theatre of Restless Dance Company as involving a process of 'turning away' from the determinations of intellectually disabled bodies in medical discourses.

In the second Interval, Barbara Kennedy helps us to bridge the gap between the live and the mediated in her exposure of the performativity of movement in Zeffirelli's film of the operatic performance, *Madama*

Butterfly. Drawing on a wide range of Deleuze's texts as well as from complexity theory, Kennedy develops what she calls 'a posthuman theory of emergent aesthetics' in which performance is no longer an object interpreted by subjects, but a process that actively institutes a becoming-biogrammatic of the body of the audience.

Finally, as we move into the opening of Act III, Timothy Murray transports us fully into the terrain of the digital, confronting the question of how we might understand Deleuze's theatres of movement and repetition 'within the context of theatre's contemporary openness to, if not its elision with, broad structures and practices of mediality, new media, and representational fields of simulacra'. Attending particularly to the *Cinema* books, Murray constructs a 'Digital Deleuze' who provides a 'creative approach to mediality' from which to consider the 'revolutionary variation of corporeality through digitality' in new-media performances by Shelley Eshkar and Paul Kaiser, Jonah Bokaer and Ashley Ferro-Murray. Next, Andrew Murphie's chapter establishes an unusual alliance between contemporary VJing, 'Chekhov's productive world-exhaustion', and 'Aeschylus and Artaud's unremitting cruelty'. The VJing event is not that which simply fulfils Debord's 'society of spectacle', Murphie argues, but a democratising performance-form that engages in combat with 'the normative configurations of image-culture'. Lastly, we close with an essay by Stamatia Portanova, founded on dancer and choreographer Merce Cunningham's view that choreography can and should follow, rather than dictate, movement. Portanova's essay uses Deleuze's and Guattari's concept of 'rhythm', and their distinction between 'numbered' and 'numbering' number, to explore how dance can recruit choreographic softwares – such as 'Dance Forms' – to allow it to take flight from its spatio-temporal stratification.

I hope to have adequately set the stage for the performances of thought that follow, each of which enacts new visions of how performance might work in Deleuze and Deleuze might work in performance – both as practice and as theory, and all things in between. The curtain rises. . .

References

Bogue, R. (1989), *Deleuze and Guattari*, New York and London: Routledge.
Bogue, R. (2003a), *Deleuze on Literature*, New York and London: Routledge.
Bogue, R. (2003b), *Deleuze on Cinema*, New York and London: Routledge.
Carlson, M. (1996), *Performance: A Critical Introduction*, New York and London: Routledge.
Deleuze, G. (1989), 'Coldness and Cruelty', in *Masochism: Coldness and Cruelty by Gilles Deleuze and Venus in Furs by Leopold von Sacher-Masoch*, New York: Zone Books.

Deleuze, G. (1994), *Difference and Repetition*, trans. Paul Patton, London: Athlone Press.

Deleuze, G. (1997), 'One Less Manifesto', trans. E. dal Molin and T. Murray, in T. Murray (ed.), *Mimesis, Masochism, and Mime*, Ann Arbor: University of Michigan Press.

Deleuze, G. and F. Guattari (1988), *A Thousand Plateaus: Capitalism and Schizophrenia*, trans. Brian Massumi, London: Athlone Press.

Derrida, J. (1978), 'The Theatre of Cruelty and the Closure of Representation', in *Writing and Difference*, trans. Alan Bass, Chicago: University of Chicago Press.

Fortier, M. (1996), 'Shakespeare as "Minor Theater": Deleuze and Guattari and the Aims of Adaptation', *Mosaic*, 29: 1–15.

Fuchs, E. (1985), 'Presence and the Revenge of Writing: Re-Thinking Theatre after Derrida', *Performing Arts Journal*, 9 (2/3): 163–73.

Hallward, P. (2006), *Out of This World: Deleuze and the Philosophy of Creation*, London: Verso.

Hollier, D. (1998), '1968, May – "Actions, No! Words, Yes!"', in D. Hollier (ed.), *A New History of French Literature*, Cambridge, MA: Harvard University Press, 1034–39.

Kowsar, M. (1986), 'Deleuze on Theatre: A Case Study of Carmelo Bene's Richard III', *Theatre Journal*, 38 (1): 19–33.

Lebel, J-J. (1968), 'On the Necessity of Violation', *The Drama Review – TDR*, 13 (1): 89–105.

Lebel, J-J. (1969), 'Notes on Political Street Theatre, Paris: 1968, 1969', *The Drama Review – TDR*, 13 (4): 111–18.

Murphy, T. S. (1992), 'The Theatre (of the Philosophy) of Cruelty in Difference and Repetition', in Joan Broadhurst (ed.), *Deleuze and the Transcendental Unconscious*. Special edition of *Pli: Warwick Journal of Philosophy*, University of Warwick, 105–35.

Puchner, M. (2002a), 'The Theater in Modernist Thought', *New Literary History*, 33: 521–32.

Puchner, M. (2002b), 'Manifesto = Theatre', *Theatre Journal*, 54: 449–65.

Rabkin, G. (1983), 'The Play of Misreading: Text/Theatre/Deconstruction', *Performing Arts Journal*, 7 (1): 44–60.

Reinelt, J. (2002), 'The Politics of Discourse: Performativity Meets Theatricality', *SubStance*, 31 (2/3), Issue 98/99. Special Issue: Theatricality: 201–15.

Schechner, R. (2006), *Performance Studies: An Introduction*, Second Edition, New York and London: Routledge.

Stiles, K. (1998), '"Beautiful, Jean-Jacques": Jean-Jacques Lebel's Affect and the Theories of Gilles Deleuze and Felix Guattari', in *Jean-Jacques Lebel*, Milan: Edizioni Gabriele Mazzota, 7–30. [References are to an unpaginated version of the essay kindly supplied by the author.]

Notes

1. Deleuze justifies this remark on the basis that he 'has trouble remaining seated so long'. We might do well to take such comments with a pinch of salt, however, given that Deleuze seems to have had no problem sitting through such epics as Syberberg's *Hitler: A Film from Germany*. See 'C for Culture' in Stivale's 'Summary of L'Abécédaire de Gilles Deleuze', available at: http://www.langlab. wayne.edu/CStivale/D-G/ABCs.html

2. As Janelle Reinelt has noted, the term 'performance' is 'related to a general history of the avant-garde or anti-theatre, taking its meanings from a rejection

of aspects of traditional theatre practice that emphasized plot, character and referentiality: in short, Aristotelian principles of construction and Platonic notions of mimesis' (Reinelt 2002: 202).

3. There are a number of different ways in which the history of Performance Studies' emergence as a discipline has been narrated. For a selection of them, see Schechner (2006). The transformation of the NYU Graduate Drama Department into the Department of Performance Studies in 1980 is generally acknowledged to be something of a turning point, as is the creation of the Centre for Performance Research by Richard Gough in Wales in 1988, and the unofficial birth of Performance Studies International in at NYU in 1990 (Schechner 2006: 19).

4. These are the core issues pinpointed by Barbara Kirshenblatt-Gimblett, another scholar who played a central role in the inauguration of Performance Studies (see Schechner 2006: 3).

5. No doubt there are geographical and institutional explanations for this, as there may be for the belated emergence of Deleuze Studies in general. Deleuze's unwillingness to travel, for instance, in contrast to Derrida's period of working in the US, might well have played a part in determining the relative speeds of dissemination of deconstruction and Deleuze-ism in the Anglophone world. For early work on Derrida and performance, see, for example, Rabkin (1983) or Fuchs (1985).

6. Timothy Murray, a contributor to this volume, translated 'One Less Manifesto' for his collection *Mimesis, Masochism and Mime*. It is this version of the text that is most frequently used by Anglophone scholars.

7. Timothy S. Murphy's essay on this area (which goes further than Foucault's 'Theatrum Philosophicum' to address Deleuze's theatricality) is an exception (Murphy 1992).

8. Bogue reports that Deleuze and Bene met sometime during September or October while the Carmelo Bene company were in residence in Paris, 'staging performances of Bene's Romeo and Juliet and S.A.D.E. at the Opera-Comique for the annual Festival d'automne. . . . Bene reports meeting with Deleuze after one of his Paris performances in 1977' (Bogue 2003a: 116).

9. With regard to this laying out of a programme of future action, Mark Fortier has argued that 'Although Deleuze's essay presents itself as an un-manifesto, with its prescriptive and proscriptive declarations, its programmatic succession of headings, . . . "One Less Manifesto" also becomes one manifesto more' (Fortier 1996: 6). The notion of 'One Less Manifesto' is an allusion both to Bene's distaste for the historical avant-garde, and to his production of Hamlet, which was entitled 'One Hamlet Less'.

10. Murphy suggests that we address these personifications in the same way that Deleuze interprets Kierkegaard's characterisation of 'the knight of faith'. 'It is necessary', Deleuze says, 'to take this philosophical indication as a director's remark, showing how the knight of the faith must be played' (Deleuze in Murphy 1992: 111). Likewise, Murphy implies, Deleuze presents us with these figures so that we might act them out.

11. For a different perspective on the relation between masochism and performance, see Deleuze's 'Coldness and Cruelty', which discusses the paradox of the masochist's self-destruction as enacted through a strictly controlled theatrical scenario of his own devising. This theatrical theory of masochism challenges appearances by presenting the 'victim' in a role that parallels that of a tyrannical director in relation to a malleable actor, or of the ventriloquist in relation to his pliant doll: 'the masochistic hero appears to be educated and fashioned by the authoritarian woman whereas basically it is he who forms her, dresses her

for the part and prompts the harsh words she addresses to him. It is the victim who speaks through the mouth of his torturer, without sparing himself' (Deleuze 1989: 22).

12. I have been unable to find out anything more about the performances of this mysterious 'Lolito', beyond what Deleuze and Guattari tell us in *A Thousand Plateaus* (1988: 274), on the basis of an account by the French journalist, Philippe Gavi.

13. This argument that Deleuze's interest in theatre is primarily a literary one is supported anecdotally by Bene's account of their meeting in his book *Opere*, which suggests that Deleuze wrote 'One Less Manifesto' without actually having seen the performance of Bene's *Richard III*. From Bene's account, related by Bogue, it seems that Deleuze's essay is based purely on a discussion Deleuze had with Bene about his project for *Richard III* when they met after one of his other performances in 1977. Bogue does not comment on this, but it does suggest a certain degree of detachment on Deleuze's part from the singularity of the performance as event. Bene says of Deleuze: '"And he writes it, without having seen the performance. And he writes *me*. And I write the text he will see in my final Roman performance at the Teatro Quirino: four months after the publication of his essay. And at the end he embraces me in the dressing room, sits down tired in the armchair, the expected enthusiasm in his eyes: '*Oui, oui, c'est la rigueur.*' And that's all (*Opere* 1166)"' (Bogue 2003a: 116).

14. On the front cover of *Desert Islands* (2003), a collection of texts and interviews by Deleuze from 1953 to 1974, we find a photograph of Deleuze on the beach at Big Sur which was taken by Lebel on this trip to the States.

15. Stiles provides a fascinating anecdote about one occasion in the early 1980s when one of Deleuze's lectures, attended by Lebel, was disrupted by 'a hostile intervention . . . by a "schizophrenic", who claimed in a phone conversation Nietzsche had informed him that Deleuze had "falsif[ied] his books"'. In order to protect Deleuze, Lebel decided to make a 'Happening intervention' of 'five intense, explosive minutes' in which he improvised a performance of invented words – partly inspired by Kurt Schwitters, partly by Artaud – which is said to have 'calmed down' the 'schizophrenic'. I want to thank Kristine Stiles for sending me an electronic copy of her article '"Beautiful, Jean-Jacques": Jean-Jacques Lebel's Affect and the Theories of Gilles Deleuze and Felix Guattari', which is otherwise available in the catalogue, *Jean-Jacques Lebel* (Milan: Edizioni Gabriele Mazzota, 1998).

16. Notably, Lebel reports that although some of the group were aware of The Living Theatre (see Herbert Blau's chapter in this volume), they were criticised for being 'too "arty" or "not directly political enough" or "non-violent" (the company was admired more as an anarchist community than as a theatre group)' (Lebel 1969: 116).

17. In fact, Guattari performed in a total of six *Polyphonix* festivals after 1979, telling Deleuze that *Polyphonix* was 'one of the only remaining "counter institutions" in the spirit of May '68' (Stiles 1998).

18. Of course, one could equally say that the artist, as 'seer, becomer', holds an exalted place in Deleuze's thought.

Chapter 1

Performing in the Chaosmos: Farts, Follicles, Mathematics and Delirium in Deleuze

Herbert Blau

Let's begin with the basics: 'It breathes, it heats, it eats. It shits and fucks.' Sounds like the body, which in a conventional theatre may have no trouble breathing or eating, or in various ways heating up, under the weight of a period costume, or angrily, passionately, or more or less imperceptibly, as in a staged embrace. But shitting and fucking, well, except in way-out kinds of performance, or scandalous body art, it's more likely to be *represented*, and where shitting is concerned, even more so than fucking, it's going to be in the wings, and even muted there, that is, the farting and plopping. Back in the theatre of ancient Rome, where unsuspecting actors were actually crucified, and sexual intercourse performed without faking it – in festive diversions from the comedies of Terence – it may have been right out there in the open, even elimination, the body or its waste. But now, whether we see it, whether we don't, what we may think of as a natural 'function' is not that at all, or so we're told in the *Anti-Oedipus* by Deleuze and Guattari: wherever we do it, whatever it is, even the eating or shitting is everywhere machines, 'real ones, not figurative ones' (and nothing like '*the* id', that egregious mistake of Freud), machines driving machines, however coupled, however connected, or spilling out of the sac, one producing a flow, menstrual, sperm, urine, that the other interrupts, 'an organ-machine . . . plugged into an energy-source-machine'. There is, to be sure, an uncertainty principle too, as with the anorexic at the mother's breast, whose mouth is wavering between several functions, not knowing 'whether it is an eating-machine, an anal-machine, a talking-machine, or a breathing-machine. . .'. And if here we're inclined to worry, because of 'asthma attacks', in Deleuze's view of performance that's not at all undesirable, indeed it's producing desire, whether wheezing, rasping, gasping, spitting up, the bronchial autoerotic, in the non-mimetic effluvium of a delirious scene (Deleuze and Guattari 1977: 1).

There is in the machinic wavering a prankish perversity (once called 'polymorphous') which emerged in an era of fetishised *play*. And even now, about the *Anti-Oedipus,* Foucault's prefatory warning serves: 'The book often leads us to believe it is all fun and games, when something else essential is taking place' (xlv). What's taking place has to do, as Foucault said, with tracking down fascisms, not only those responsible for our genocidal history, but the petty ones that, in the paranoia-machine after 9/11, still constitute the embittering tyranny of everyday life. In a later book, Deleuze separated his own writing into *Essays Critical and Clinical,* but even there, in the space-*between,* where (we're told) the god of theatre presides, the vigilant Dionysus, over the *'trajectories and becomings'* (Deleuze 1998: 67), the implications for performance seem what they always were, the autoerotic on automatic in runaway machines, given over to pure expenditure in the libidinal economy – which doesn't seem much concerned, as on Wall Street today, with the prospect of recession, or stagflation. Yet, while 'continually producing production' (Deleuze and Guattari 1977: 7), these amniotic desiring-machines, with their pure naked intensities globalising delirium, are by no means part of the production apparatus of the bourgeois theatre, about which Deleuze was even more jaundiced than Brecht – and so, too, about the dramaturgy of the unconscious, its Freudian *mise-en-scène,* which Deleuze restaged in his essay 'What Children Say' as a 'milieu' of subjectivity, a subversive labyrinth confounding the Oedipal structure, with wandering lines, loops, reversals and unpredictable 'singularities'.

In this milieu, where 'it is not a matter of searching for an origin, but of evaluating *displacements',* parents find themselves positioned 'in a world . . . not derived from them' (Deleuze 1998: 61–2) – mommy and daddy mere walk-ons in a dominant children's theatre. With the enlivening performativity of their hand-flapping forgettings and rockabye repetitions, 'nothing is more instructive than the paths of autistic children' (61), the stammering, stuttering, tantrums and babbling echolalia – as if the primal prototype for the vocal experiments and body language of the clamorous 1960s. As for the multiplicities, disjunctures, flows, inconsequent juxtapositions, subtractions and amputations – cannibalising the body, putting its organs up for grabs – they still seem fun and games, while acquiring an ecstatic mission from the messianism of Artaud. It's as if Artaud's Cruelty, with the metastasising rapture of its miraculated intensities, totalised in the Plague, were absorbed into the Deleuzian *chaosmos* as another universe. If we can put anything of such dimensions into a philosophical perspective, it was the chaosmos which, according to Deleuze, superseded the world, by disrupting the pre-established harmony (defined by Leibniz) of all existing things, thus emancipating the virtual into a kind of spectral history, an atemporal miasma of passing presents and dubious pasts. This in turn produced, in a performative anti-aesthetic, what might be thought as a new music of the spheres, all harmony gone, but the replenishing dissonance of unresolved chords. Or descending from the spheres to *A Thousand Plateaus*, 'a nonpulsed time for a floating music', in which 'forms are replaced by pure modifications of speed'. That's how Pierre Boulez described it, but amidst the modifications, 'movement and rest, speed and slowness, floating affects' (Deleuze and Guattari 1987: 267), the exemplary figure is John Cage, raising the question of *how* you hear them, when and what, as with the notorious performance of *4'33'* of silence – that suspended music, floating, much admired by Deleuze. We wouldn't expect, of course, that in the void of such a performance, or the performative void, nonpulsed, nonplussed, there'd be any reason for reason, but in the Deleuzian chaosmos you never rule anything out.

Having started, then, with the basics, let's space out to the cosmological: that the universe is rational, or that the idea of rationality is inherent in the cosmos, was held to be true – as we tend to forget – before or without monotheism. Pythagoras saw nature as numbers a century or so before Plato's transcendent realm of Ideal forms, those perfected circles and galaxies of which the material world is merely a flawed reflection. What's nevertheless surprising today is to encounter scientists, whether among subatomic particles or in astrophysics, whose views of an orderly universe appear to be Platonic, as when they speculate, for instance, that mathematics does not describe the universe, but rather that the universe is, by nature or design, mathematical. This would have hardly surprised Artaud, whose hallucinatory states or swarms of images in the brain, its 'inexhaustible mental ratiocination' (Artaud 1958: 63), are there – as through the swirling circles and galaxies of the Balinese theatre, its flights of elytra, sudden cries, detours in every direction – with a 'mathematical meticulousness' (57), without which there'd be no pure theatre of Ideal forms, yet umbilical, larval, gestures made to last, '*matter as revelation*' (59). (As for the faith-based folly of the wrong Ideal, it should be apparent that – in the 'wholly materialized gravity' (65) of it all, 'a new and deeper intellectuality' (91) – Artaud is not talking of Intelligent Design.) Thus, as we may gather from Stephen Hawking, in *A Brief History of Time*, which can no longer be defined by mere succession, nor space by coexistence or simultaneity, there's a mental ratiocination in *equations*, restless, heuristic, an inexhaustible desire, which won't be satisfied without a universe to describe, and with the universe at its service – and a tempting metaphysics, 'like indrafts of air around these ideas' (Artaud 1958: 90) – mathematics is on fire (Hawking 1998). And so it is with 'Creation, Becoming, and Chaos, . . . all of a cosmic order' (Artaud 1958: 91), what Artaud insisted upon was the forgotten domain of theatre, that temporal form in space, given to disappearance, but oneirically remembered as timeless, and rehearsed again by Deleuze.

What comes as no surprise, because for him it's the wrong equation, is Deleuze's attitude towards *mimesis*, an impediment to becoming, which is 'always incomplete', no mere copy or imitation, in which *this* resembles *that*, but a process, rather, of always being formed, 'a passage of Life that traverses both the livable and the lived'. If there were an 'objective' to becoming, as in the Stanislavski Method, the infinitive phrase would be: *to free Life* from what imprisons it. Or, at another performative level – more abstruse, but with a fastidious grammar – 'to find the zone of proximity, indiscernibility, or indifferentiation where one can no longer be distinguished from *a* woman, *an* animal, or *a* molecule' (Deleuze, 1998: 1), the indefinite article's power 'effected only if the term in becoming is stripped of the formal characteristics that make it say *the* ("the animal in front of you. . .")' (2). More could be said (and I've said it) about what's inside that parenthesis, as if a proscenium theatre, its unregenerate scopophilia, and what's in front of you there, visibly invisible, dying in front of your eyes. As it happens, and for all the incessant becoming, the spirals, wanderings, reversals, or ambiguous fibrillations, keeping life from being imprisoned, Deleuze has faced it, too, whatever face he put upon it: before his suicide, his own problem in breathing, and the ominous weaknesses of others, Spinoza's frailty, Nietzsche's migraines, the something in becoming that's unbearable in being (for Beckett, *the* Unnamable), whatever it is 'that has put on them the quiet mark of death' (Deleuze and Guattari 1994: 172) – the living insignia of theatre, seen unseen, its troubling materialisation from whatever it is it is *not*.

Are we trapped, then, by mimesis? Or is becoming, really, some repetition of being? In the performativity of Deleuze, as in his prose, repetition acquires the value that the word has in French: *répétition*, rehearsal, trying this, trying that, also a form of testing, thus making something new of repetition itself. Or as Deleuze saw it in Nietzsche, each time round extracting something *other*, 'the brutal form of the immediate', from the Eternal Return. Kierkegaard, too, felt the immediacy of repetition, but as an infinite power of consciousness; in Nietzsche's case, it becomes a matter of *will*, which is to be liberated 'from anything which binds it by making repetition the very object of willing'. In that regard, repetition would appear to be a redemptive double bind: 'if we die by repetition we are also saved and healed by it' (Deleuze 2004: 6). For both Nietzsche and Kierkegaard, repetition is also a double condemnation, of both habit and memory. But – as if condemned, then – to be free becomes the thought of the future (8). Which doesn't quite set the stage for the theatre of existentialism, as we saw it in Sartre and Camus, which is still, in dramatic form, a conventional theatre of representation. What's imagined, rather, as Deleuze derives his theatre of repetition from Nietzsche and Kierkegaard (though the latter's God is not exactly kin to the former's Dionysus), is a 'metaphysics in motion, in action', without any mediation, 'vibrations, rotations, whirlings, gravitations, dances or leaps which directly touch the mind'. And all of this is occurring in an empty space filled by signs, masks, 'through which the actor plays a role which plays other roles' (11), in a Big Bang of pure forces, the dynamics of space itself, spirals of colour and sound, a language that speaks before and through words, gestural, spectral, phantasmic, the desiring forces of repetition with an unexpected power, yet necessarily *what it is* in the going beyond itself.

If death has its dominion, which saves and heals, it's also important to observe that Deleuze's notion of becoming as forever incomplete will have undergone a revision through the 'dizzying and slippery perspective' of Artaud's alchemical theatre, and its reimagining of 'the Orphic Mysteries which subjugated Plato' and must have evoked, with its hallucinatory psychology, the density of it, 'the passionate and decisive transfusion of matter by mind' (Artaud 1958: 52). Meanwhile, in a shift from the indefinite article to the subatomic becoming, its particle physics, there is the seemingly oppositional nature of quantum mechanics, according to which randomness is all, or at least at the heart of (the) matter, those elementary particles which seem to be everywhere or anywhere, or in a Deleuzian way *nowhere*, until some mathematical measurement arrests promiscuous flux or shapes inscrutable waves, confirming the 'hidden variable' theory of the later Einstein, distressed by randomness, about God not playing dice.

It might appear to be chancy still, but with 'time *out of joint*', unhinged, constituted only '*by a vertigo or oscillation*' (Deleuze 1998: 31), Deleuzian performance still has, in its aleatoric vitalism, not only the clinical, but calculating moments, as in his equation for 'foreign words', which are to the tower of Babel as 'chains of atoms' to the periodic table (17). If there's some guesswork in that equation, so it is, too, with the conundrums of cosmology, where 'law of nature' is either deferential to 'truth', mathematically down-to-earth, or for the vertigo up above, a problematic phrase. I don't want to get lost in the cosmos, where the whole world is a stage, or down there in the cellarage, its molecular substructure, but that, indeed, is how Deleuze conceives it, from the 'multiplicity of nerve fibers' (Deleuze and Guattari 1987: 8) performing in all of us to the rhizomatics of theatricality on the thousand plateaus, where each of us is several, or more, with nothing like 'character' in the becoming of non-identity, through the proliferous space of the epistemological in between. Or rather like Genet's Grand Brothel, where life is not only a dream, but with everything betrayed at once, in the becoming of what-it-is-not, an irreverently enacted 'nightmare-dream' (Deleuze 1998: 117), which requires in its spatial dynamism 'a double theatricality'. With image compounding image in the profoundest subjectivity, thus destroying the ego, there is nothing like the extrusion of abstract ideas, which 'are not dead things' – certainly not in Genet's theatre, as Deleuze perceives it – but part of 'a secret cipher marking the unique chance', and here we're back to 'a dice throw': if God is not playing, 'a Will that throws the dice' (119–20).

As for the scientific view of the scattering of randomness – or the compacting of it, by intensified gravity, into a black hole – we now hear of a contingent inclination to far-out inquiry, or deep within, that is neither timeless nor absolutist, and if not a secret cipher, virtually Deleuzian in its 'law without law'. So too, in string theory, there is the project of 'random dynamics' in which physical laws are 'derived' as a consequence of 'a random fundamental "world machinery"' (Overbye 2007: D4); surely the mind-bending matrix of any desiring-machine. And I can say this because of physicists who concede that if, with all the quantum uncertainties, there *are* laws of nature, they might very well have emerged from primordial chaos by fibrils or inchling aeons of cosmological chance, what – like a Deleuzian follicle, the merest 'mite' of an energy source – they call 'it from bit' (Overbye 2007: D4). All of this is further complicated by the web-spidering of bots in a world of information, where the intrinsic randomness is such that, on any given day, who knows (God knows?) what will turn up online: everything possible, incessant novelty and sameness at once, a fecund universe that in its digitisation might be what Foucault meant when he said, 'perhaps one day, this century will be known as Deleuzian' (Foucault 1977: 165). Which, unfortunately, can also be profoundly boring. But such is *Life* (his capitalised version of it, revolving *it* from bit – It? [*Pause.*] It all, as Beckett might say) in the vicissitudes of the cosmos, where string theory, the alleged theory of everything under the sun, or in the eternal dark, apparently has 10^{500} solutions. If that's an Einsteinian nightmare, it disarranges, ramifies, aporetically scatters, the world of performance for Deleuze, where, of course, the law of no law *is* a law.

So it is in the theatre apotheosised by Deleuze, conceived in 'subtraction' by Carmelo Bene, who detested 'all principles of consistency or eternity', no less 'textual permanency'. Charged with narcissism, obscenity, blasphemous kitsch, Bene created a theatre with no other purpose than the process of its creation, about which he said: 'The spectacle begins and ends at the same moment it occurs' (Deleuze 1997: 240). For Bene, as for Deleuze – and the two of them collaborated on a book together – the birth of a possible theatre requires divesting it of any complicity with power. If that sounds *echt* Brecht, the 'operation' in Bene (he wouldn't use the word 'technique') is not to distance by alienation, but 'to *amputate* the elements of power' (Deleuze 1997: 241) which, even when represented critically, enforce the law, so long as theatre is dependent upon the apparatus of representation. Deleuze declares that in Bene's theatre representation is cut off 'at the same time as the actor ceases to be an actor'; the amputation 'gives birth to and multiplies something unexpected, like a prosthesis. . . . It is a theatre of surgical precision' (239), which exceeds that of the A-effect (or V-effect), where the actor calls attention to the fact that s/he is acting. In using the pronoun slash himself – 'S/he is an operator' – Deleuze is pointing through Bene to a theatre surging forward with a political function in 'the strength of a becoming'; instead of magnification, as in traditional stagings of Shakespeare, 'a treatment of minoration', as in Bene's subtraction of *Hamlet*, or amputation of Romeo that liberates Mercutio from a textual death into the non-dying subject of quite another play. Yet there's measure for measure here, since 'to minorate' is a term (Fr., *minorer*) 'employed by mathematicians' (243). So, then, let's be precise: if 'minority' represents 'nothing regionalist, nor anything aristocratic, aesthetic, or mystical', it is not, for Deleuze, ideological either, no mere identity politics, but rather in the presentness of the presenting 'a minority consciousness as a universal-becoming' (255–6).

With his own consciousness of the countercultural aftermath of May '68 – brought on by the Living (the French said it without Theatre, as if it were Life),[1] when it disrupted the Festival of Avignon, left-wing to begin with, but becoming touristy – Deleuze concludes his defence of Bene's 'operation' (he refused to be called a director) by saying, 'It is truly a matter of consciousness-raising, even though it bears no relation to a psychoanalytic consciousness, nor to a Marxist political consciousness, nor even to a Brechtian one' (256). Nor does Bene have any patience with the formulas of the avant-garde; thus, the title of Deleuze's essay on the 'maker', 'controller', 'mechanic', undeniable 'protagonist', but *not* actor or director, of a minoritarian theatre: 'One Less Manifesto'. That said, let's remember what was posited at the onset of the essay: that in giving birth to the unexpected, with no formula there, just the stammerings and variations, the theatre is a 'critical theatre', with the fabrication of lessness (Bene's, not Beckett's): less 'character', less text, no dialogue in performance, but voices superimposed, aphasic, plosive 'playback', and with no drawn-out predictable plot, for audience expectations, even a populist audience (like Dario Fo's), a severe reduction of time. Bene's plays are very short, but 'this critical theatre is constitutive theatre. Critique is a constitution' (239). Yet, swear by it as you will, whatever it is that is constituted by the groundlessness of subtraction, the haunting question remains: *why* theatre, if what you're after is critique? And despite the disclaimer about the avant-garde, the Deleuzian paradox of his 'One Less Manifesto' is that as he superimposes his own voice, there and elsewhere, on the stammerings, stutterings, lapses, parapraxes, aphasia, in what children say, he is not subtracting from but adding to the avant-garde legacy, even the Ubuesque (Bene staged Jarry's play), and when autistic, there is not only Futurist noise, but – along with Tzara's manifesto that disavows manifestos – some Dada too.

Think of those 'nomadic singularities' of the organless body, 'its 'mad or transitory particles', or the follicles of strata on the thousand plateaus, where 'God is a lobster' (like Ubu?), 'double pincer, double bind' (Deleuze and Guattari 1987: 40). The double bind is that the pincer seems derived from the Futurist Marinetti's 'fiscofollia', or 'body madness' (Marinetti 1986: 183), while the feverish insomnia of his Variety Theatre, with nothing impelling performance but a logic of sensation, sets out the game plan for Deleuze's 'phantasmaphysics', the term created by Foucault for precisely that logic, its 'fibrils and bifurcation' (Foucault 1977: 166), which return us through a 'reversed Platonism', or converted, subverted, perverted, to an insidious displacement within. In searching out, within the Platonic milieu, ascending to purest Form, then descending to 'its smallest details, . . . as far as its crop of hair or the dirt under its fingernails – those things that were never hallowed by an idea' (168), we come upon those again who wouldn't know it if they had one, and hallowed by Deleuze for that. There, in that impromptu nether region, antidoxological, diapered, undiapered, the milieu of infantility, the reversal occurs at that other orifice, the mouth, 'the canal where the child intones the simulacra, the dismembered parts, and bodies without organs, the mouth in which depths and surfaces are articulated' (179). And then moving into the nexus between Futurist performance – its *Zang-Tumb-Tumb* (*parole in libertà*) or its machinic 'noise' – and the 'indescribable vibration' (Artaud 1958: 52) of the alchemy of Artaud, requiring an actor who has not forgotten how to scream: 'The mouth where cries are broken into phonemes, morphemes, semantemes: the mouth where the profundity of an oral body separates itself from incorporeal meaning' (Foucault 1977: 179), as in 'the complete, sonorous, streaming naked realization' of the theatre of Cruelty (Artaud 1958: 52).

Phonemes, semantemes, whatever the realisation, this is not quite the Mouth of Beckett's *Not I*, where the orifice, the canal, is a 'godforsaken hole', with the 'speechless infant' there, 'parents unknown . . . unheard of' (Beckett 1984: 216), and speaking of machines, 'the whole machine', asking the mouth to stop, 'and the whole brain begging' (220), maybe to end desire, desire not desiring, 'the words . . . the brain . . . flickering away like mad . . . quick grab and on' (222), which suggests that even delirium has its critical variations, as it does even in Brecht. As regards that canal, or other forsaken hole, Deleuze might have been more responsive to the early Brecht's *Baal*, and the corrosive seriality of its orgiastic hero, who lives deliriously by nature or choice, and with cruelty too, flaunts his nakedness and vice, always ready to 'Have some fun or bust! / What you wish, says Baal, is what you must! / And your shit's your own, so sit and have a ball. . .' (Brecht 1964: 21). Here too the warped appearance of fun and games, the elephantiasis of it, with Baal outdoing Ubu, bloated in copulation, could be misunderstood, as it apparently was when the play was first produced. The filthy behaviour of Baal, unconscionable, even murderous, had, according to Brecht, its political agenda, his worst reflexes mirroring what was worse: again an equation of fascism with the tyranny of everyday life, and what in compliance or self-contempt we imposed upon ourselves. Or, ready to scream, life as a piece of shit, holding it all in.

'Why such a dreary parade of sucked-dry, catatonicized, vitrified, sewn-up bodies', wrote Deleuze with Guattari, having just invoked Artaud's declaration of war against organs – '*To be done with the judgement of god*', which will not even let you 'experiment in peace'. In their judgement – like another manifesto, in *A Thousand Plateaus* – all kinds of experimentation, 'not only radiophonic, but also biological and political [incurred] censorship and repression', whereas 'the BwO is also full of gaiety, ecstasy, and dance'. And so it was in the '60s, that paradisal era of the '*hypochondrial body*', '*the schizoid body*', '*the drugged body*', '*the masochist body*' (Deleuze and Guattari 1987: 150), sodomised too, in the 'epidermic play of perversity', or the new dispensation of Sade, where 'a dead God and sodomy are the thresholds of a new metaphysical ellipse' (Foucault 1977: 171). The ellipse was a trajectory through the chaosmos, with a celebrative detour through the theatre: the Living, the Open, the Ontological-Hysteric, Grotowski's psychophysics, the enraptured stasis and distensions in the stagings of Robert Wilson, *Dionysus in '69* at the Performance Garage, and with 'the door off its hinges' (Deleuze 1997: 27), as if Deleuze had loosened a screw, the audience dancing out, taking over performance, in a participatory mystique, drugged out, even fucking, right there on the streets.

What followed in the academy, for over a generation, was a discourse on the body, the all-knowing body, which brought performance to theory, but increasingly ideologised, with deference to sex and gender, race, class, ethnicity. Not all of it was in extremis, like the *Anti-Oedipus*, where the mystique was really contingent upon a derangement of body and thought, as if the asyntactic delirium, its fractures and disjunctures, or schizoid *jouissance*, were what T. S. Eliot never imagined or dared when, with the advent of high modernism, he recovered the metaphysical poetry of the seventeenth century, albeit with mixed feelings about its 'dissociation of sensibility' (Eliot 1934: 288). For the emotions they had in mind, Deleuze and Guattari, there was nothing like an 'objective correlative', the absence of which, for Eliot, made *Hamlet* an artistic failure; as for Bene's *Hamlet*, its subtraction, his 'one less *Hamlet*' (Deleuze 1997: 239), it might have been a prosthesis, claiming non-representation, but whatever there was on stage, or amputated there, it was unlikely to be the correlative of the performative body in the imaginary of Deleuze. Or that banished Oedipal body, not-there in wish-fulfilment. 'Is it really so sad and dangerous', we were asked in *A Thousand Plateaus*, 'to be fed up with seeing with your eyes, breathing with your lungs, swallowing with your mouth, talking with your tongue, thinking with your brain, having an anus and larynx, head and legs?' (Deleuze and Guattari 1987: 150–1). Sadly perhaps, though up for danger, when this ethos came on the scene, I was sufficiently aligned with Brecht to concur with his Galileo, when he said in defence of reason, though not unsensory, that he believed in the brain. Which, with all the fibrillations, ventricles, basal ganglia, within the arachnoid mater – the membrane that covers the cerebral cortex – is hardly disembodied.

So it was in the 'ghosting' and 'burrowing' of my KRAKEN group,[2] where we were susceptible to, even impassioned by, a synaesthesia of organs and body parts, like listening with a kneecap, humming with a thumb, the eyelids avid as taste buds, images there in your gut, or for that shitty matter, no mere fun and games, lifting the elbow to let out a fart. 'Why not walk on your head', was the early Deleuzian challenge, 'sing with your sinuses, see through your skin, breathe with your belly: the simple thing, the Entity, the full Body, the stationary Voyage,

Anorexia, cutaneous vision, Yoga, Krishna, Love, Experimentation'
(Blau 1982: 151). We were not all that countercultural, but indeed, we
did it all: instead of Yoga, I taught the Tai Chi Ch'uan, and the actors
in the group could perform through contortions or backflips or, with
stammerings, stutterings, howls (indeed, I was an 'expert witness' at the
Howl trial[3]), up the nose, down the lungs, corporeal incantations, off-
the-wall explosive sounds, with text, without text, but eventually back to
words – words words words – complexly associational, an always ellipti-
cal score, while standing on their heads, or speaking of 'playback', with
ideographic acrobatics and choral precision too, in a surge of disparate
voices, high-pitched, guttural, logorrheic machines, or machine-gunned
utterance, as fast as words could move, with syllables divided across the
length of the playing space, not randomly, by chance, but in the mathematics of ghosting, with exactitude.

Words, body, playback, it was certainly autoerotic, but inquisitional
too. And there was method in the madness: at whatever selvedge of
feeling, in the linguistic abyss or derangement, it was still a matter of
thought – that thinking with the body, which internalises delirium
or projects hallucination, without indulging fantasy (the vice of psychoanalysis, according to Deleuze) nor the programmatic (his name for
experimentation which is antipsychiatric). What we were doing might, in
the hysterical passing from one code to another, scramble all the codes,
but the burrowing (Kafkaesque) or the ghosting (Hamletic) was a rigorous way of knowing, a formation of ideas, with shifts of singularity and
multiple affect, but when push came to shove, at the extremity of performance, where there were actual bodily and psychic risks – the actor
could really get hurt – the commitment was conceptual, we wanted to
understand, whatever the psychophysics, with belief in the brain.

Thus, as others have written about it, my difference with Deleuze. But
with difference and repetition, it could be a subtle difference. '"Give me
a body then"', wrote Deleuze, with his eye on film, in *Cinema 2*:

> This is the formula of philosophical reversal. The body is no longer the
> obstacle which separates thought from itself, that which it has to overcome
> to reach thinking. It is on the contrary that which it plunges into or must
> plunge into, in order to reach the unthought, that is life. Not that the body
> thinks, but obstinate and stubborn, it forces us to think, and forces us to
> think what is concealed from thought, life. (Deleuze 1989: 189)

But here's the difference: what forces us to think even more is that it
remains concealed, which thus gives life to (the) theatre, which wouldn't
exist if you could see it; that is, if the absence of transparency weren't,

through some ontological fault of becoming, in every fibre, follicle, nerve-end of being – where the truth of the matter is, '*matter as revelation*', we can't tell *it* from *bit*. And that will be no less true, with all those *bytes*, in the age of information.

As for the BwO, that legacy from Artaud – '*No mouth. No tongue. No teeth. No larynx. No esophagus. No belly. No anus*' – it is like Nietzsche's Dionysus, *essentially* imageless, having nothing to do with the body itself, 'nor what remains of a lost totality' (Deleuze and Guattari 1977: 8). And since it's not a projection, resisting being imaged, it can't be represented, though somewhere there's 'a God at work' with the intention of 'messing it all up or strangling it by organizing it' (9). Well, let it be blessed by the truer God of Artaud – but despite the ecstatic vanity of his vision of an anti-theatre, its excruciating mystery, with apparitions from beyond, there is no performance without the always vulnerable, material body; or in its absence, as on an empty stage, the expectation of it, some projection of the body, as in the detritus of its absent being, mournfully there, appalling – what Beckett conveys in *Breath*. If the body without organs is the body without an image, model of 'the death instinct', as Deleuze insists, he also insists 'that is its name, and death is not without a model. For desire desires death also, . . . just as it desires life, because the organs of life are the *working machine*' (8). Whatever the model may be, it has been said about death that it can't be represented, but if you think of it in the theatre it can only be represented. As for the machine, whatever it may be desiring, it works *as theatre* only with the body there – even in its absence, you can smell it in the wings, that smell of mortality, which may come upon us in delirium, as with King Lear on the heath; or surreptitiously, insidiously, as in Strindberg's *Ghost Sonata*; or inexhaustibly in Beckett, giving birth astride of a grave. Double pincer, double bind: God may be a lobster, but 'down in the hole, lingeringly, the grave-digger puts on the forceps' (Beckett 1954: 58), while reminding us that mortality is the unseeable substance of theatre, there, not there, which in the consciousness of its vanishing endows it with Life.

References

Artaud, A. (1958), *The Theatre and Its Double*, trans. M. C. Richards, New York: Grove Press.
Beckett, S. (1954), *Waiting for Godot*, New York: Grove Press.
Beckett, S. (1984), 'Not I', in *Collected Shorter Plays*, New York: Grove Press.
Blau, H. (1982), *Take Up the Bodies: Theatre at the Vanishing Point*, Urbana: University of Illinois Press.
Brecht, B. (1964), 'Prologue to *Baal*', trans. E. Bentley and M. Esslin, in *Baal, A Man's A Man* and *The Elephant Calf*, New York: Grove Press.

Deleuze, G. (1989), *Cinema 2: The Time-Image*, trans. H. Tomlinson and R. Galeta, Minneapolis: University of Minnesota Press.

Deleuze, G. (1997), 'One Less Manifesto', trans. E. dal Molin and T. Murray, in T. Murray (ed.), *Mimesis, Masochism, and Mime: The Politics of Theatricality in Contemporary French Thought*, Ann Arbor: University of Michigan Press.

Deleuze, G. (1998), *Essays Critical and Clinical*, trans. D. W. Smith and M. A. Greco, London and New York: Verso.

Deleuze, G. (2004) *Difference and Repetition*, trans. P. Patton (London / New York: Continuum)

Deleuze, G. and F. Guattari (1977), *Anti-Oedipus: Capitalism and Schizophrenia*, trans. R. Hurley, M. Seem and H. R. Lane, New York: Viking Press.

Deleuze, G. and F. Guattari (1987), *A Thousand Plateaus: Capitalism and Schizophrenia*, trans. B. Massumi, Minneapolis: University of Minnesota Press.

Deleuze, G. and F. Guattari (1994), *What is Philosophy?*, trans. H. Tomlinson and G. Burchell, New York: Columbia University Press.

Eliot, T. S. (1934), 'The Metaphysical Poets', in *Selected Essays*, London: Faber and Faber.

Erlich, J. W. (1961) (ed.), *Howl of the Censor*, San Carlos, CA: Nourse Publishing.

Foucault, M. (1977), 'Theatrum Philosophicum', trans. D. F. Bouchard and Sherry Simon, in *Language, Counter-Memory, Practice: Selected Essays and Interviews*, Ithaca, NY: Cornell University Press.

Hawking, S. (1998), *A Brief History of Time*, New York: Bantam.

Marinetti, F. T. (1986), 'The Variety Theatre', trans. V. N. Kirby, in Michael Kirby (ed.), *Futurist Performance*, New York: PAJ Publications.

Overbye, D. (2007), 'Laws of Nature, Source Unknown', *The New York Times (Science Times)*, 18 December.

Notes

1. The Living Theatre, an experimental group founded by Julian Beck and Judith Malina in 1947, and based at first in New York, became the emblematic theatre of the '60s, thanks to its radical politics and confrontational stagings, eventually inducing the audience to perform – as in *Paradise Now*, the archetypal production of that dissident period with its participatory mystique. In the latter part of the '60s, the group toured chiefly in Europe, and were even more anarchist and pacifist than before. Wherever they could, as at Avignon, their productions were meant to be disruptive, violating social taboos, including nudity, and always challenging the established order.

2. See Chapters 3–5 of my book, *Take Up the Bodies* (Blau 1982).

3. Because Allen Ginsberg's *Howl* contained references to illicit drugs and sexual practices, in 1957 customs officials seized copies of the poem as it was being imported from the printer in London. Shortly afterwards, Lawrence Ferlinghetti was prosecuted because the book was published and sold through his City Lights Bookstore. Nine 'literary experts' testified on his behalf at the obscenity trial, an account of which, with recorded testimony, can be found in Erlich (1961). Erlich was the defense attorney, and Ferlinghetti won the case – Judge Clayton Horn deciding that the poem was of 'redeeming social importance'.

ACT I

Deleuze on Theatre: Artaud, Beckett and Carmelo Bene

Chapter 2

I Artaud BwO: The Uses of Artaud's *To have done with the judgement of god*

Edward Scheer

> I, Antonin Artaud, am my son, my father, my mother, and myself . . . I don't believe in father or mother, don't have papa-mama. (OC XII: 65, 70)[1]

> For I am the father-mother, neither father nor mother, neither man nor woman, I've always been here, always been body, always been man. (OC XIV**: 60)

These fragments taken from late Artaud texts, *Ci-Gît* (Here lies) and *Suppôts et suppliciations* (Henchmen and torturings), written in 1946 and 1947 respectively, represent a singular version of the twentieth-century avant-garde contestation of the world as it appears to be. They represent the artist claiming the right to be the author of himself, to create a more authentic version of the self. They have also become familiar for readers of Deleuze and Guattari's own avant-garde adventure throughout the two volumes of *Capitalisme et schizophrénie*: *L'anti-Oedipe* and its sequel *Mille Plateaux*. Artaud's apparent acknowledgement and denial (disavowal) of the Oedipal law resonates powerfully with the anti-Oedipal themes of these works. It is a theme he returns to in the later writings:

> Between the body and the body there is nothing, nothing but me. It is not a state, not an object, not a mind, not a fact, even less the void of a being, absolutely nothing of a spirit, or of a mind, not a body, it is the intransplantable me. But not an ego, I don't have one. I don't have an ego . . . what I am is without differentiation nor possible opposition, it is the absolute intrusion of my body, everywhere. (OC XIV**: 76)

In Deleuze and Guattari, Artaud's extravagantly performative style is presented as an experiment in thought, both fully mad *and* entirely credible: 'How could this body have been produced by parents', they say, 'when by its very nature it is such eloquent witness of its own self-production, of its own engendering of itself?' (Deleuze and Guattari 1983: 15). They recognise that he is not simply describing things but *acting them out* in language, that he is not merely talking about dissociation nor presenting symptoms for the schizoanalyst to dissect, but *performing* the schizophrenic production of reality:

> It might be said that the schizophrenic passes from one code to the other, that he deliberately scrambles all the codes, by quickly shifting from one to another, according to the questions asked him, never giving the same explanation from one day to the next, never invoking the same genealogy, never recording the same event in the same way. When he is more or less forced into it and is not in a touchy mood, he may even accept the banal Oedipal code, so long as he can stuff it full of all the disjunctions that this code was designed to eliminate. (15)

Deleuze and Guattari perform this same trick themselves in a tactical deployment of the language of psychoanalysis for the purpose of de-potentiating it, rendering it as an intellectual toy, a plaything of artists, philosophers and creative nutters of all persuasions. It is highly amusing to them that Artaud's radical refusal of the lack inscribed by the Oedipal culture of family, church, clinic and society as index of normative desire, would seem, in psychoanalytic terms, to give him no ground for desire. Artaud produces excess: there is too much signification, too much potential in his ideas. His body, he says, is everywhere, so he is not lacking anything nor is he a passive product of his culture. So what *does* Artaud want, they ask?

In *Anti-Oedipus* Deleuze and Guattari assemble a variety of responses. What Artaud wants, they say, is the body without organs, the pure becoming of schizophrenia and, of course, the theatre of cruelty. In this chapter, I will try to track these topics in forming a picture of Artaud's aesthetics and of Deleuze and Guattari's thought. The aim will be first to establish the conceptual links between them and the linguistic tropes connecting these enterprises and then to examine their sites of divergence in terms of the different practices of Deleuze and Guattari and Artaud. As a focalising point I will look at a particular performative production of Artaud's and the uses to which it has been put by Deleuze and Guattari in the first instance and more recently by a number of artists in contemporary performance culture.

The use of Artaud in *Anti-Oedipus* and *A Thousand Plateaus* is in some ways a unique confluence: of the work of a radical writer and artist with two brilliant thinkers, all dedicated to a culture of experiment, 'an act the outcome of which is unknown' (John Cage, quoted in Deleuze and Guattari 1983: 371, fn.). While there is a playfulness to much of this writing in and around Artaud, it cannot conceal the seriousness of the enterprise, which represents a fundamental contestation of everything that is accepted as foundational to society. It is a contest because Artaud, along with Deleuze and Guattari, is not content to describe that which is the case, but dares to generate alternative images and concepts for others to use.

In this sense they are all, as Timothy Murphy says, acting out the 'conflict between the dogmatic and generative forms of thought' (Murphy 1992: 117). But while there are a number of structural analogies between Deleuze and Guattari's work and that of Artaud, they are not reducible to one another. For one thing, Artaud is an artist not a philosopher. His area of production includes writing but also drawing, making radio pieces, and public performances. In these works – the flak of fragments and scraps rescued from states of extreme dissociation – he is acting out not only thought experiments, but actual experiences of what Foucault termed 'unreason' (Foucault 1961).

It is an experience which Deleuze himself describes in *The Logic of Sense* (1969) as:

> a pure becoming without measure, a veritable becoming-mad, which never rests. It moves in both directions at once. It always eludes the present, causing future and past, more and less, too much and not enough to coincide in the simultaneity of a rebellious matter. (Deleuze 1990: 1–2)

The shifting and elusive quality of this 'rebellious matter' provides an apt image for Artaud's oeuvre, but the point is that, whether understood as the radical suspension of the 'frame-setting message' (Bateson), or the complete absence of any metanarrative, Artaud's 'madness' is, as Derrida says, 'simultaneously more and less than a strategy' (Derrida 1967: 291). It is a resource he uses throughout his oeuvre and which, for Deleuze and Guattari, is fundamental to it.

Appropriately, they deploy some of Artaud's most colourful phrases throughout their own work, not as evidence of a generic schizophrenia, but in what Foucault describes in his preface to *Anti-Oedipus* as a 'mobile arrangement' of those ideas. It is an arrangement around which an entire set of experimental practices can be elaborated. Perhaps the most ubiquitous Artaudianism in the work of Deleuze and Guattari, and the one which resonates most powerfully as a concept for and of performance, is the 'body without organs'. It achieves such a currency in their work that it appears in shorthand throughout the second volume of *Capitalisme et Schizophrénie* as the BwO.

The Original BwO

The concept of BwO is introduced in the first chapter of *Anti-Oedipus* as 'the unproductive, the sterile, the unengendered, the unconsumable.

Antonin Artaud discovered this one day, finding himself with no shape or form whatsoever, right there where he was at that moment' (Deleuze and Guattari 1983: 8). Where he was at that moment (22–29 November 1947) was in a recording studio in Paris. Here Artaud, with several others, was recording his performance piece in five parts *Pour en finir avec le jugement de dieu* (To have done with the judgement of god), to be broadcast on national radio in February of the following year. The others included Roger Blin, the theatre director; Maria Casarés, a celebrity actress; and Paule Thévenin, who would become the executor of Artaud's estate and the editor of the *Oeuvres Complètes* for Gallimard. The broadcast was ultimately banned by the director of Radio Diffusion Française, Wladimir Porché, on the grounds that it was 'obscene, inflammatory and blasphemous' (Barber 1993: 157). For Deleuze and Guattari this is always the price of true experimentation, 'not only radiophonic but also biological and political, incurring censorship and repression. Corpus and Socius, politics and experimentation. They will not let you experiment in peace' (Deleuze and Guattari 1988: 150).

There are five sections to the piece, based on readings of Artaud's text interspersed with percussive sounds and screams. These latter sections punctuate the performance of the text and follow each section of the written piece. In the first section, Artaud rails against an official state practice he claims to have discovered, by which children are made to donate sperm to the American government for the manufacture of soldiers. 'Why are the Americans such a warlike people?' he asks. The themes of anti-war, anti-state, anti-ontogeny are thereby introduced from the beginning.

The second section consists of drums and screams which fade into the text performed by Maria Casarés. 'Tutuguri, le rite du soleil noir' is an interpretation of a ritual dance of the Tarahumara Indians, which Artaud witnessed on his visit to Mexico in 1936, and reads as directly opposed to the Christian myth of the crucifixion: 'le ton majeur du Rite est justement L'ABOLITION DE LA CROIX' (the major tone of the Rite is precisely THE ABOLITION OF THE CROSS) (OC XIII: 79). The authority of the Christian god and the myths that sustain it is the overt object of critique in this section. The performance by Casarés is suitably over the top and matched by Blin in his reading of section three, which develops the discussion of the conditions for the abolition of God's judgement. In this section, voiced by Blin, all extant creation is described as abject:

> And where does this filthy abjection come from? From the fact that the world is not yet constituted, or that man has only a faint idea of the world and he wants to protect it forever? It comes from the fact that, one fine day, man stopped the idea of the world. Two roads were open to him: that of

the infinite outside, that of the infinitesimal inside. And he chose the infinitesimal inside. (OC XIII: 85)

The acceptance of the body such as it is, of life and of the world such as they are, constitutes for Artaud a betrayal of the creative impulse, a betrayal of the active consciousness which would renew and sustain a vital idea of the world, and a betrayal of the infinite potentials of the body. This bad faith amounts to accepting God's judgement. Language is also an index of this abjection. To rely on a relentlessly second-hand language and to enunciate words which have already been chewed over by millions of other mouths is an abjection which is countered in this text by Artaud's *glossolalia* or invented language:

> o reche modo
> to edire
> di za
> tau dari
> do padera coco
> (OC XIII: 87)

Artaud seems to be trying to locate a vehicle for expression not concurrent with the symbolic order and to express his thought *authentically* by reconnecting language with the body. Blin's forceful reading of this, with sudden pitch shifts and a staccato rhythm, provides a performative accompaniment to Artaud's notion that language produces not only sense, but immediate physiological effects on the body of the listener, creating a body as an intensive state and not an accumulation of behaviours, practices, articulations; in other words, creating a body without organs. In his theatre writings Artaud insisted on this aspect of language, which could be utilised in theatre, or on radio and film, to work at the level of the body of the listener, and to transform it. To restrict oneself to the everyday use of language and to its function as description or as conversation is another act of bad faith.

In the next section, 'La question se pose de', performed by Paule Thévenin, Artaud counters this bad faith with

> the thundering manifestation of this explosive necessity: to dilate the body of my internal night, of the internal nothingness of my self which is night, nothingness, irreflection, but which is explosive affirmation that there is something to make space for: my body. (OC XIII: 94)

This latent and potential body needs to be activated by the theatre of cruelty to achieve a 'pure becoming without measure' which, for Deleuze and Guattari, will express the total repudiation of social being. The use of terms such as *explosive necessity* and *affirmation* is typical of Artaud in his attempt to perform the effect he is describing. They embody his aesthetic of action and vitality, of urgency and forcefulness.

The final section, performed by Artaud himself, stages an imagined interview between Artaud and a nameless character who insists that Artaud is mad and should be silenced and tied down. This is the famous declaration that the human form is the carrier of a divine virus and that to liberate man it will be necessary to rebuild him without the organs which are the instruments of God's oppression in the human form – measuring it, structuring it, articulating it; in other words, judging it:

> For tie me down if you want to, but there is nothing more useless than an organ. When you have made him a body without organs, then you will have delivered him from all his automatisms and restored him to his true liberty. Then he will re-learn how to dance inside out . . . and that will be his true side. (OC XIII: 104)

For Artaud, organs are useless in terms of the production of vital energy (which is, after all, what bodies are for) and they sap the body's creative potential, forcing it to perform the menial tasks of biological *functions*. Organs render the body as slave rather than master. Artaud's image of the body without organs therefore contests not only the ways that bodies are structured, but the ways in which they perform, biologically and socially. This is why the theatre was the key site for Artaud's vision: it permits the imaginative reconfiguration of these bodily forms, comportments and behaviours and allows the body to act in ways that are profoundly anti-social. However, this is also why Artaud's development of radical potentials for physical expression and reception in performance could never be subsumed within Western theatrical institutions.

The End of Theatre

Nevertheless, Artaud was acutely aware of the theatrical and aesthetic context of his time and of the necessary performative components of theatrical form (characters, roles, normative behaviours or functions) which delimited the terrain of his work. Of the anecdotes which survive of his years with Charles Dullin's Atelier in Paris in 1922–3, his student performance of Charlemagne as an ape suggests more than an anti-naturalistic approach to character, conveying as clearly as his subsequent writings his contempt for the concept of role. Although role gives definition to a function that might otherwise be random, it also restricts possibilities for behaviour and performance. But the forms of theatre available to Artaud at the time were inconceivable without role – that is, without the representational aspect of performance which requires that an actor must present elements of character. This was still some years before the Happenings and the untitled events of the 1950s and '60s, which took place with the benefit of Artaud's challenges to this convention.

Indeed received conventions of form, such as the primacy of role in theatre, are the point of departure for all aspects of his artistic production of texts, performances, recordings and drawings. Artaud's work in these various media is always directed at a critique of the foundational terms in which they operate, that is, their accepted forms. In traditional theatre, the received wisdom is representation: its form requires an observance of some concept of role. The archetype of this arrangement for Artaud is the body itself. Its form cannot be sustained without the organs. So the body without organs defies not only particular instances of the body, but the entire matrix of representations within which bodies, forms and roles are circulated and define each other. In other words, it is a critique which also operates at the level of society and culture and cannot simply be confined to a discussion of the design of the human body.

The notion that Artaud perceived, and which Foucault would elaborate, is that physical comportment represents and performs social coding, and hence that one way to recode society is to start with the body. The body without organs is an important *aesthetic* contribution to this area of radical thought which today is echoed in the work of a number of performance artists such as Marina Abramovic, Stelarc, Mike Parr and in the surgical interventions performed by Orlan. All of these artists provoke the limit of the body and, as Artaud did, demonstrate both the contingency of its construction and its significance in culture. We read Artaud's trace in any aesthetic practice where actual bodily changes are made by the performer as a gesture of defiance of the notions of the socialised restriction of bodily behaviours and of biology conceived as origin or destiny.

But what kind of biology? If the BwO sounds like an attack on the body, Deleuze and Guattari helpfully observe that:

> the BwO is not at all the opposite of the organs. The organs are not its enemies. The enemy is the organism. The BwO is opposed not to the organs but to that organization of the organs called the organism. It is true that Artaud wages a struggle against the organs, but at the same time what he is going after, what he has it in for, is the organism . . . The judgment of God, the system of the judgment of God, the theological system, is precisely the operation of He who makes an organism . . . because He cannot bear the BwO. (Deleuze and Guattari 1988: 158)

They seem to be saying that the BwO challenges the primacy of natural creation (the organism) and by extension, the (natural) subalternity (insufficiency and inferiority) of representations in culture. We know from Artaud's theatre writings that representational practices such as theatre or visual, acoustic and text-based media should not be content to record or register reality, even those things for which we have no language, but should instead contest and combat the existing order of things. The components of this creation (organs) are therefore crucial to the challenge, which is based on a radical re-deployment of them.

This observation has implications for Artaud's entire oeuvre. To maintain the perpetual combat against the existing order of things, Artaud needs a battlefield, and this is the significance of the organs of the body and their cultural correlatives: aesthetic form, syntax and language, representation and the theatre itself. Without these, there remains only the silence of collapse, surrender and 'the absence of a voice to cry out'. The theatre of cruelty is where the body without organs is made. It is opposed to all forms, since they are forms of social production, but also opposed to silence and surrender. So it will need to appropriate forms, to invade them, inhabit them, to distort them and render them useless.

Theatre of Cruelty

The materials of Artaud's combat are what he finds in language: letters, characters, phoneticisation and signification; in representation: the page, the pencil, the line; and in theatre: the spectators, performers and venue. They are the particles of all received forms which must be registered, re-enacted and rejected: all 'ceux qui n'ont pas gagné d'être vivants par eux-mêmes' (those who didn't earn the right to be the living by themselves), therefore: 'Lettre sans lettre, mot sans mot' (Letter without letter, word without word) (OC XIV**: 23) and even 'les nombres ne sont jamais réductibles à un chiffre' (numbers are never reducible to a digit) (OC XXIII: 203). The material of the number, letter, word – in short, form itself – has to be reworked to constitute a body without organs: a zone that is not already infected with the disease of organic closure.

It is neither a question of re-introducing form, nor one of definitively surpassing it: 'Je ne crois pas aux formes initiales à la forme, et à la non-forme (bien entendu, ah non, pas bien entendu), mais je crois à la non-forme encore moins' (I don't believe in the initial forms of form or non-form [as is well known, or rather as is not well known], but I believe even less in non-form)' (OC XXIII: 304). You have to use whatever is at hand. This is why, as Artaud indicates here, a double movement, an appropriation or re-enactment is necessary, such as in the therapeutic tactic of 'acting out' where an episode is re-enacted, but differently, to enable a different outcome for the re-enactor. For Artaud, the work of acting out these forms consists in making them contingent, in disestablishing the autonomy of their base. In the radio piece, Artaud says, in a smugly condescending tone of voice: 'Vous délirez Monsieur Artaud. Vous êtes fous!' He is playing the role of the judge, the clinician or psychiatrist, and ultimately the 'normal man', in refuting the self-evidently 'bizarre' claims Artaud is making here about American imperialism, the judgement of god and the body without organs by questioning the sanity of their author. But in appropriating this position, Artaud is not so much empowering himself as showing how contingent these positions are, and that their existence can be seen to depend on principles which are themselves conditional, even theatrical:

> All beings intoned a theatre and a liturgy directed against me alone, alone against everything, this is how god was formed, he formed himself but like a sect and a theatre and the universe is a theatre, the representation of a tragedy which is ending and not a founding fact. (OC XIV**: 204)

If the universe is already a theatre, then the theatre of cruelty has to set itself against the institutionality of theatre as an art form, since this only expresses a fake and forfeited form of life: 'the representation of a tragedy which is ending'. The theatre of cruelty has to begin making the BwO, freeing life of its inauthentic attachment to representation and reconnecting it to the forces that underlie all forms. The theatre of cruelty is not therefore a theatre as such, but an entity defined by a fundamental *conflict* with theatre, a critique of all the institutional practices (the organs) of the theatre in the name of a principle of vitality that dissolves '*notre petite individualité humaine*' (our trivial human individuality). As such, it approaches the efficacy and liminality of ritual and will, therefore, be a constant challenge to anything that takes the name of theatre. For Artaud, life is crisis and necessitates rituals that can transcribe this crisis, embody it and make it liveable. Cruelty is liminality.[2] Theatrical performance, for him, is a ritual preparation for this kind of cruelty which, separated from the world and divorced from the body as a docile instrument of power, permits the emergence of the new and gives shape to new historical circumstances.

In a later essay, 'Pour en finir avec le jugement', Deleuze calls this liminal response to crisis the 'système physique de la cruauté' which consists of the non-organic vitality of the BwO, as described above, and the affective athleticism of the theatre of cruelty. The physical system of cruelty is a useful way of describing what is at stake here because it can be seen to operate in all Artaud's work and does not return us too quickly to the problem of theatre. Deleuze reads Artaud's work as forming an active and vital system opposed to organisms such as literary masterpieces. It is 'écriture de sang et de vie qui s'oppose à l'écriture du livre, comme la justice au jugement, et entraine un véritable inversion du signe' (writing of blood and of life which is opposed to the writing of a book, like justice opposes judgement, and carries out a real inversion of the sign) (Deleuze 1993: 160).

An inversion of the sign would involve the substitution of the signifier for the thing itself, the physical gestural acts of signification – Artaud's late texts were dictated while he hammered rhythmically on a block of wood – for the words on the page. For performance, this means the theatricalisation of life rather than the life of the theatre; the simulation of acting out rather than the representation of character in acting; the abandonment of narrative or dialogue for the language of incantation:

> to make language express what it doesn't usually express is to make use of it in a new, exceptional and unaccustomed way, to return it to its possibilities of physical disturbance, to divide it and release it actively in space . . . to turn against language and its basely utilitarian, one could say alimentary, sources, against its origins as a hunted beast, and finally to consider language in the form of Incantation. (OC IV: 69)

Incantation is the act of calling forth that which had been latent, of manifesting the potentials of language in a measured chanting which can transform states of consciousness and the body's autonomic nervous system. Again, this is leading us to a consideration of ritual as the only form that can respond to these ideas. The problem for the Western world, as Artaud was only too well aware, is that we have outsourced our ritual functions to the institutions of art and religion, in order to contain and commodify the liminal experience. So, once more we are forced to confront, as in Artaud's time, the theatre and the judgement of god.

The Judgement of God

What does this notion 'to end the judgement of god' mean in a contemporary context? Deleuze sees it in the critique of the Judeo-Christian tradition in the work of Nietzsche, D.H. Lawrence, Kafka and Artaud considered as Baruch Spinoza's *grandes disciples*. Deleuze's reading of Artaud as a disciple of Spinoza comes more clearly into focus in his book on the latter, in which Deleuze delineates a Spinozan diagnosis of the world:

> a humanity bent on self destruction, multiplying the cults of death, bringing about the union of the tyrant and the slave, the priest, the judge and the soldier, always busy running life into the ground, mutilating it, killing it

outright or by degrees, overlaying it or suffocating it with laws, properties, duties, empires – this is what Spinoza diagnoses in the world, this betrayal; of the universe and of mankind. (Deleuze 1988: 12)

This passage suggests that the basis for the relation between Spinoza and Artaud is that both perceived, and wanted, to counter the global death wish which Artaud labelled 'the judgement of god'.

Deleuze perceived that Artaud had suffered greatly 'du jugement sous sa forme la plus dure, la terrible expertise psychiatrique' (under the most severe form of judgement, the terrible expertise of psychiatry) (Deleuze 1993: 158). Yet Artaud 'ne cessera d'opposer à l'infini l'opération d'en finir avec le jugement de Dieu' (would never cease to oppose to the infinite, the operation of having done with the judgement of God) (159). This is a telling observation, since it links the ongoing nature of combat in Artaud, as in the production of the body without organs and the sustained vitalism of the theatre of cruelty, with the forces that Artaud saw everywhere under the sign of theological condemnation: the requirement to live an inauthentic life, to represent something or to speak or write in a language that must always be second-hand.

For Deleuze, the principle of immanence is coterminous with Artaudian cruelty, which involves, as Artaud specifies in his theatre writings, a cruel – in the sense of rigorous or disciplined – attitude towards the self. Deleuze opposes this cruelty to the 'supplice infini' (infinite torture) of the doctrine of judgement, which he illustrates through reference to a number of texts from Greek tragedy. In these texts, the gods were said to assign to men their 'lot' in life, which then predetermined lives in terms of their natural 'organic' ends or appropriate forms. This system resulted in two modes of judgement: the false judgement of hubris, which resulted from men overestimating their gifts, and the redistributive judgement of the gods. This bifurcation was subsequently internalised as the judgement of the self *by* the self.[3] A significant example in Deleuze is, of course, Sophocles' Oedipus tragedies and their place at the inauguration of the Freudian enterprise of psychoanalysis, a key site of the normative exercise of judgement.

As I've argued above, Artaud combats the Oedipal form of judgement (the judgement of Freud or God) by engaging in a process of 'abreaction'[4] in which he precipitates the judgement and brings it down on himself in order to have done with it, even creating an Oedipal protagonist with an oddly familiar back-story:

And just as I was crucified on Golgotha two thousand years ago, I was also poisoned throughout my entire existence by the family in which I was living and who lyingly pretended to have given me life. It was these bewitchments and nothing but them, which made of me . . . this stammering cripple perpetually engaged in the neuropathic search for my self. (OC XIV**: 147)

This could appear, on one level, to be pure and simple delusion but, according to those who knew him well, like Marthe Robert, Artaud frequently carried on like this in conversation, continuing until his friends asked him to drop it.[5] We see this in Artaud's performance of his essay on the theatre and the plague at the Sorbonne in 1933, of which Anaïs Nin wrote so eloquently, but that was widely perceived at the time to have been a moment of pure psychotic breakdown. As soon as everyone had walked out in disgust, Artaud approached Nin and asked if she wanted to go for coffee. This event is illustrative of how Artaud negotiated the terrain of the social: he saw it as bad theatre and responded in kind, but always leaving behind him a sense of the indeterminate. Infuriatingly incapable of reproducing expected comportment, he was forever generating alternative behaviours: often bizarre and completely inappropriate ones.

Deleuze and Guattari describe the philosophical equivalent of this creative approach to social behaviour as 'event-thought' or 'problem-thought' as opposed to 'essence-thought'. Only event-thought is capable of bringing 'something incomprehensible into the world' (Deleuze and Guattari 1988: 378). For Deleuze, as for Artaud, the event-thought is not a work unless it is at the same time a new mode of existence. And no new modes of existence are possible without cruelty; that is, without necessity, rigour and urgency. Such works threaten the doctrine of judgement since they bring themselves into being, whereas judgement insists on repetition, as Artaud's entire critical trajectory illustrates, and on pre-existent criteria which are, apparently, universally applicable.

Of course, Artaud's playful 'event-thought' had a tragic dimension. The controversial electroshock treatments he was subjected to at the asylum in Rodez were administered in spite of his claims that he was assuming roles, playing out positions, acting out the symptoms of mental anguish as any good writer would do: 'Qu'est-ce qu'un poète sinon un homme qui visualise et concrétise ses idées et ses images plus intensément et avec plus de juste bonheur et de vie que les autres hommes et qui par le verbe rhythmé leur donne un caractère de fait' (What is a poet if not a man who visualises and concretises his ideas and images more intensely and with more justifiable delight and liveliness than other men and who, through the rhythmic word, gives them a factual character) (OC XI: 11).

Instead of reading his work as the elaborate dramaturgy of a writer, critics from Jacques Rivière (who initially rejected his early poems before agreeing to publish them as examples of their intriguing conversation) to Porché at Radio France (banning the broadcast he had commissioned) and the clinicians at Rodez (denying the status of Artaud's statements as art and insisting that they were symptoms) enact a system of judgement based on what is perceptible at any given moment and assumed to be the case. They tell him he is doing fine, and will sort it all out, one fine day when he is more himself. Deleuze and Guattari lay the blame on Freud:

> The error of psychoanalysis was to understand BwO phenomena as regressions, projections, phantasies, in terms of an image of the body. As a result it only grasps the flipside of the BwO and immediately substitutes family photos, childhood memories, and part-objects for a worldwide intensity map. It understands nothing about . . . a continually self-constructing milieu. (Deleuze and Guattari 1988: 165)

In a series of heart-rending letters to his doctors at the asylum of Rodez: Gaston Ferdière and Jacques Latrémolière (especially the latter, who was directly responsible for administering the treatment, and particularly in the letter dated 6 January 1945), Artaud asserts his right to be treated as a writer and artist rather than a madman. Artaud begs Latrémolière to stop the shock therapy and appeals to his awareness that 'ce n'était pas un traitement à me faire subir, et qu'un homme comme moi n'avait pas à être traité mais au contraire aidé dans son travail' (this was not a treatment I should have to undergo, and that a man like myself need not be treated but on the contrary helped in his work) (OC XI: 12–3). In the midst of the life-threatening experience that was the electro-shock therapy, Artaud continues to denounce the judgement underlying it that gives rise to it, with a staggering lucidity and courage:

> I am disgusted with living, Mr. Latrémolière, because I perceive that we are in a world where nothing lasts, and where anything may be held up to ridicule and accused of unreason according to the state of mind at that moment or on that hour and the unconscious of the accuser, of which he himself, who takes himself to be judge, is totally unaware. (OC XI: 12)

The contingency of judgement and the delegitimisation of unreason is what concerns Artaud, even as a vertebra is smashed by the shock treatment he endured at that time. In another letter, from January 1945, also addressed to Latrémolière, the terms are even more explicit:

> Love, intelligence, the rarest affective intuition represent us, and then one day all this is changed and swept aside, and all that remains in us is the shadow of the eternal discriminator who imagines that he always judges with the same consciousness as beforehand, but no longer has it. (OC XI: 29)

The immense pathos in the letters of this period, just at the end of the war, before Artaud was to be released from the asylum, would be interchanged at times with a more ludic tone such as in the letters to André Breton. This latter relation was always an ambiguous one. Breton repeatedly emphasised the literary or theatrical aspects of Artaud's work in an attempt to eclipse the shadow of insanity, which, for Breton, hovered over Artaud and always obscured the truly artistic. For Breton the 'convulsive beauty' of art was always constituted as such more by the doctor applying the electrodes than by the suffering patient. Of course this interpretation of Artaud's work serves to return its radically skewed trajectory too quickly to the categories of the aesthetic, those very categories Artaud worked so hard to multiply beyond functionality. These correspondences all manifest the judgement that fetishises pure categories (is Artaud mad or a man of the theatre?) over complex vital arrangements (he is neither and both); the judgement that does not allow for the existence of the new, its emergence or even its perception.

What Deleuze discovers in Artaud's theatre writings is, oddly enough, not the taint of insanity but the use of the symbol, though as always this concept takes an unusual shape in Deleuze's reconfiguration. The symbol, he says, is 'an intensive composite which vibrates and extends itself, which doesn't mean anything, but makes us whirl around in all directions until we pick up the maximum possible force, of which each element receives a new meaning in relation with the others' (Deleuze 1993: 167–8). Artaud's cruel imagery in *Le Théâtre et son Double*, his allegories of plague and alchemy, of incest and cosmic disturbances, of revitalised culture and metaphysics, of affective athleticism and hieroglyphic language, of oriental dance and incantation, are symbols in precisely this sense. They are not attempts to appropriate or subjugate the forms of otherness, for example the practice of the Balinese dancers into Western theatre styles, but on the contrary to fracture their mutually exclusive identities in order to release a transfiguring force in which 'chacune des deux forces redouble et relance l'autre' (each of two forces intensifies and relaunches the other) (Deleuze 1993: 168). In Deleuze's earlier work with Guattari, this process would have been described as *deterritorialisation* or *destratification*, the lateral metastasis of the *rhizome*, but here it is more simply the basis of the struggle against oppressive systems of judgement.

As I have already argued, only a fistful of pseudo rituals remain to us in the West, so we are bound to return to the institutions of religion and the judgement of god. We see judgement around us everywhere, even if we don't experience it as Artaud did: ultimately, as a violent, state-sanctioned attack on his own body. But we also return, for the same reason, to the institutions of the aesthetic, and perhaps, to the theatre. But to what kind of theatre should we return? Alongside certain practices in performance art of the kind mentioned briefly above I would also like to consider some of the various performative uses of Artaud's text *To have done with the judgement of god*.

Conclusion: Performing *To have done with the judgement of god*

After the banning of the piece in 1948 it was not heard on the airwaves until 1973, when René Farabet, the director of the Atelier Création Radiophonique at Radio France, finally broadcast it. The master copies had been erased but Blin allowed his own copy to be circulated so, although it was not officially released on a label until Harmonia Mundi's version of 1986, the recording itself did not entirely disappear in the meantime.

One pirate copy reached Hijikata Tatsumi the founder of Butoh in Japan, and became 'one of Hijikata's most treasured possessions' (Holborn 1987: 14), which he played to guests such as Susan Sontag even as late as 1986, just months before his death. The links between the development of the language of Butoh in the 1960s and the theories of Artaud, first translated into Japanese in 1965, were substantial and have been explored in other places,[6] but the significance to Butoh artists and audiences of *To have done with the judgement of god* in particular is worthy of note. In 1984, Hijikata choreographed Min Tanaka in a piece called *Ren-ai Butoh-ha Teiso* (*Foundation of the Dance of Love*), which was performed to the sound of Artaud's voice in *To have done with the judgement of god*. Tanaka continued to use the recording in subsequent performances (Daly 1998: 15–23). Despite its rather dated production values and mediocre sound quality, the recording of Artaud's voice still entrances audiences and artists, not only Butoh audiences.

It is as if his ideas about incantation are finally realised in this work, though of course it is only a sketch of these ideas. How far would Artaud have taken them had he had access to contemporary amplification and equalisation technologies? The sound artist Scott Gibbon, working along-side Romeo Castellucci and the Socìetas Raffaello Sanzio in *Genesi: From the Museum of Sleep* (1999), gives an indication of this with his manipulation of Artaud's voice in Act II of this work. Entitled *Auschwitz*, this Act responds to the text of Artaud's piece in some detail and explores the full horror of judgement from the perspective of the holocaust:

Dressed in long white tunics with cowls, the children play in a large, light room, the soft fabrics waving in the wind. There is a gentle breeze. Gentleness, calm, apparently, unless it's only a lull. Or the false intimacy of an already stolen childhood, ready to be sacrificed to men. . . . Behind the veil, the smooth coldness of a clinical world breaks through. A world where life no longer counts at all. Here the purpose is not to save lives, but to analyse their anatomy. In the depths of the room, a new Adam Lucifer, invisible, has got it into his head to become God again. He removes the organs of children to manufacture eternal life. Eternity for the executioners . . . It's Antonin Artaud: I'm not crazy, I'm not delirious, I'm not.

(Castellucci 2001)

Discernible fragments of Artaud's voice rise and repeat throughout the latter part of the scene. Taken from the first and the last sections of *To have done with the judgement of god*, the voice seems to comment on the threatened innocence of the children on the stage and the atrocity which, to chilling effect, the piece does not attempt to represent.

Disembodied, threatening, hallucinatory – the voice haunts these productions with all that they cannot contain. The voice is a fetish, a reminder of a phantasmatic relation to a theatre that cannot be and to an artist whose death sixty years ago has done little to diminish the potency of his ideas.

References

Artaud, A. (1976–), *Oeuvres Complètes*, 26 vols (of 30 prepared), Paris: Gallimard. See especially: *Suppôts et suppliciations* (comprises volume 14 of the OC in two parts: XIV* and XIV**); *Pour en finir avec le jugement de dieu* (OC XIII: 65–104); *Héliogabale ou l'anarchiste couronné* (OC VII: 13–137); *Ci-Gît* (OC XII: 75–100); and *Le Théâtre et son double* (OC IV).
Artaud, A. (1996), 'Letter to André Breton, 28 February 1947', trans. Yvonne Houlton, *Interstice*, 2: 33–4.
Barber, S. (1993), *Antonin Artaud: Blows and Bombs*, London: Faber and Faber.
Castellucci, R. (2001), 'Fragments of Beginnings', available at http://www.theatre-contemporain.net/spectacles/genesi/indexus.htm
Daly, A. (1998), '*Dancing: A Letter from New York City*', TDR, 42 (1): 15–23.
Deleuze, G. (1979), 'The Schizophrenic and Language: Surface and Depths in Lewis Carroll and Antonin Artaud', in J. Harari (ed. and trans.), *Textual Strategies*, New York: Cornell University Press.
Deleuze, G. (1993), 'Pour en finir avec le jugement', *Critique et clinique*, Paris: Minuit.
Deleuze, G. (1990), *The Logic of Sense*, trans. M. Lester with C. Stivale, edited by C. V. Boundas, New York: Columbia University Press.
Deleuze, G. (1988), *Spinoza: Practical Philosophy*, trans. R. Hurley, San Francisco: City Lights Books.
Deleuze, G. and F. Guattari (1983), *Anti-Oedipus*, trans. R. Hurley, M. Seem and H. R. Lane, Minneapolis: University of Minnesota.
Deleuze, G. and F. Guattari (1988), *A Thousand Plateaus*, trans. B. Massumi, London: Athlone Press.

Derrida, J. (1967), 'La Parole Soufflée', in *L'Écriture et la Différence*, Paris: Seuil.
Foucault, M. (1961), *Folie et déraison: Histoire de la folie à l'age classique*, Paris: Plon.
Holborn, M. (1987), 'Tatsumi Hijikata and the Origins of Butoh', in M. Holborn and E. Hoffman (eds), *Butoh: Dance of the Dark Soul*, New York: Sadev/Aperture.
Kazuko, K. (1986), 'Butoh Chronology: 1959–1984', *TDR*, 30 (2): 127–41.
Kurihara, N. (2000), 'Hijikata Tatsumi: The Words of Butoh', *TDR*, 44 (1): 10–28.
Murphy, T. S. (1992), 'The Theatre (of the Philosophy) of Cruelty in Difference and Repetition', in Joan Broadhurst (ed.), *Deleuze and the Transcendental Unconscious*. Special edition of *Pli: Warwick Journal of Philosophy*, University of Warwick, 105–35.
Turner, V. (1986), *The Anthropology of Performance*, New York: PAJ Publications.

Notes

1. References in the text are to Artaud's *Oeuvres Complètes* (1976–), abbreviated as OC followed by volume number.
2. One can usefully compare Victor Turner's 'collective response to hazards such as war, famine, drought, plague, earthquake, volcanic eruption, and other natural or man-made disasters' with any of the various metonyms for the theatre which Artaud mobilises in *Le Théâtre et son Double* (Turner 1986: 101).
3. Augusto Boal's theatrical exploration of the 'cop in the head' syndrome in his forum theatre experiments would be a contemporary example of a response along these lines. In this exercise, a situation of conflict with authority is re-enacted by the actor (often the victim of abuse) with different outcomes suggested by the spectators who may intervene to change the course of events. The purpose of this is to suggest that the situation could have been resolved otherwise and that the perceived power relation interpolated by the actor (the cop in their head) can be altered.
4. The term 'abreaction' comes from Freud's early work with Joseph Breuer published in the paper 'On the Psychical Mechanism of Hysterical Phenomena: Preliminary Communication', of 1893. In this they argue for the necessity of reactions adequate to traumatic events as a way of discharging the affect provoked by these traumatic episodes. Stifled reactions may need to be 'abreacted' later on. Abreaction appears here for the first time as the active constituent of catharsis. More precisely it denotes the end state of a process of 'living out' or 'acting out' a 'previously repressed experience' with the attendant discharge of affect. In the clinical application of abreaction the events in the patient's repressed memory are precipitated and re-rehearsed in order to de-potentiate 'the affectivity of the traumatic experience'. The process involves the simultaneous action and activation of memory with the anticipation of future trauma.
5. Conversation between the author and Sylvère Lotringer, who knew Marthe Robert.
6. Artaud-kan (the house of Artaud) was one of the first Butoh groups. It first performed in 1966 and was active throughout the 1960s and '70s. Hijikata's *Revolt of the Flesh* (1968) was based on Artaud's *Heliogabalus*. Indeed the Paris-based critic and choreographer Sumako Koseki defined Butoh as 'the voice of Artaud at the end of his life', a reference to the recording (Koseki quoted in Barber 1993: 5).

Chapter 3

Expression and Affect in Kleist, Beckett and Deleuze

Anthony Uhlmann

Given that Beckett's apparent desire for control over the performances of his plays during his lifetime, and the subsequent ongoing insistence of the Beckett Estate that his stage directions be closely adhered to, are well known, I will, in this chapter, move away from what has become the standard debate – wherein the interests or intentions of the author are opposed to the creative freedom of producers, actors and directors – towards a different point of focus. This will involve an examination of the concepts of 'expression' and 'affect' which Deleuze develops through his reading of Spinoza and Leibniz on the one hand, and the work of the German Romantic dramatist Heinrich von Kleist on the other. I will then seek to compare these to Beckett's statements regarding his own strong interest in the work of Kleist in order to develop an understanding of the *external* nature both of expression itself and of the affect in his work, and the implications of this for performance practice.

In order to begin it is useful to again detail the control Beckett extended over productions of his work while he was alive. Both Kenneth Tynan – when he changed the script of *Breath* – and JoAnne Akalaitis – when she tampered with the stage directions to *Endgame* – were threatened with legal action (Bair 1990: 640–1, Brater 1989: 84, 107). In his letter to Akalaitis, who had changed the setting of *Endgame* to an abandoned New York subway car for her 1984 production, Beckett stated that 'Any production which ignores my stage directions is completely unacceptable to me' (Brater 1989: 107). Indeed, the stage directions to his plays, especially those written after *Happy Days* in 1961, have been seen to further emphasise Beckett's desire for control. Some of these plays include diagrams explaining movements of the characters, and detailed instructions on the level and pitch of voice desirable. It is almost as if the plays have been 'blocked' within the text. As Enoch Brater notes: 'Stage directions multiply as Beckett begins to challenge the theater's traditional

function as a collaborative and interpretive art' (107). To quote from
Deirdre Bair:

> For Beckett, the perfect stage vehicle is one in which there are no actors or
> directors, only the play itself. When asked how such theatre could be made
> viable, Beckett replied that the author had the duty to search for the perfect
> actor, that is, one who would comply fully with his instructions, having
> the ability to annihilate himself totally. 'Not for me these Grotowskis and
> Methods', Beckett storms. 'The best possible play is one in which there are no
> actors, only the text. I'm trying to find a way to write one'. (Bair 1990: 544)

How might one account for such an apparently violent response?
Clearly, Beckett's concepts of dramatic production seem antagonistic to
those which have dominated twentieth-century practices, such as those
developed by the Russian director and theorist Stanislavski, through
which the actor is asked to look within him or herself to find the reality
of the part (i.e., their own unapologetically subjective understanding) in
order to express a real subjectivity on stage. It is important to remember, then, that a second, minor tradition of acting co-existed for a time
with that developed by Stanislavski. Writing in 1911, and strongly
influenced by Heinrich von Kleist's 1810 story (or essay in story form)
'On the Marionette Theatre', the English director and theorist Edward
Gordon Craig suggested that when ruled by emotion (as is the case with
Stanislavski's 'realist' approach) actors lose control over their bodies
and their voices, and, accordingly, what they produce is no more than a
series of, perhaps interesting, accidents. As an alternative to 'realism' he
envisaged the 'uber-marionette':

> The uber-marionette will not compete with life – rather it will go beyond it.
> Its ideal will not be the flesh and blood but rather the body in trance – it will
> aim to clothe itself with a death-like beauty while exhaling a living spirit.
> (Craig 1956: 84–5)

While Craig's ideas add little to those already apparent in Kleist's short
story, and while Craig dismissed his own idea of the uber-marionette as
'an impossible state of perfection' (Innes 1983: 124) and further stated
that he was looking to the actors to perfect their own craft, the ideas
he draws from Kleist nevertheless offered possibilities for the theatre,
a certain kind of theatre, which simply could not be realised through
Stanislavski's techniques. Indeed, this was something which Stanislavski
himself recognised. Christopher Innes notes that:

> By 1907 Stanislavski was . . . in search of a deeper kind of realism that
> would reflect 'the life of the human spirit'. But his experiments with symbol-
> ist drama . . . had been unsuccessful. The acting techniques he had developed

for internalizing emotion and translating unexpressed thoughts into physical action were useless for plays that had abstract figures and no subtext. . . . Maeterlinck had complained [to Stanislavski] that the mystical level of his *Bluebird* fantasy was totally missing [from Stanislavski's production]. So, prompted by Isadora Duncan . . . and impressed by the first copy of [Craig's book] *The Mask*, Stanislavski invited Craig to direct *Hamlet* for the Art Theater. (Innes 1983: 149–50)

Samuel Beckett professed admiration for Kleist's story 'On the Marionette Theatre' on more than one occasion and indicated that he was seeking to develop some of its insights into his own performance practice. James Knowlson tells us Beckett visited Kleist's grave in 1969, and knew lines from *The Prince of Homburg* by heart (Knowlson 1996: 569). He also outlines how Beckett made use of and referred to 'On the Marionette Theatre' while rehearsing the production of *Happy Days* he directed at the Schiller-Theatre in Berlin in 1971, in arguing that 'precision and economy would produce the maximum of grace' (584). Then again, in 1975, while assisting at the production of his television play *Ghost Trio*, Beckett spoke with both the principal actor, Ronald Pickup, and with Knowlson about the importance of Kleist's Marionette story to understanding what he was attempting to do in this piece. As Knowlson describes it, Beckett more or less recounted Kleist's story in total. First, he outlined how the principles of grace and harmony, related to the puppets which are detailed in the story, might be applied to the processes he was attempting to develop. Then he recounted the third part of Kleist's story concerning the bear whom, in lacking self-awareness, and so human self-consciousness, therefore possesses both a more precise grace and a more comprehensive intuition with regard to the movement of bodies than any self-conscious person might (632–3).

I will develop a reading of Kleist's story below, considering how it might help us to understand how a different kind of theatre – one which moves away from the inner world of an actor in favour of developing affects which express an external composite world, which includes but is not limited to the actors (who also offer externalised expressions) – is possible, and has been realised in Beckett's works. Yet in order to do this it is at first necessary to define more precisely what is meant by the concepts of 'expression' and 'affect'.

In *Marxism and the Philosophy of Language*, V. N. Volosinov (who may or may not have been a mask used by Mikhail Bakhtin; see Volosinov 1986: Translator's Preface, ix) develops a strong critique of the traditional manner in which the term 'expression' is used, both in the philosophy of language, and more generally in philosophical idealism.

He argues that there are 'two trends of thought in the philosophy of language', though the second does not interest us here. He calls the first 'individualistic subjectivism' and argues that it is linked to a 'romantic' view of language. This notion of self-expression, I would argue, is closely aligned with the understanding developed by Stanislavski. Volosinov criticises individualistic subjectivism's choice of the subject as source by critiquing the conception of expression it presupposes. Individualistic subjectivism requires two elements within the concept of 'expression'. Expression moves from inside the speaker to outside. Thus there has to be something inside which needs to be and can be expressed: an internal something is expressible, and it is an outward objectification of this expressible which is expressed. Yet, if the expressed involves signs, then this concept of the expressible seems to imply a meaning which is prior to signs. To quote Volosinov: 'any theory of expression inevitably presupposes that the expressible is something that can somehow take shape and exist apart from expression; that it exists first in one form and then switches to another form' (84). Volosinov argues that such a theory is built on spiritualistic and idealistic grounds: 'Everything of real importance lies within'; the subject is the source, and language is considered the more or less inadequate messenger of the soul. A false dualism of inside and outside is in this way fabricated. This concept of expression sees expression as always proceeding from inside to outside, requiring interpretation to proceed contrariwise from the outside to the inside.

Volosinov categorically states that such a theory of expression is 'fundamentally untenable', offering the following reasons:

> The experiential, expressible element and its outward objectification are created, as we know, out of one and the same material. After all, there is no such thing as experience outside the embodiment of signs. Consequently, the very notion of a fundamental, qualitative difference between the inner and the outer element is invalid to begin with. Furthermore, the location of the organizing and formative center is not within (i.e., not within the material of inner signs) but outside. It is not experience which organizes expression but the other way around – *expression organizes experience*. (85)

Having developed this critique, Volosinov abandons the use of the term 'expression' altogether. Elsewhere he tends to disparage it by associating it with an understanding of linguistics which draws upon aesthetics, stating that any 'sort of expression is, at the root, artistic' (52). What Volosinov passes over here is that he has, in effect, developed, or rather rediscovered, a different concept of expression; one which involves the purely external rather than a movement from the internal towards the external; one in which expression does indeed organise experience. In the late 1960s Gilles Deleuze, no doubt not thinking of Volosinov's critique (whose work he nonetheless knew well and spoke of in approving terms[1]), describes a concept which seems very similar to that which Volosinov has identified and abandoned, one which Deleuze argues has a long tradition stretching back to the Renaissance.

This concept is developed in Deleuze's reading of Spinoza and Leibniz in *Expressionism in Philosophy: Spinoza*. Here Deleuze outlines an ontological understanding of expression which *does* understand expression as an 'external' process, or at least one in which everything is laid out upon the same plane of immanence (Spinoza's Substance as it is expressed by its attributes, thought and extension). This surface, however, might be folded so that not everything appears visible, through processes of involution and evolution, implication and explication (see Joughin's preface in Deleuze 1990). An understanding of what might be meant by such an externalised concept of expression is important to developing a better knowledge of what is at stake in the ideas of performance apparent in Beckett's practice, which he in turn explained by comparing them to ideas Kleist puts forward in 'On the Marionette Theatre'.

Deleuze outlines how expression is a basic concept for both Spinoza and Leibniz, one which allowed them to overcome difficulties they found in Descartes' system (difficulties which stem from cutting a mechanistic system off from a created world). Deleuze contends that the concept of expression allows them to 'restore a Philosophy of Nature'. He states: 'In Leibniz as in Spinoza expression has theological, ontological and epistemological dimensions. It organizes their theories of God, of creatures and of knowledge' (Deleuze 1990: 17). 'Expression' then, both involves and explains the very process of creation, through which a perfect and absolutely infinite Being (Spinoza's Substance or Nature) expresses itself first through its infinite attributes and then through the infinite number of finite modes which are in turn expressed by the attributes:

> Substance first expresses itself in its attributes, each attribute expressing an essence. But then attributes express themselves in their turn: they express themselves in their subordinate modes, each such mode expressing a modification of the attribute. . . . the first level of expression must be understood as the very constitution, a genealogy almost, of the essence of substance. The second must be understood as the very production of particular things. (14)

The concept of expression, then, is developed to help us to understand the extremely difficult process through which Substance might work through Attributes (Thought and Extension being those we know) to produce particular things. This concept of expression is not founded upon the opposition of an internal and an external; rather, it implicates, or folds in, the idea of that which creates *with* that which is created: the One expresses the many through being 'complicated' (or interfolded) within them. The internal and external, in so far as they are brought into play, are folded out, implicated with one another in ways that make them virtually indistinguishable.

These are challenging ideas, and move us towards highly technical lines of argument. The concept, however, is extremely important to us here, as it allows us to begin to consider how an 'expression', in this case, the staging of a performance, might be viably understood to involve the externalisation of meaningful elements throughout the work; an externalisation which requires each component of the work to function as a part of an interconnected, complicated, single expression. Such a form of performance would not fit well with a theory of acting which sought to embed a series of different and perhaps contradictory individualistically subjective expressions (in Volosinov's sense) within the performance.

I would argue that Beckett drew upon Kleist to better develop his works as univocal expressions (in Deleuze's sense): expressions which, at least ideally, would be absolutely unified within a performance, expressions which would not be diffused by carrying several discrete examples of reinterpretation (the inner meanings judged to exist by the actors) within them. The German actor Ernst Schroeder recounted something of Beckett's attitude to such processes of reinterpretation within the whole:

> Of course I occasionally tried to entice a comment out of the taciturn man as to the psychology of the part. I finally told him that the actor in a rehearsal is studying not only the part, he's also studying himself under the magnifying-glass of the part. And finally, that this magnifying-glass, in this case, was especially obscured by the filter of the author. Beckett, smiling, agreed this was so. (McMillan and Fehsenfeld 1988: 239–40)

Yet even if one were to concede that a practitioner like Beckett might conceive of his works as univocal and externalised expressions, it is apparent that such a practitioner is clearly not working in the manner of Spinoza's Substance. The connection between the performance practitioner and Substance is meant analogically, but this does not mean that it involves a loose metaphor. The word analogy, used rigorously, involves the translation of a thing existing in one medium into a thing existing in a different medium. This translation, in turn, takes place through a proportional equivalence, or ratio, which is maintained across both media. Just as Spinoza's Substance expresses its essence through its attributes in producing its modes through Reason (ratio), or laws of causation, so too a practitioner might be understood to develop a univocal and externalised expression of a given set of ideas, images or affects through the rational ordering and interconnection of all of the elements in play within the performance piece. A cursory reading might consider that this analogy returns us to the misery of the ancient identification of the artist and God, but I would challenge this reading which in any case, would be talking about a different conception of God, and a different conception of the artist to those developed here. As Stephen Dedalus suggests in *Stephen Hero*: 'For Stephen art was neither a copy nor an imitation of nature: the artistic process was a natural process' (Joyce 1963: 171).

The question of how a performance practitioner or any other artist might develop a univocal externalised expression presents itself. Deleuze's understanding of 'affect', which is also developed in part through his reading of Spinoza, helps us to see how this might be possible.

In *What is Philosophy?* Deleuze and Guattari distinguish between three kinds of thought each in its own way capable of creation: philosophic, scientific and artistic. The three forms exist as three separate planes. The philosopher creates concepts on the plane of immanence; the scientist lays down functions on the plane of reference or coordination by creating figures or undertaking partial observations; the artist creates affects or sensations on the plane of composition by describing percepts. These three forms of thought are understood as the three active responses of the human brain faced with the chaos of Being; active and necessarily ongoing responses laying down planes on which their concepts, affects and functions are constantly in movement. These forms are distinguished from 'opinion', a reactive response which pretends that chaos can be tamed once and for all by insisting that concepts, functions and affects can be forever fixed in place. The three forms not only define themselves against chaos then, they are also in constant conflict with opinion which strives to limit their creation.

So, according to Deleuze and Guattari, the artist seeks to create affects (which are not to be confused with emotions). The emotions that the actor brings to bear in performing can behave as a kind of interference to this process. They are interference because they do not relate to the affects which the work itself is seeking to convey. We might line these terms up here with the two understandings of expression detailed above. An affect here refers to an external expression while an emotion refers to an individualistically subjective expression. Therefore a performance might require an actor to suppress extraneous emotion so that an audience might be carried along by the external affects produced by the work as a whole. In the worst cases what is at stake might be related to the struggle between the artistic affect and opinion. In 'finding a character' a method actor might tap into a reservoir of emotions that are readily accessible; a kind of common knowledge. A familiar, easily recognisable emotion might be extracted and projected so that the audience do not sense the unfamiliar affect of the work but rather recognise the familiar emotion offered by the actor: they are thereby comforted in the belief that they have grasped the 'meaning', and the play fails to affect them in the least.

It is worth attempting to develop our understanding of affect more fully here by returning to Spinoza, in relation to whom Deleuze develops his own concept of affect. In Part 3 of Spinoza's *Ethics* an affect is defined as 'the affections of the Body by which the Body's power of acting is increased or diminished, aided or restrained, and at the same time, the ideas of these affections' (Spinoza 1985: 493). In Part 2 of the *Ethics*, these affections are understood to involve our Body's perceptions of the contact it undergoes with other bodies (as for example when light strikes our eyes, a sound strikes our ear drums, something touches us, or when an image of another body occurs to us). An affect, then, is brought about through a causal chain. Just as bodies are caused by other bodies in a chain of cause and effect in Spinoza and, in parallel to this, ideas cause other ideas, so too affects (those sensations of our power increasing or decreasing which come about through the contact with other beings we encounter) develop lines of cause and effect.

One of the radical implications of Spinoza's model of causation, which extends causation into the human mind (and all other modes of the attribute of thought) as well as to all physical things (within the attribute of extension), is that it lays out a line of causation, as it were, on a surface. Spinoza is himself very clear about this idea and the implications of it. Everything is laid open to the laws of causation, the laws of nature, and this includes the human mind and what it thinks, and the human body and what it feels:

> Most of those who have written about the Affects, and men's way of living, seem to treat, not of natural things, which follow the common laws of nature, but of things which are outside nature. Indeed they seem to conceive man in nature as a dominion within a dominion . . . [Yet] nature is always the same, and its virtue and power of acting are always one and the same, i.e., the laws and rules of nature. . . . The Affects, therefore, of hate, anger,

envy, etc., considered in themselves, follow from the very same necessity and force of nature as the other singular things. (491–2)

An affect, then, in a sense similar to that applied to attributes, might be thought to be an expression, a modal expression, which, rather than coming from an inside and moving out, is both caused by what is external and becomes involved with the nature of the person through whom it is expressed (not as something which is simply 'internal' to that person, but which, in effect, allows that person to perceive their self). We can see this more clearly if we turn again to Part 2, Proposition 16 of the *Ethics*, where Spinoza explains how the affections we experience, the idea of being affected by something else (i.e., of coming into contact with something else) involves both the nature of our body and the body we touch. That is, the knowledge we have of anything else (the knowledge of the first kind, from the senses for example) is really, and first and foremost, a knowledge of ourselves, and of how we have been affected: it does not give us a clear idea of the thing we perceive. Yet there is necessarily another way of seeing this: in so far as we do understand ourselves, we can only understand ourselves through the contact we make with other bodies. Our very thought, then, is determined from the outside.

Deleuze offers another way of understanding the same idea of exteriority through his reading of Spinoza's contemporary, Leibniz. In his *Monadology*, written in 1714, Leibniz defines a conception of the individual, the monad, which is individuated from other monads by perceptions of what is external. Each monad reflects the primary monad: the originary simple substance that is God. Only God does not correspond to a compound substance, only God is mind independent of matter. As each monad reflects the infinite monad that is God, the whole of the infinite universe is reflected or perceived within each of the monads. It is something like a hologram which is reputed to contain the whole image within each fragment. Yet each monad is distinct and distinguishes itself through its perceptions. While each perceives everything, each (with the exception of God) perceives most things confusedly. Its power and its nature are defined by what it perceives clearly.

Monads then, are distinguished by perception, which is understood as an internal process, but it is a peculiar kind of internal process as it is completely oriented towards the external. The monad, therefore, somehow seems to come between the dichotomy internal/external, interpreting what is other so that it can distinguish what is the same or the self; and this process is unceasing, since the monad (that which is unchangeable in its parts) changes in accordance with what it perceives.

Its perceptions in turn are equated with its affections. To quote Leibniz from *Principles of Nature and of Grace*:

> one monad, in itself and at a particular moment, can only be distinguished from another by internal qualities and activities, which can be nothing else but its *perceptions* (that is to say, the representations in the simple of the compound or of that which is outside) and its *appetitions* (that is to say, its tendencies to pass from one perception to another), which are the principles of change. (Leibniz 1992b: 195)

What then, are some consequences of this for theatre? In Kleist, according to Deleuze, the self is an illusion created by the jumbling together of minute unrelated perceptions. And this confusion (remembering the chaos evoked in *What is Philosophy?*) is primary, preceding the order that creates transcendent subjects. To quote Deleuze from *The Fold: Leibniz and the Baroque*:

> The prince of Homberg, and all of Kleist's characters, are not so much Romantic as they are Baroque heroes. Prey to the giddiness of minute perceptions, they endlessly reach presence in illusion, in vanishment, in swooning, or by converting illusion into presence. . . . The Baroque artists know well that hallucination does not feign presence, but that presence is hallucinatory. (Deleuze 1993: 125)

What is involved in such a state of affection? The affect of the work of art is unfamiliar: the kind of giddiness or uncertainty with which we are at first threatened is analogous to a kind of death. To quote Leibniz from the *Monadology*:

> But when there are a very great number of small perceptions with nothing to distinguish them, we are stupefied, just as it happens that if we go on turning round in the same direction several times running, we become giddy and go into a swoon, so that we can no longer distinguish anything at all. And death can throw animals into this state for a time. (Leibniz 1992a: 182)

For Deleuze, art should affect rather than be understood, if understanding means only recognising the opinions which accompany the clear interpretations required of method actors, and the subjects they create, in so far as they only express themselves by showing the world commonplace, conflict-free emotions: such emotions will in no way affect us, in no way modify our perceptions (which would involve, following Leibniz, the modification of our souls).

The automatic emotion kills the affect which such a work attempts to create: the audience fails to see beyond the familiar and so are unable to be astonished by affects which are unknown to them. The automatic emotion is safe, by definition it is not new, it is easily recognisable, whereas the unfamiliar and defamiliarising affect is capable of taking the ground away.

These are the kinds of affects Deleuze and Guattari describe in the work of Kleist, where:

> feelings become uprooted from the interiority of 'subject,' to be projected violently outward into a milieu of pure exteriority that lends them an incredible velocity, a catapulting force: love or hate, they are no longer feelings but affects. . . . Affects transpierce the body like arrows, they are weapons of war. The deterritorialization velocity of affect. . . . This element of exteriority – which dominates everything, which Kleist invents in literature, which he is the first to invent – will give time a new rhythm: an endless succession of catatonic episodes or fainting spells, and flashes or rushes. Catatonia is: 'This affect is too strong for me,' and a flash is: 'The power of this affect sweeps me away,' so that the Self (Moi) is now nothing more than a character whose actions and emotions are desubjectified, perhaps even to the point of death. Such is Kleist's personal formula: a succession of flights of madness and catatonic freezes in which no subjective interiority remains. (Deleuze and Guattari 1987: 356)

In Kleist's *The Prince of Homberg*, the eponymous character is swept away by a euphoric affect which drives him to an act of heroism. Later, on being condemned to death for the disobedience this heroism requires, he is lain low by an affect which reduces him to the most pathetic cowardice. In both cases the affect seems to come from outside: first it is caused by the battle which fills him with heroic affection, and then it is caused by seeing the grave that has been newly dug for him, which suffuses him with cowardly affection. Further, the Prince is able to change from one role to the next in a trice in relation to the affect generated by an external situation. This is shown when a notion of fine behaviour sweeps him up in an affect which would, if it were allowed to, lead him to martyrdom.

An understanding of an 'external' expression might help us to begin to judge what Beckett perceives in Kleist's 'On the Marionette Theatre'. In Kleist's story the narrator meets an old friend, a classical dancer, in a park and remarks that the friend seems to be spending a lot of time watching a low-brow puppet show. He wonders what attraction this could possibly have. The friend explains that some of the dance movements performed by the puppets have an extraordinary grace. Agreeing to this point, the narrator wonders why this might be, and the friend replies that this grace can be explained in mathematical terms. The puppet master does not need to control every aspect of the puppet because the movements themselves have a centre of gravity, and the puppets are machines which allow a movement in a straight line to be translated in perfect ratio into a curved movement. Further, these curved movements turn about the true centre of gravity: that is, they are in perfect harmony with the purely physical logic of the movement. The friend further suggests that the relationship between the movement of the puppeteer and the puppet can also be understood in mathematical terms; that is, in terms of ratios or proportions:

> [He said] '. . .there's a subtle relationship between the movements of his fingers and the movements of the puppets attached to them, something like the relationship between numbers and their logarithms or between asymptote and hyperbola'. (Kleist 2003)

When asked to explain what benefits these puppets might have over human dancers, the friend indicates that the first advantage is a negative one: that it would never be guilty of self-consciousness.

Spinoza indicates that we fall into error when we confuse the manner in which causal relations proceed. This occurs when we make mistakes through the first kind of knowledge: we see some other body, for example, and think we understand it because we see it. Yet all that comes to us from that other body through our sight is an image of that other body. Furthermore, when we come into contact with that image, it tells us more about our own selves than it does about that body itself. We fall into error, then, when we attempt to understand through an image of something. This is because an idea can only be understood through another idea; an idea cannot be understood through a body.

This notion might also be seen to be clearly exemplified in Kleist's story. The friend and the narrator continue their discussion and they begin to focus on the idea of self-consciousness. The narrator indicates that he understands very well how self-consciousness might 'disturb natural grace'. He then goes on to describe a young man he knows who possessed a wonderful natural grace, yet once he became conscious of that grace himself and tried to deliberately reproduce it, he simply lost the grace altogether. This happened because he saw himself in the mirror performing a graceful movement. This image of his own movement seemed to offer the first consciousness of his own grace: in Spinozan terms we could say that the image from the mirror is a body which impresses itself on the young man. The young man sees the grace, which is his own grace. He then attempts to reproduce it by repeating the movement in the mirror. This is an error because he is, in effect, attempting to understand the grace of the movement of his body through an image of that movement (what he has seen). He is then unable to reproduce that movement because he did not have any understanding of it before, and the image of the movement cannot give him access to a true understanding of the thing. We can consider this in another way. The young man is like an actor performing a part in a self-conscious manner: that is, creating his movements through imperfect understanding, he falls back on clichés. On the other hand, the work which attempts to create an external expression requires an actor to lose all such self-consciousness, to allow the body, as it were, to follow its own logic without trying to impose an interpretation: to identify centres of gravity around which movements should naturally proceed.

One might interpret the movement of the puppets and the young man when he was unselfconscious, and the bear who is the third example offered in the story, as examples of bodies which move in accord with the laws of nature which have made those bodies. There is an idea which corresponds to the idea of the body and the idea of the movement of the body, but this is not an idea of which any of these three are conscious. In order to fully understand this point, it is important to underline how Spinoza develops a distinction between the attribute of thought and consciousness. In 'On the Difference Between The Ethics and a Morality' Deleuze discusses the devaluation of consciousness (in favour of the attribute of thought) in Spinoza (Deleuze 1988: 17–22). For Spinoza our consciousness itself is always based only on inadequate knowledge. We exist due to the interconnection of an infinity of causal relations: we can only sense at all, think (consciously) at all, because of the incredibly complex interaction of these causes. But we are never really aware of these causes; rather, we only become aware, we only become conscious, in so far as we experience the effects of these causes. Our consciousness of what is real then, is partial and incomplete. We only ever get a mutilated view of the whole, a tiny incoherent fragment. What is truly real is what we are not conscious of: the true interrelationship of causes which allows us to experience effects. When Kleist indicates that the three examples involve a lack of self-consciousness, he allows us to understand how such an unselfconscious entity might develop a movement which is more elegant than that of a person who is consciously attempting to perform such a movement. So too, drawing on Spinoza, Deleuze shows how there is a logic which is proper to bodies and this logic is pure when we attempt to simply perform movements in line with that innate logic. Spinoza also allows us to see how we cannot understand a body (which is in the attribute of extension) through an inadequate idea of that body (which is in the attribute of thought). Deleuze underlines this point in emphasising Spinoza's insistence that 'we don't even know what a body can do' (17–18). In struggling to comprehend our bodies we develop a false or inadequate understanding of ourselves. This in turn is intuitively recognised by others and usually categorised as involving self-consciousness (when it in fact betrays an absence of genuine understanding). This further explains why, following Kleist, in order to return to an equilibrium through which our bodies and minds are perfectly in harmony, we would have to gain either perfect knowledge, or totally rid ourselves of knowledge. The puppet is more perfect because it has no consciousness: the unfallen Adam would also be perfect because he would understand his own body perfectly.

One element that no doubt appealed to Beckett in Kleist's story is the strong interest in how the proportions and ratios of mathematics and geometry might be applied to art. While much work remains to be done on Beckett's use of mathematics, it is clear that he was deeply interested in mathematics and seemed to draw upon it in developing certain of his works. This is apparent in some prose works like *Murphy* with its biscuits, *Molloy* with its sucking stones, and *The Lost Ones* (Beckett 1990) with its crushed cylinder related to pye, but is still more clear in many of the works for theatre and TV, such as *Quad* (Beckett 1995), which involves the exhaustion of a square, or plays such as *What Where* and *Come and Go* (Beckett 1995), which involve the permutation of protagonists. Protagonists are identified by abstract traits such as colour or movement, for example, rather than through particular traits. Beckett is an artist who, as everybody immediately understands, moved further and further towards abstraction as his career developed. It might be argued that this movement towards abstraction was itself a mathematical tendency or involved a growing interest in mathematics. Such a tendency might be reconciled with his own understanding of Spinoza, a philosopher he read but struggled with. In a well-known letter concerning another philosopher, Spinoza's contemporary Arnold Geulincx, Beckett indicates his interest in 'the conviction that the *sub specie aeternitatis* vision is the only excuse for remaining alive' (cited in Knowlson 1996: 219). Beckett was reading Spinoza in Latin and French at the time, which explains this direct citation from Spinoza, drawn from the statement in Part 2 of the *Ethics* that 'It is the nature of Reason to perceive things under a certain species of eternity [*sub specie aeternitatis*]' (Prop. 44).

It is Reason, then, which perceives things under a certain species of eternity, and Reason, as Spinoza also shows us in Part 2, proceeds through abstraction. In Part 2, Prop. 38, we are told that the foundations of Reason are the common notions; that is, those abstract things that every one of us shares in common. On the other hand, Reason has nothing to do with those particular things that make each of us uniquely who we are.[2] Rather, it proceeds from abstract notions (such as the idea of extension itself, the idea of movement and stillness, speed and slowness, the idea of number and proportion, for example). Beckett seems, then, to have been interested in this aspect of Reason, this aspect of the mathematical: the play of cause and effect which takes place at an abstract level. This understanding of Reason, and its role is also, in turn, linked to the concept of expression Deleuze perceives to be at work in Spinoza's system: 'The mind conceives things *sub specie aeternitatis* through having an idea that expresses the body's essence from this point of view. Spinoza's conception of the adequacy of ideas seems always to involve this expressive character' (Deleuze 1990: 15).

A crucial point, felt by many who witnessed Beckett's direction of his own plays, is that the tiny details he attended to were replete with significance: that this minute control was crucial to Beckett's own vision of what his plays were, as much as what they were 'about'. In the introduction to *Beckett in the Theatre: The Author as Practical Playwright and Director*, McMillan and Fehsenfeld note how some sections of their book:

> are concerned with details of text and production – changes of single words, stage diagrams, light and sound cues – which might at first seem intended only for specialists. That is not the case. For Beckett, these details give his plays their shape, which is so important to him. (McMillan and Fehsenfeld 1988: 12)

The word 'shape' alludes to Beckett's well-known statement that in his work he is interested in the shape rather than the substance of ideas (McMillan and Fehsenfeld 1988: 58–9). Perhaps this line of thought is best summarised by the French actor Pierre Chabert, who played Krapp in the 1975 production at the Petite Salle, Theatre d'Orsay:

> Beckett is director long before he actually takes over rehearsals or works with the actors. In this respect he represents a unique example – perhaps even a limit – in the history of the theatre. The actual staging of the play is always written into his texts. They are characterized by a theatrical form of writing in which speech is never dissociated from space or from the concrete language of the stage. Speech is never conceived as being separate from gesture, movement, place, physical position and bodily posture. (Chabert 1980: 85–6)

As Knowlson has noted, Beckett's notebooks 'reveal a careful choreography of word and gesture, sound and silence, movement and stillness . . . all the different elements that are involved in staging a play . . . are . . . intricately integrated with the play's thematics' (Knowlson 1985: 13).

He was attempting to stage a space: the gestures, the qualities of light and voice as well as words and presence. The performance is no longer textualised by the actors and a director, the text extends to the limits of the stage and involves the development of a univocal externalised expression. Time and space are inscribed with 'fundamental sounds' (Schneider quoted in McMillan and Fehsenfeld 1988: 14–15) and motions. Speaking to Rosette Lamont in Paris in 1983, when asked how he began to write drama, Beckett replied: 'When I was working on *Watt* I felt the need to create for a smaller space, one in which I had some control of where people stood or moved, above all of a certain light. I wrote *Waiting for Godot*' (McMillan and Fehsenfeld 1988: 15).

Because of his interest in developing a univocal expression, Beckett, when he directed his own plays, had no choice but to see his actors as 'puppets' akin to Kleist's. That is, he had no choice but to elude the actor's questions concerning the *meaning* of their actions and words. His elusiveness on these points is well documented (see McMillan and Fehsenfeld 1988: 184; Asmus 1975: 20, 24; Chabert 1980: 91, Whitelaw 1978: 87; Schneider 1975: 31). His breaking with Stanislavskian methods is crucial to the development of a univocal expression. Method actors want to know why they do things, they crave motivation, the need to make sense of the character's actions. This approach not only makes it difficult to control the pace of a performance (which is important to the musical structure of the works [see Esslin 1975: 99]), but is highly disruptive within a univocal system.

References

Asmus, W. D. (1975), 'Beckett Directs Godot', *Theatre Quarterly*, V (19): 19–26.
Bair, D. (1990), *Samuel Beckett: A Biography*, London: Vintage.
Beckett, S. (1955), *Molloy*, New York: Grove Press.
Beckett, S. (1957), *Murphy*, New York: Grove Press.
Beckett, S. (1983), *Disjecta: Miscellaneous Writings and a Dramatic Fragment*, edited by Ruby Cohn, London: John Calder.
Beckett, S. (1990), *The Complete Dramatic Works*, London: Faber and Faber.
Beckett, S. (1995), *The Complete Short Prose*, edited by S. Gontarski, New York: Grove Press.
Brater, E. (1989), *Why Beckett*, London: Thames and Hudson.
Chabert, P. (1980), 'Samuel Beckett as Director', trans. M.A. Bonney and J. Knowlson, in J. Knowlson (ed.), *Theatre Workbook 1, Samuel Beckett: Krapp's Last Tape. A Theatre Workbook*, London: Brutus Books.
Craig, E. G. (1956), *On the Art of the Theatre*, New York: Theatre Arts Books.
Deleuze, G. (1988), *Spinoza: Practical Philosophy*, trans. R. Hurley, San Francisco: City Lights.
Deleuze, G. (1990), *Expressionism in Philosophy: Spinoza*, trans. M. Joughin, New York: Zone.

Deleuze, G. (1993), *The Fold: Leibniz and the Baroque*, trans. T. Conley, Minneapolis: University of Minnesota Press.

Deleuze, G. and F. Guattari (1987), *A Thousand Plateaus*, trans. B. Massumi, Minneapolis: University of Minnesota Press.

Deleuze, G. and F. Guattari (1994), *What is Philosophy?* trans. H. Tomlinson and G. Burchell, New York: Columbia University Press.

Esslin, M. (1975), 'Review: "Godot", the Authorized Version' (Schiller Theatre Company at the Royal Court Theatre), *Journal of Beckett Studies*, 1 (Winter): 98–9.

Innes, C. (1983), *Edward Gordon Craig*, Cambridge: Cambridge University Press.

Joyce, J. (1963), *Stephen Hero*, New York: New Directions.

Kleist, H. von (2002), *The Prince of Homburg*, trans. N. Bartlett, London: Oberon.

Kleist, H. von (2003), 'On the Marionette Theatre', trans. I. Parry, *Southern Cross Review*: http://southerncrossreview.org/9/kleist.htm

Knowlson, J. (ed.) (1985), *Happy Days: Samuel Beckett's Production Notebook*, London: Faber and Faber.

Knowlson, J. (1996), *Damned to Fame: The Life of Samuel Beckett*, London: Bloomsbury.

Leibniz, G. W. (1992a), 'Monadology. 1714', trans. M. Morris and G. H. R. Parkinson, in G. H. R. Parkinson (ed.), *Philosophical Writings*, London: J. M. Dent.

Leibniz, G. W. (1992b), 'Principles of Nature and of Grace. 1714', trans. M. Morris and G. H. R. Parkinson, in G. H. R. Parkinson (ed.), *Philosophical Writings*, London: J. M. Dent.

McMillan, D. and M. Fehsenfeld (1988), *Beckett in the Theatre: The Author as Practical Playwright and Director. Volume 1: From 'Waiting for Godot' to 'Krapp's Last Tape'*, London: John Calder.

Schneider, A. (1975), '"Any Way You Like, Alan": Working with Beckett', *Theatre Quarterly*, V (19): 27–38.

Spinoza, B. (1985), *The Collected Works of Spinoza*, Volume 1, trans. E. Curley, Princeton, NJ: Princeton University Press.

Volosinov, V. N. (1986), *Marxism and the Philosophy of Language*, trans. L. Matejka and I. R. Titunik, Cambridge MA: Harvard University Press.

Whitelaw, B. (1978), 'Practical Aspects of Theatre, Radio and Television: Extracts from an unscripted interview with Billie Whitelaw by James Knowlson. A television recording made on 1 February 1977 for the University of London Audio-Visual Centre', *Journal of Beckett Studies*, 3 (Summer): 85–90.

Notes

1. Deleuze and Guattari indicate that Volosinov's book, *Marxism and the Philosophy of Language*, offers 'a theory of enunciation that goes beyond the traditional categories of linguistics' (Deleuze and Guattari 1987: 523, fn. 5).

2. It is interesting, then, that Beckett, in his later work, might be thought to be turning away from what seemed a fundamental premise at the beginning of his career. One which he outlined in his first published essay, 'Dante . . . Bruno. Vico . . . Joyce': that 'Poetry is [most perfect] when concerned with particulars' (Beckett 1983: 24).

Chapter 4

A Theatre of Subtractive Extinction: Bene Without Deleuze

Lorenzo Chiesa

I'd like to be Watson. . . . Watson doesn't understand a fuck, whenever he acts he does it at random. He is inactive even in the action that runs him. Being unable to enjoy the inorganic (it looks like it is not possible), maybe Watson is the thing that has so far been able to bewitch and enchant me. The most complete insignificance. Have you seen the vacuous faces they foist on the various Watsons, while all the other actors are always a bit hypertensive? Yes, I'd like to be Watson. (Bene and Dotto 1998: 279–80)

Sì proviamo con la vita
quotidiana e si vedrà!
Al lavoro del piacere
senza remora e decoro
il piacere del lavoro
basta qui sostituir!
(Bene 2002: 323)

In the introduction to *Difference and Repetition* (1968), Deleuze singles out Kierkegaard and Nietzsche as two thinkers of repetition who have introduced radically innovative means of expression into philosophy by elaborating an anti-representational notion of movement. These authors invent a philosophy that directly proposes itself as a theatrical philosophy, a philosophy in the guise of theatre. For Kierkegaard and Nietzsche, it is a question of 'producing within the [philosophical] work a movement capable of unsettling the spirit outside of all representation; it is a question of making movement itself a work, without interposition' (Deleuze 1994: 8). Such movement should therefore be contrasted with Hegel's 'abstract logical' movement, a 'false movement', which is itself represented in that it dialectically relies on opposition and mediation. While Kierkegaard and Nietzsche intend to set philosophy as such in motion *as* a theatre of 'immediate acts', Hegel is unable to go beyond the much simpler idea of a philosophical theatre:

he cannot 'live', as a philosopher, 'the problem of masks . . . the inner emptiness of masks' (8).[1]

Deleuze's interest in the anti-representational power of theatre as real movement re-emerges punctually ten years later in 'One Less Manifesto' (1978), the text he dedicates to the controversial Italian dramatist Carmelo Bene. For Deleuze, Bene's irreverent interpretations of theatre's great figures, Shakespeare in particular, promote a theatre of 'non-representation', that is to say, 'unleash . . . an always unstable non-representative force' that presents without representing, 'renders a potentiality present and actual' (Deleuze 1997: 241–2, 256, 254).[2] In this later article however, Deleuze stresses the importance of the *subtractive* method adopted by Bene's pursuit of the real movement of anti-representational theatre. On the one hand, *Difference and Repetition* identifies the 'essence' of (theatrical) movement in nothing other than repetition: 'The theatre of repetition is opposed to the theatre of representation, just as movement is opposed to the concept and to the representation which refers it back to the concept' (Deleuze 1994: 10). On the other hand, 'One Less Manifesto' assumes that the perpetual motion of what Deleuze repeatedly calls here 'continuous variation' – also understood in terms of 'lines of flight' and the 'power of a becoming' – is initiated and sustained by subtraction (Deleuze, 1997: 247, 255).[3]

Deleuze observes that Bene's adaptations invariably begin by subtracting an element from the original work they critically interpret. For instance, in his *Romeo and Juliet*, Bene does not hesitate to 'neutralise' Romeo: this amputation makes Shakespeare's original work oscillate but, at the same time, it allows Bene to develop the character of Mercutio – who dies very early on in Shakespeare. Beyond mere parody, subtraction thus paves the way to the gradual constitution *on stage* of an otherwise mostly virtual character, un-represented in and by the text. More importantly, according to Deleuze, such constitution challenges the very notion of representation inasmuch as what we witness on stage is an unrelenting process of deformation, an anamorphic movement. This is especially clear in Bene's S.A.D.E., where the prosthetic character of the slave tirelessly 'seeks himself, develops himself, metamorphosizes himself, experiments with himself . . . in relation to the deficiencies and impotencies of the master' (Deleuze 1997: 240). The de-formed subjectivity of the slave – who in vain keeps on changing his dresses and masks in order to stimulate the sexual apathy of his master – is subordinated to and dependent on movement and speed. In the end, the subtractive creation of the Benean character amounts to a perpetual de-formation that avoids representation precisely in so far as it follows a line of continuous variation.

Moving from these premises, the purpose of this chapter is twofold. First, I aim to question Deleuze's tacit replacement of repetition with subtraction as the key notion in his account of anti-representational theatre, and especially to see whether his own interpretation of this notion is appropriate to understanding Bene's work. Second, I intend to problematise the way in which such a shift towards subtraction runs parallel to a *politicisation* of Bene's theatre – the title of the final and most crucial section of 'One Less Manifesto' is, significantly enough, 'Theatre and its Politics'. Here, Deleuze seems more interested in investigating philosophically the politics of theatre rather than focusing on theatre as philosophy and philosophy as theatre as he did in *Difference and Repetition* – where his main concern was 'a theatre of the future' that is at the same time 'a new philosophy' (Deleuze 1994: 8). I shall argue that Deleuze politicises Bene's theatre in an untenable way; I shall also show how an analysis of the philosophical presuppositions of such a misleading political interpretation throws some light on the reasons why Deleuze shrinks away from the notion of repetition in 'One Less Manifesto'.

It is doubtless the case that, in 'One Less Manifesto', Deleuze returns to theatre in order to develop his earlier critique of dialectical opposition as mediation and to dwell on the notion of anti-representational 'immediate acts'. According to him, 'Bene's theatre never develops itself in relations of . . . opposition', it shuns the representation of conflict, 'regardless of its "toughness" and "cruelty"'; any relation of opposition would indeed necessarily lead him back to a traditional 'system of power and domination' (Deleuze 1997: 248–9).[4] Such a system is precisely what Bene politically subtracts from the stage: or better, it is that which in being subtracted supports relations of variation that are anti-oppositional. The pre-emptive neutralisation of master characters, the representatives of power, causes the emergence of a continuous variation in minor characters – epitomised by the slave in *S.A.D.E.* More concretely, this anti-oppositional variation corresponds to the continuous hindrances by which Bene's handicapped minor characters are defined in the act of their de-formative creation (for instance, 'costumes limiting movement instead of aiding it, props thwarting change of place, gestures either too stiff or excessively "soft"') (248).

We could argue that continuous variation – for instance, 'the costume that one takes off and puts back on, that falls off and is put back on' (248) – is itself repetitive, that repetition as real anti-oppositional movement still silently informs Deleuze's reading of Bene. As such, the notion of subtractive continuous variation would be nothing else than a specification of the 'multiplication' of the 'superimposed masks' with which, according to *Difference and Repetition*, Nietzsche fills in the 'inner emptiness' of the 'theatrical space' of subjectivity (Deleuze 1994: 9). The 'gesture in perpetual and positive imbalance' that, for Deleuze, effectively captures continuous variation in Bene's theatre, clearly echoes the 'gestures which develop before organised bodies, masks before faces, spectres and phantoms before characters' of what *Difference and Repetition* calls a 'theatre of repetition' (Deleuze 1994: 10; 1997: 248). Having said this, we should nevertheless bear in mind that Deleuze's discussion of Nietzsche and Kierkegaard in the very same introductory pages explicitly deems repetition to be incompatible with the operation of subtraction, understood here in terms of extraction. Quite bluntly, for Deleuze, one must not subtract/extract anything from repetition – repetition as 'something new' – given that 'only contemplation, the spirit that contemplates from the outside, "extracts"'; one should 'act', not subtract/extract, if one wishes to undo representation (Deleuze 1994: 6).[5] Without entering into the manner in which these passages could hint at the presence of a presumed turning point in Deleuze's thought, I would like on the contrary to further complicate this apparent inconsistency assuming – beyond terminological confusion – a substantial continuity in his work of the decade 1968–78. It is precisely because, as we have just seen, we could easily speak of an anti-representational theatre of subtractive repetition and repetitive subtraction with regard to 'One Less Manifesto' that Deleuze's avoidance of the term repetition – never mentioned in the entire article – becomes all the more intriguing and significant.[6]

Among the virtues of Deleuze's interpretation of Bene's theatre is the way in which it characterises it as an anti-historical theatre of the immediate (Deleuze 1997: 242, 254). For Bene, what is immediate – the time *Aion* – is the act that suspends the actions of history – the time *Kronos*. Theatre must be anti-representational in so far as it needs to recuperate the anti-historical elements of history. As Bene has it, 'the history we live, the history that has been imposed on us, is nothing other than the result of the other histories that this very history had to oust in order to affirm itself' (Attisani and Dotti 2004: 90, 20–21). The principal task of theatre is therefore to 'wage war' on history. Theatre must stage the 'historical possibilities' that are unmediated by history, and these may well include the potentialities of a written text (for instance, the life of Mercutio). Such staging is literally ob-scene, Bene says, since it lies 'outside the scene', outside the representations of official history and its literature, in spite of being materially put on stage (90). In other words, Bene's theatre intends to remain non-performable (*irrappresentabile*), and in this way avoid representation, while nevertheless creating a performance (*spettacolo*) (21). Deleuze is thus correct in emphasising that Bene's characters – first and foremost the slave in *S.A.D.E.* – are in continuous variation precisely because they do not 'master' their role on stage. 'The slave hinders and impedes himself in the continuous series of his own metamorphoses, because he must not *master* his role of *slave*' (Deleuze 1997: 248).[7] As Bene himself has it in his introduction to *S.A.D.E.*, far from being a parody of Hegel, this play 'mortifies', 'liquidates and un-puts on stage' the Hegelian dialectic of master and slave (Bene 2002: 275; Bene and Dotto 1998: 320). In not mastering himself as slave, the slave *does not represent* 'the reverse image of the master, nor his replica or contradictory identity' (Deleuze 1997: 240, 248). Like Deleuze's philosophy, which condemns Hegelian creation since it 'betrays and distorts the immediate' (Deleuze 1994: 10) to the extent that – as summarised by Peter Hallward – it 'concedes too much to history' (Hallward 2006: 100), Bene's theatre of immediate acts against actions refuses dialectical mediation and the notion of history that goes with it.

A further merit of Deleuze's reading lies in his identification of subtraction with the method by means of which Bene's theatre achieves the suspension of actions and the subsequent emergence of acts. As we have seen, Deleuze tracks down the subtractive method in Bene's pre-emptive elimination, or neutralisation, of the representatives of power (and history) – for example, the master's impotence that supports the basic plot of *S.A.D.E.* In the introductions to his plays as well as in his numerous theoretical writings, Bene repeatedly acknowledges that, for him, staging a performance corresponds to a 'removing' from the scene (Bene 2002: 275). He even often uses the very term 'subtraction': for instance, he concedes that 'a man of theatre who practices anti-theatre . . . subtracts' (Bene and Dotto 1998: 149). Similarly, what is truly obscene in theatre is 'by definition what subtracts itself from the concept', *in primis* the historical concept of stage representation (31); in other words, the staging of the anti-historical elements of history always depends on subtraction (234–5).

Having said this, the problem is that, according to Bene, subtraction should aim at what he succinctly defines as an 'intestinal and visceral zero' (149). Is this subtraction towards the inorganic, which I will call a subtraction towards *extinction*, compatible with Deleuze's use of the notion of subtraction in 'One Less Manifesto'? I would suggest that it is not, despite Bene's display of unconditional admiration for Deleuze in general – 'Gilles has been the greatest thinking machine of this century' (326) – and his grasp of theatre in particular – 'the author of *Difference and Repetition* is *naturaliter* a lucid connoisseur of theatre' (Bene 2002: 1166). Deleuze reads Bene through a vitalist notion of subtraction, one that aims to achieve an 'intensive variation of affects' as the 'one and the same continuum' by excluding any negation whatsoever (Deleuze 1997: 249, 251). This kind of subtraction where every elimination and amputation always already unleashes a proliferation of 'potentialities of becoming' without any intervening negative gap is as such inapplicable to Bene (242).[8]

As a matter of fact, one of the most recurrent motifs in Bene's writings is the idea that the human being is an excremental living abortion: 'Life ends there where it begins. Everything is already written in the fetid state, not the foetal one. What remains is only flesh that is going off' (Bene and Dotto 1998: 7, 9, 18–19). For Bene, the individual body exclusively pursues its de-individuation since life is nothing other than continual putrefaction: the apparatus of representation – which ultimately serves the reproduction of the human species to the detriment of individuals – prevents most people from acknowledging this state of affairs before they reach a terminal state. ('They need a metastasis to realise it. They do not feel in metastasis any earlier, when they "flower"' [14, 36].) Against such perverted dissimulation, obscene theatre as the *o-skenè* that undermines the field of representation by subtracting itself from it intends to promote the 'freezing of the species' (34–5). In this context, Bene elaborates an original notion of porn: porn is ob-scene, but not erotic. While on the one hand, following Schopenhauer, the sighs of lovers are actually the whimpering of the species, on the other, porn is 'what cadaverises itself, what makes itself available as mere object. In porn [there] are only two objects that annihilate themselves reciprocally. Can you imagine two stones copulating? It gives you an idea.' For this reason, Bene concludes, there is no desire in porn: the two must be clearly distinguished; correcting a suggestion made by his friend Klossowski for whom 'porn is the beyond *of* desire', Bene concludes that porn is rather 'what exceeds desire' and is thus unrelated to it (35).[9]

It seems to me impossible to reconcile the porn aspirations of such an ob-scene theatre of inorganic de-individuation, and eventually extinction, with the philosophical prominence that Deleuze grants to desire. In 'One Less Manifesto', he curiously never associates the 'intensive variation of affects' set free by Bene's subtractive theatre to desire, yet it goes without saying that this very variation inevitably implies 'an immanent conception of desire with no aim outside its own active deployment and renewal, an affirmative force' (Schuster 2008: n.p.).[10] Deleuze is at his best when he accounts for Bene's subtractive method in terms of the continuous variation of gestures and language dictated by apraxia and aphasia. In Bene's plays, an aphasic work on language converges with a work of obstruction on things and gestures. 'Costumes never ceas[e] falling off . . . one must always surmount objects instead of using them', while, in parallel, diction is 'whispered, stammered, and deformed', sounds are either 'barely audible or deafening' (Deleuze 1997: 248). Yet, for what we have just said about Bene's theatre of porn obscenity, Deleuze goes completely astray when he equates subtractive apraxia and aphasia with the political quest for an affirmative *ars erotica*. Without knowing it, 'the initial stammering and stumbling' pursue 'the Idea [that] has become visible, perceptible, the politics [that] has become erotic' (251).[11] Even more problematically, given his detailed analysis of *S.A.D.E.* in 'One Less Manifesto', Deleuze remains strangely silent on the telling conclusion of this play, which, in my opinion, should be taken as a paradigm of Bene's theatre. The slave continually varies his hindered camouflages, aiding the transgressive situations he simulates to stimulate an erection in his master; yet such transformations, such subtractive developments, are ultimately aimed at *his own* extinction. The extinction of the master as master, his decision to close down his firm and go bankrupt in order to finally work and enjoy – as Bene has it, 'only Work can give Monsieur some sort of erection' (Bene 2002: 325)[12] – is followed in the finale by the literal cancellation of the slave. Taking off his make-up, the slave actually 'cancels his face' while reading the following words: 'Thou shalt stop making a spectacle of yourself' ('*Non darai piu' spettacolo di te*') (349). This sentence must be mumbled, Bene specifies, 'in the guise of a funeral service or a lullaby for the void'. The play then ends.

At this stage, it should be clear that the concept of continuous variation is insufficient to adequately understand Bene's anti-representational theatre. Subtraction cannot be confined to the initial elimination of the representatives of power – for instance, the reduction of the Sadean master to an impotent 'masturbatory tic' – nor, conversely, can it be fully exhausted by the positive un-mastered becoming of minor characters that benefit from such amputation. Rather, Bene's subtraction amounts to a negative and finite becoming towards extinction as de-individuation. For Deleuze, variation must never cease: as he points out in 'One Less Manifesto', 'it is necessary that variation never stops varying itself' (Deleuze 1997: 254);[13] Deleuze thus indirectly admits that subtractive variation is after all a form of endless repetition. On the contrary, for Bene, variation eventually stops at the point of extinction: repetition as subtraction is only possible within the domain of the signifier and its theatrical distortion. There are no intensive forces, no becoming, at the level of the inorganic porn, the ideal goal of theatre that would also correspond to its demise.

In both 'One Less Manifesto' and the dense pages he dedicates to Bene's cinema in *L'image-temps*, Deleuze seems finally to acknowledge that Benean subtraction is always oriented towards extinction when he dwells on what Bene himself calls 'the "secret" of dis-grace' (Bene and Dotto 1998: 222). Deleuze proposes that Benean subtraction corresponds to the 'operation of grace' as dis-grace: we escape representation, 'we save ourselves, we become minor, only by the creation of a dis-grace', a series of corporeal (aphasic and apraxic) deformities (Deleuze 1997: 243).[14] Disgraceful subtraction as the 'power to disappear' gives us a body that is no longer visible – that is, represented – and eventually leads us to the achievement of the 'Schopenhauerian point [as] the point of non-desire [*non-vouloir*]' (Deleuze 1989: 191).[15] Here, Deleuze does not discuss the way in which aphasic and apraxic subtraction can be regarded as both the becoming invisible of the body and – as previously noted – the becoming visible of the Idea. But even more problematically, he then suggests that the dis-graceful point of non-desire is followed in Bene's characters by a 'starting all over again' (*reprendre tout*) (190).[16] I must say I find this conclusion utterly unconvincing. While it may well be the case that, even for Bene, life as continual putrefaction knows no extinction, given what we have seen, how could his theatre aim at a new beginning? What about the *o-skenè* of inorganic porn as the '*freezing* of the species'?

In the chapter of *Out of This World* devoted to the concept of creative subtraction, Peter Hallward has elegantly shown that, for Deleuze, the path of extinction – entirely dependent on the intervention of grace in mystics such Eckhart – should at all costs be opposed to that of subtractive individuation (Hallward 2006: 84–5). Only the latter can be truly creative: as Hallward has it, 'creation would cease to be creative if it collapsed into extinction' (84). I would suggest that, in stark contrast to this position, Bene attempts to elaborate an anti-representational theatre where creation is *only* possible as subtraction towards *de*-individuating extinction. The trajectory of the slave in *S.A.D.E.* perfectly exemplifies how repeated subtractive acts are indispensable to actively reach de-individuation. Yet, moving beyond theatre, complete de-individuation – the obscenity of porn – remains asymptotically unreachable before natural death occurs. Precisely in so far as de-individuation should be an active process towards the inorganic that must not be reduced to the vague idea of natural death – remember, 'life ends where it begins' – but will anyway be passively imposed on us by death, all we can do to be creative is to accompany putrefaction. As Bene writes, 'we are shit, no metaphor intended. The important thing is to know it. Take cognisance of this [*prendere atto*] and flush the toilet, that is, transform it into act [*trasformare in atto*]' (Bene and Dotto 1998: 87).

Passages like this should keep us from confusing Bene's subtraction oriented towards de-individuating extinction with Deleuze's subtraction oriented towards the virtual. When Bene speaks of life as a 'mis-deed' that continually 'escapes itself' and in which 'what matters is never realised', he is not in the least hinting at the virtual, an underlying creative power of life that would be enclosed by the representational apparatus of the actual. For him, life is rather a misdeed in the sense that, again, 'life is your own death that plunges down on you hour after hour' (86–7). Even if we sympathise with Hallward's argument according to which the essence of the Deleuzian notion of creation lies in the process of counter-actualisation, there remains an insurmountable difference between Deleuze and Bene on this issue. Both authors believe that only the actual can counter-actualise, that is to say, counter-actualisation does not depend on a sudden emergence of the virtual. However, if on the one hand, for Deleuze, counter-actualisation is, as Hallward observes, creative 'like everything else' – and 'counter-actualisation will thereby become indistinguishable from the virtual' (Hallward 2006: 87, 83) – on the other, for Bene, *only counter-actualisation is creative*. Bene himself perfectly captures this subtle but crucial point when he specifies that what is ultimately at stake in flushing the toilet that we are – or counter-actualisation – is the issue of *creative defecation*. In opposition to any 'vitalist artifice', any 'daydreaming about a flesh that is different from that available' – any anti-Oedipal body without organs, we may add – we should readily admit that we are nothing other than black holes and attach a '*creative* paternity to defecation' (Bene and Dotto 1998: 256–7).

It should, then, come as no surprise that Bene also understands subtraction towards asymptotic extinction, the only possible creative process, in terms of *addition*. The '"secret" of dis-grace' is nothing other than the inversely proportional relation between subtractive and additive methods: 'The more you add, the more you take away. A plus equals three times minus. *Additions-subtractions*' (222). With specific regard to theatre, this means that Bene's ob-scenity cannot be limited to the continuous variation of gestures and language dictated by apraxia and aphasia. These explicitly subtractive methods are indeed paralleled and boosted by additive ones: for instance, the use of lyrical archaisms, a more general adoption of literary and poetical clichés, as well as the very privileging of classics (Shakespeare *in primis*) over the avant-garde. As noted by Giancarlo Dotto, additive grace as subtractive disgrace means that, in Bene, 'a kind of abused indulgence in lyricism is reversed into the "deformity" of a paradoxical and untreatable writing' (221). Bene himself is quite clear on this point when he refuses to confine the 'secret' of dis-grace to 'the Artaudian or Rabelaisian somersaults on language'. In so far as only the actual can counter-actualise, subtraction can and must also be gained by subjecting oneself to 'the yoke of the *bello scrivere*, to style' (222). Lyrical additive 'exasperation' is what most effectively allows us to 'subtract a given topic from the banality of what is actual' (245).[17]

Here, it is important to stress that, given the overlapping of addition with subtraction *within subtraction itself*, Bene's theatre relies on an original notion of *creative negation* through repetition, one that should not be associated with any conciliatory synthesis in spite of its emphasis on extinction. The 'additions-subtractions' repeatedly operated on the signifier by theatrical acts as im-mediate events 'must forget the finality of [the] actions' they disrupt and, most importantly, the finality of disruption itself. Im-mediate acts carry out a form of negation that is first and foremost vain, gratuitous, and hence repeated. As suggested by Maurizio Grande, Bene is primarily interested in the 'greatness of missing the aim' (*a grandezza del non andare a colpo*) (237). What is more, even though the 'additions-subtractions' may hypothetically achieve organic extinction, the latter amounts to an anti-vitalist – and non-repetitive – continual putrefaction which can in no way be regarded as synthetic.

In his recent article 'In Praise of Negativism', Alberto Toscano has noted that while 'Deleuze's vision of art qua resistance is . . . famously pitted against the negativity of lack and the dialectic', it is also at the same time 'shot through by a profound destructive impetus' (Toscano 2008: 62). This component emerges clearly in the treatment of Melville's Bartleby as a work (and a character) that unleashes, in Deleuze's own words, 'a *negativism* beyond all negation' (Deleuze 1998: 71).[18] Why then is Deleuze unprepared to acknowledge a negativist dimension in Bene's theatre? Why does he read Bene's subtraction as continuous variation without ever referring to negation or negativism? And, most crucially, why is such negativist variation never explicitly related to repetition? This is all the more puzzling considering the fact that, moving outside the domain of art and leaving aside the analysis of theatrical repetition carried out in *Difference and Repetition*, Deleuze had already extensively dwelled upon the relation between creative negation and repetition in the 1962 book on Nietzsche. In this text, Nietzsche's eternal return of the same is conceived as an affirmation that *must* contain negation: indeed, 'a yes that is not able to say no . . . is a false yes' (Deleuze 1983: 178). I would thus suggest that Deleuze's reading of Bene skilfully avoids thinking the connection between subtraction and creative negation on the one hand (as elaborated in *Essays Critical and Clinical*) and between creative negation and repetition on the other (as elaborated in *Nietzsche and Philosophy*). In so far as Bene's anti-vitalism lies at the intersection of these two relations, their open thematisation – not to mention an analysis of their reciprocity, that is, the fact that subtraction is repetitive and repetition is subtractive – would have obliged Deleuze to assume the primacy of negation over affirmation in Bene's theatre. From this would have also followed the impossibility of appropriating it for a minor vitalist politics. We should always bear in mind that what is ultimately at stake in 'One Less Manifesto', but also in *Essays Critical and Clinical,* is in one way or another the ontological 'power of a becoming' that, following Toscano, 'allow[s] literature' and art in general 'to issue into Life' (Toscano 2008: 66).

Bene's rejection of a vitalist understanding of life as the continuous variation of 'pure forces' – the 'terrible power' (*puissance terrible*) that, according to *Difference and Repetition*, accounts ontologically for the theatre of repetition (Deleuze 1994: 10) – is unquestionable. Not only, as we have seen, is life nothing other than perpetual putrefaction, but this very process cannot even be understood in terms of movement; according to Bene, conceiving of life as becoming already presupposes the adoption of the standpoint of representation. The inorganic does not move, it does not become; 'everything that moves, produces itself, is vulgar', while 'what is inanimate is never vulgar even if it stinks'. Thus, the negative creations of anti-representational theatre are not real movements: anti-representational theatre rather recovers 'traces of putrefaction', it shows how a simple 'hair, burp, or fart suffice to move from a circumscribed damage to metastasis'. Everything else is just 'essays on life that replace life . . . Doctor Heidegger's ontological farts' (Bene and Dotto 1998: 88).

In this context, it is plausible to suggest that Bene tacitly postulates a fundamental and twofold impotence that is inherent to human life as such: as we have seen, representation ultimately serves reproduction and the preservation of the species, but why is representation needed in the first place? Why can humans not simply reproduce while increasingly de-individuating themselves as organisms like all other animals? Although Bene never explicitly asks himself this question in his writings, he seems to start off from the general premise that *homo sapiens* is characterised, as a species, by a biological handicap which is itself both compensated for and redoubled by a symbolic handicap, that is, the apparatus of representation and language. From this standpoint, creative negation via subtraction would amount to actively giving oneself up to the anti-representational component of language, being spoken by the signifier. Such forsaking would itself ultimately achieve, outside of any predetermined finality, the extinction of the species and the abolition of representation along with it.

In order to substantiate this point, which is in my opinion crucial for a correct understanding of Bene's ob-scene theatre, we should pay particular attention to what he says about Lacan's notion of the signifier and the fact that discourse never 'belongs' to the speaking being (Bene and Dotto 1998: 334). Bene's theoretical works abound with illuminating references to Lacan. In one instance, he goes as far as proposing that his entire theatrical enterprise revolves around the question of the signifier: 'Ever since my early performances . . . I have put the question of the "signifier" to myself, even before taking note of Jacques Lacan's enormous work' (138). While Bene deliberately adopts Deleuzian terminology in renaming the actor as an 'actorial machine', he does not hesitate to understand the de-individuating process enacted by this very machine – its catalysis of the 'vocation for the inorganic' – as, first and foremost, an 'abandonment to the whims of the signifier' (137). In other words, machinic de-individuation is not a vitalist line of flight; rather, machinic de-individuation corresponds to acknowledging that we are always spoken by the signifier and, more importantly, *actively* surrendering to our predicament. (What Lacan would have seen as the impossibility of *choosing* psychosis as a way of being *fully* spoken by the signifier.) As Bene writes, since 'we are *handicapped* by this mass of signifiers that we ourselves put on stage, all we can do is abolish ourselves as signified, both in the body and the voice' (138).

Judging from sentences like this, Deleuze would then be correct in focusing on the centrality of aphasic and apraxic handicaps in Bene's theatre. Furthermore, it would seem to be inevitable to equate Bene's handicapped performances – in which 'stammering, hampering one's saying' is seen as synonymous with 'genius' (146) – with what Toscano defines as the creative 'achievement of a kind of speechlessness' (Toscano 2008: 62) in Deleuze's artistic minor heroes (Bartleby, Beckett, Artaud, Gherasim Luca, etc.). However, Bene importantly specifies that such stammering and hampering indicate in the end nothing else than a vital 'damage' (*guasto*): the ingeniousness of being 'at the mercy of signifiers' is therefore always already a 'regression to idiocy' (Bene and Dotto 1998: 146, 221). In a rare passage that seems to be criticising precisely Deleuze's idea of art, Bene further contends that all 'literature, major *and minor*, is . . . a *simulation of life* [that] avoids surgery', perpetual putrefaction – in other words, minor literature as a departure from life as putrefaction remains an 'inconsiderate therapy of impotent inertia' (122, emphasis added). In contrast, Bene prefers to understand his theatre as anti-therapeutic in the wake of Lacanian psychoanalysis. Just as in Lacan's 'analytic theatre . . . the anxious demands of the patient-spectator are never attended to or healed but . . . left to suffer', so in Bene's theatre the tormenting crux of human life as vital damage 'is sent back to the sender and amplified to the point of rendering it intolerable. Spectators witness my gestures (apraxia) and my words (aphasia) insofar as they find there their own disguised dilemma' (332).

Further evidence of Bene's unrelenting anti-vitalism can be recovered in his critique of transgression. Anti-therapeutic theatre 'transgresses transgression', Bene says (334). The anti-anti-Oedipal master in *S.A.D.E.* cries out 'I want to *marry* my daughter!' precisely because incest without marriage transgresses nothing, it does not cure his impotence (Bene 2002: 297, emphasis added). (Human) life is also damaged in the sense that it lacks enjoyment, independently of the restrictions imposed by the Law. Rather, in Bene's theatre, enjoyment is only possible *within* the limits of Law: this is the principal message underlying the master–slave anti-dialectic relation in *S.A.D.E.* Throughout the first act of the play, the slave attempts to arouse the master's lust by involving him in a long series of simulated transgressions of the Law. Nothing works: stealing, feeling remorse for having burnt one's city, systematically destroying one's own family (committing incest and selling one's wife and daughter) are not even sufficient to induce an erection. His hand frantically moving in his pocket, the master is reduced to an unproductive masturbatory tic. In the end, it is only when a girl is persuaded to steal and then reported to the police that the master is able to ejaculate: as specified by Bene, the only sadistic act that makes the master enjoy is achieved '*in the name of the Law*' (276). Transgression is successful only when it becomes *inherent* transgression, the Law's own transgression; therefore transgression is ultimately not transgressive at all: as Lacan had already noted, the Sadean hero exclusively enjoys for the Other, that is, he enjoys as a masochist.[19] Thus, Bene's impotent libertine who can literally ejaculate only in the face of the slave disguised as policeman refutes the general Sadean fantasy of a Nature that enjoys through the continuous succession of generation and destruction imposed by the sadist on the human body. Against Sade's law of desire, against his impossible imperative to transgress the Law and always enjoy more, Bene relocates enjoyment within the dialectic of Law and desire.

How could we ever relate such an anti-vitalist notion of desire as always subjected to the Law with Deleuze's reading of Bene's 'minor' theatre as the battleground of a political conflict between two forces, the power of the law (its desire) and the desiring 'outside' that always exceeds it? (In their book on Kafka, Deleuze and Guattari speak even more explicitly of artistic minority in terms of a recovery of desire *in the place* of the law: '*Where one believed there was the law, there is in fact desire and desire alone*' [Deleuze and Guattari 1986: 49].) In other words, how can Deleuze speak of Benean theatre as a theatre for which 'minority indicates the power [*puissance*] of a becoming' as distinct from a 'majority that indicates the power [*pouvoir*] or *impotence* of a state'? (Deleuze 1997: 255, emphasis added).[20] Deleuze clearly overlooks the fact that, for Bene, impotence is a precondition for *both* the master who does not subtract himself from representation *and* the slave who develops subtractively in order to attain his own anti-representational extinction. Like the master, the slave only enjoys masochistically for the Other, that is, he enjoys doing everything possible to help Monsieur to come – we are told that, on this level, 'the cause of his master is his own cause' (Bene 2002: 311). Yet, while the master still needs to accept that enjoyment is always given within the limits of Law, the slave has already realised this, and uses this very realisation to subtract himself from the Law and ultimately abandon it. There is no doubt that the slave's extinction, which is, significantly enough, only possible after the master has himself enslaved his desire to the Law, will at the same time put an end to his own enjoyment.

In a little-known 1976 interview with Gigi Livio and Ruggiero Bianchi, Bene commends Deleuze and Guattari's book on Kafka for the way in which it evinces that 'there is no subject that delivers a statement or subject whose statement is being delivered'. At the same time, he nevertheless reproaches them for 'not fully assuming anti-historicism' (Attisani and Dotti 2004: 55–6). Although Bene does not further substantiate this criticism, I think he is here indirectly pointing at a fundamental difference between his method of creative subtraction towards putrefying extinction and Deleuze's (and Guattari's) method of creative subtraction towards an infinite proliferation of intensive Life. As we have seen, Deleuze correctly interprets Bene's theatre as an anti-historical theatre of the immediate act that suspends the actions of history.

The problem is that, for Bene, such suspension should affect both the past and the future: to put it simply, not only does anti-representational theatre recuperate the anti-historical elements of history – the 'other histories' ousted by history – but it also prevents them from *becoming* historical. ('Everything that *is* future *is* already past, it is not the beginning of something, it is already the just after the end [*il subito dopo della fine*]' (Bene and Dotto 1998: 219). In other words, in criticising Deleuze's vestiges of historicism, Bene is also necessarily denouncing his residual teleology. As observed by Toscano, the creative resistance of Deleuze's artistic heroes always underlies an 'orientation towards the outside, the veritable teleology which governs the mechanisms of extraction'. On the one hand 'the procedural exhaustion of the possible is supposed to make possible a renunciation of "any order of preference, any organization in relation to a goal, any signification"'. On the other hand, such '"becoming that no longer includes any conceivable change" is clearly the terminus of the procedure-process that allows literature to issue into Life' (Toscano 2008: 65–6).[21]

More specifically, I would suggest that what Bene cannot accept is Deleuze's teleology of *vitalist production* and the supposedly anti-capitalist emancipatory politics of unbridled invention that it evokes. Subtraction must be active and creative – we must indeed assume the paternity of creative defecation – yet never productive, since *pro*-duction is inherently finalistic. '*Lavorio*' should always remain excremental ('*Lavorio* is self-demolition'; 'Man is born to work on himself') and cannot be confused with '*lavoro*' ('A worker is not a man'; 'Freedom means liberation from work, not occupation') (Bene and Dotto 1998: 70; Attisani and Dotti 2004: 53–4). Whether additive *or* subtractive, for Bene, production is nothing else than accumulated work, which is inevitably recuperated by the apparatus of capitalist representation. While life as such is continual putrefaction, represented life – what Bene calls '*vita quotidiana*', everyday life – is just work. Turning to *S.A.D.E.*, it is therefore not a coincidence that, frustrated by the impossibility of attaining enjoyment through transgression, the master concludes the first act of the play with a desperate scream: 'I want to live! I want to work!' (Bene 2002: 321). This also shows how Bene's critique of production as work is at the same time a critique of work as the only possible means of enjoyment. Significantly enough, the slave introduces the second act singing '*al lavoro del piacere . . . il piacere del lavoro basta qui sostituir*' (323). It is first necessary to replace the non-existent 'work of pleasure' with the all-pervasive 'pleasure of work' for the master to be later able to ejaculate in the name of the law. As a matter of fact, the slave sets up for his master the simulation of everyday sadomasochistic office life: he hires a prostitute who is said to embody 'the woman-object' of the master and tellingly 'lets herself be *invented*' (330, 332, emphasis added). Conversely, moving his hand frantically in his pocket, the master now becomes 'prey to vitalism *tout court*', Bene says, and treats the prostitute as a 'décor of flesh' (325). He starts using her as a filing-cabinet (he opens a drawer by pinching her hard on the hip; he closes it by slapping her bottom), she then in turn becomes his mail (he flips through it by dishevelling her hair), his phone (he twists her wrist, a receiver, and brings it to his ear), an ashtray (he extinguishes a cigarette in the palm of her hand), a business suitcase (he ties her with a belt and drags her), an open window (he gags her), etc.

Would it be exaggerated to read such a caricature of late-capitalist production in terms of a faithful portrayal of Deleuze's vitalist becoming? Are we not witnessing here the becoming-drawer/mail/phone/ashtray/suitcase/window of the secretary-prostitute? After all, in 'One Less Manifesto', Deleuze problematically goes as far as suggesting that 'the woman-object in *S.A.D.E.*, the naked girl . . . connects her gestures according to the line of a variation that allows her to *escape* the domination of the master' (Deleuze 1997: 249, emphasis added).[22] Is Bene's caricature not thus providing us with a possible concrete configuration of radical capitalist deterritorialisation as expounded in *Anti-Oedipus*? Remember, in the capitalist field of immanence there are no longer masters and slaves 'but only slaves commanding other slaves' (Deleuze and Guattari 1977: 254). The universalisation of capitalism would achieve absolute deterritorialisation, a limit at which production would equate with immediate vital creation. Beyond this limit, to be regarded as inescapable, we would find a 'nomadic or schizophrenic subject, one worthy of the end of history or the end of actuality' (Hallward 2006: 103). In this way, as Hallward has observed, what Deleuze and Guattari add to Marx's analysis of the trajectory of capitalism is 'a new eschatology' (103). But, in a few words, is not such an eschatological end of actuality precisely what all of Deleuze's artistic heroes – most of whom are indeed schizophrenics – have in common?

S.A.D.E. makes clear that, for Bene, there is nothing remotely reassuring or vaguely progressive about capitalist deterritorialisation: the transformation of the traditional despotic master into a hyperactive and hypertensive office manager. In parallel, Bene refuses to accept pathological figures such as Bartleby, Wolfson and Artaud as ethico-political models of aesthetic resistance.[23] The scrivener's 'I would prefer not to' is just no longer effective in today's late-capitalist coercively inventive ideological constellation. One cannot simply reply 'I would prefer not to' to the compulsive sadomasochistic enjoyment imposed by contemporary work: 'One asks to be neglected, but it's impossible. . . . One cannot escape being *entertained*' (Bene and Dotto 1998: 82). Instead of Bartleby, Wolfson and their peers, Bene can only advance the theatrically ob-scene figure of the slavish Watson, in his opinion, the closest one can get to inorganic porn, the Schopenhauerian point of non-desire. 'I'd like to be Watson. . . . Watson doesn't understand a fuck, whenever he acts he does it at random. He is inactive even in the action that runs him. Being unable to enjoy the inorganic (it looks like it is not possible), maybe Watson is the thing that has so far been able to bewitch and enchant me' (279). Beyond Wolfson's aphasic stumbling through which language ultimately pursues an eschatological communion with the pure forces of life, Watson's impotent vacuity perfectly overlaps immediate acts with the most radical form of being acted upon by the signifier.

References

Attisani, A. and M. Dotti (eds) (2004), *Bene crudele*, Viterbo: Stampa Alternativa.

Bene, C. (2002), *Opere*, Milan: Bompiani.

Bene, C. and G. Dotto (1998), *Vita di Carmelo Bene*, Milan: Bompiani.

Deleuze, G. and F. Guattari (1977), *Anti-Oedipus: Capitalism and Schizophrenia*, trans. R. Hurley, M. Seem and H. R. Lane, Minneapolis: University of Minnesota Press.

Deleuze, G. (1983), *Nietzsche and Philosophy*, trans. H. Tomlinson, Minneapolis: University of Minnesota Press.

Deleuze, G. (1989), *Cinema 2: The Time-Image*, trans. H. Tomlinson and R. Galeta, London: Athlone Press.

Deleuze, G. (1994), *Difference and Repetition*, trans. P. Patton, New York: Columbia University Press.

Deleuze, G. (1997), 'One Less Manifesto', trans. E. dal Molin and T. Murray in T. Murray (ed.), *Mimesis, Masochism, and Mime*, Ann Arbor: University of Michigan Press.

Deleuze, G. (1998), *Essays Critical and Clinical*, trans. D. W. Smith and M. A. Greco, London: Verso.

Deleuze, G. and F. Guattari (1986), *Kafka: Towards a Minor Literature*, trans. D. Polan, Minneapolis: University of Minnesota Press.

Hallward, P. (2006), *Out of This World: Deleuze and the Philosophy of Creation*, London: Verso.

Lacan, J. (2008), *The Seminar of Jacques Lacan: The Other Side of Psychoanalysis*, London and New York: Norton.

Schuster, A. (2009 forthcoming), 'Is Pleasure a Rotten Idea? Deleuze and Lacan on Pleasure and Jouissance', in D. Hoens, S. Jöttkandt, G. Buelens (eds), *Tickle Your Catastrophe: On Borders, Cuts and Edges in Contemporary Theory*, London: Palgrave.

Toscano, A. (2008), 'In Praise of Negativism', in S. O' Sullivan, S. Zepke (eds), *Deleuze, Guattari, and the Production of the New*, London: Continuum.

Notes

1. My translation.
2. My translation.
3. My translation.
4. My translation.
5. My translation.
6. In other words, I shall henceforth deliberately leave aside the fact that, in *Difference and Repetition*, Deleuze uses the verb 'to extract' (*soutirer*) to signify a notion of subtraction that is mutually exclusive with the notion of subtraction as expounded in 'One Less Manifesto', and focus exclusively on the way in which subtraction/extraction is understood in the latter text.
7. My translation. See also page 240.
8. My translation.
9. As an example of what should *not* be taken as porn, Bene refers to Lewis Carroll's little girls and their 'morbid mental perversions' (Bene and Dotto 1998: 16).
10. With regard to Deleuze's aprioristic equation of lack and negativity with impotence, Schuster further asks himself a crucial question: 'Why not view lack as something "good" and plenitude, positivity, chaotic multiplicity, etc. as the real terror?'
11. My translation.
12. See also Bene (2002: 343).
13. My translation.
14. See also Deleuze (1997: 249).
15. It is worth noting that Bene recurrently praises Schopenhauer in his writings: 'My permanent educator is called Arthur Schopenhauer' (Bene and Dotto 1998: 23).
16. My translation.
17. On the topic of Bene's manipulation of stereotypes, Klossowski writes the following: 'Having appeared under the stereotypical aspect of the [*dramatis*] *persona*, Carmelo does not try to maintain it *as such before the spectator*, he rather tries to unveil the aspect of it that has been concealed by traditional interpretations. This does not amount to a secret that, according to the plot, the character would deliberately hide . . . but what *he cannot say or know* . . . the unexpectable that the character brings with him' (P. Klossowski, 'Cosa mi suggerisce il gioco ludico di Carmelo Bene', in Bene 2002: 1470–1).
18. Turning to Deleuze's analysis of Francis Bacon, Toscano adds the important specification that such negativism 'requires an initial abandonment to the cliché' (Toscano 2008: 63) – which Deleuze recovers in Bacon's relation to photography as a reaction against abstract art. This could easily be related to Bene's use of lyrical 'exasperations'.
19. See especially Lesson IV of *The Seminar of Jacques Lacan: The Other Side of Psychoanalysis* (Lacan 2008). The slave in *S.A.D.E.* makes exactly the same point when he sings: 'Ci vuol altro al mio padrone / per godere, lo si sa! / Altro! Altro! Altro! Altro! (*S.A.D.E.*, in Bene 2002: 302).
20. My translation.
21. In 'One Less Manifesto', Deleuze himself unashamedly acknowledges that 'becoming minor is a *goal*, a goal that concerns everybody' (Deleuze 1997: 255, my translation, my emphasis).
22. My translation.
23. As Grande suggests, for Bene, 'going beyond Artaud means going beyond the idea of . . . the actor-martyr [and] the advent of a language-without-writing. In other words, one must carry out a process of parodistic evacuation of sense' (Bene and Dotto 1998: 312).

Interval

Chapter 5

Performing, Strolling, Thinking: From Minor Literature to Theatre of the Future

Daniel Watt with a Response from Julian Wolfreys

> I am not at home.
> True, I am sacked by skin but something is not right.
> I'll walk a while
> without the least hope of finding a way out
> or in.

This begins, as does *Anti-Oedipus*, with a schizo stroll.

I am imagining Heidegger. He is walking in those dark woods that surround 'die hütte' at Todtnauberg in the Black Forest. It is winter and there is a heavy snowfall. The thick canopy of branches has protected the *Pathmarks* but, deep in thought, he is still some way *Off the Beaten Track*. These mountain tracks – or to use the German of Heidegger's book: *Holzwege* – are dead ends (as we shall examine later). They are paths that end abruptly, seemingly leading nowhere. In *What is Philosophy?* Deleuze and Guattari discuss the territory of philosophy, and the ground upon which its foundations shakily rest. Heidegger is obviously a very particular thinker of a very particular thinking of territory:

> Heidegger lost his way along the paths of the reterritorialization because they are paths without directive signs or barriers. Perhaps this strict professor was madder than he seemed. He got the wrong people, earth and blood. For the race summoned forth by art or philosophy is not the one that claims to be pure but rather an oppressed, bastard, lower, anarchical, nomadic, and irremediably minor race. . .
> (Deleuze and Guattari 1994: 109)

It is this bastardly minor race of philosophers and artists that this chapter addresses. Does this new 'race' ever find a place to 'dwell' adequately? Is it doomed to the anarchic nomadism of sites without places, habitation without dwelling, and bodies without organs, identities or even minds (save those assailed by a schizo-thought that keeps them in perpetual motion)?

Identities blur and faces fade in and out. Perhaps it is the cold distorting reality and memory. Heidegger fades into Beckett, or perhaps it is Beckett as Molloy, circling the forest in an attempt to escape it. From the pained logic of this circulatory resistance Artaud emerges, but the imagined Artaud from the radio broadcast *Pour en finir avec le jugement de dieu*, and it is more his face I think of, contorting itself around the screams and sounds of that performance. There are others, and as with any reverie many things are omitted, nothing quite discernible. Kafka seems to offer some way out – through the door of the hut, perhaps, and then again a dissolution of forms and we are back in the forest, with all these faces somehow pinned to trees; the wood overflowing with posters for the missing – and there are so many missing in the dark woods of Europe.

You will find other signs on branches as you proceed. They are memories; other's interjections, thoughts from the outside, nothing more, or less. There are animal sounds in the distance. These are unidentifiable and unrecognisable, if indeed animals they are. There will be houses, homes, bridges and pathways. There will be a lot of walking for which we are unprepared, naked and cold. There is history, but one of the future: all the old gods are dead.

Some 'directive signs' first.

This chapter engages with the trajectory of Deleuze's work on philosophy, literature and performance with a view to elaborating the potential offered for a future theatre based on the work of Bene, Beckett and Artaud. But whilst all three are important examples for Deleuze, they by no means constitute a new canon of 'minor' theatre. Rather they point to the inherently radical, rhizomatic and often deranged sensibility of performance which wanders through dark woods of thought, to emerge bruised and disoriented at some point in the future. The chapter traces a route from the work on 'minor literature' in *Kafka: Towards a Minor Literature*, to the political possibility of the body without organs which offers a resistance to the homely conception of 'dwelling', and the post-war implications of 'building'.

So: 'Now that we know where we're going, let's go there. It's so nice to know where you're going, in the early stages. It almost rids you of the wish to go there' (Beckett 1979: 20).

Excursus 1

So, now that we know where we're going it is probable that we shall make a detour immediately.

What is it in the work of Deleuze that seems so proximal to the work of the theatre? It can perhaps be found in the fascination with movement in the work of philosophers such as Nietzsche, whose own writing takes on the character of an environment, a space of performance, rather than a process of thought strung along some teleological thread of time. Deleuze clearly states in *Difference and Repetition* that it is in the performative aspect of movement that philosophy finds its moment of becoming:

> . . . it is a question of producing within the work a movement capable of affecting the mind outside of all representation; it is a question of making movement itself a work, without interposition; of substituting direct signs for mediate representations; of inventing vibrations, rotations, whirlings, gravitations, dances or leaps which directly touch the mind. This is the idea of a man of the theatre, the idea of a director before his time. In this sense, something completely new begins with Kierkegaard and Nietzsche. They no longer reflect upon the theatre in the Hegelian manner. Neither do they set up a philosophical theatre. They invent an incredible equivalent of theatre within philosophy, thereby founding simultaneously this theatre of the future and a new philosophy. (Deleuze 1994: 8)

And Deleuze's own work, when frequently writing on matters 'theatrical', cannot be said to be reflective. It does not simply consider the work of theatre but rather enacts it, following in the tracks of Kierkegaard and Nietzsche here. His thinking moves through the new environment that is neither 'a philosophical theatre' nor a 'theatre within philosophy', but a 'theatre of the future'.

The theatre of the future does not achieve itself. It is a movement. It is a mode of being that is in process. It is characterised most notably as having no place in which to dwell because it no longer finds its home in the theatre. In 'One Less Manifesto', Deleuze offers the passionate possibility of theatre's transformation, in the context of the work of Carmelo Bene:

> Theater will surge forward as something representing nothing but what presents and creates a minority consciousness as a universal-becoming. It forges alliances here and there according to the circumstances, following the lines of transformation that exceed theater and take on another form, or else that transform themselves back into theater for another leap. (Deleuze 1997: 256)

Theatre here takes on its transformative capacity by adapting and relating. It forms a symbiosis, briefly, with other forms of art or 'bastardly' activity; writing, walking, thinking. What is most interesting in this quotation concerns the 'minority consciousness as a universal-becoming'. The question of the 'minor' is at the heart of the Deleuzian enterprise, or the movement that fuses a certain philosophy with a certain theatre. The potential offered by the 'minor' is one of an openness to change, to new surroundings, and emerges from the sort of schizo-stroll which focuses purely on passage through, not direction towards. In fact it may go further, by working in reverse, for as Deleuze notes, again about Bene:

> The theatre maker is no longer an author, an actor, or a director. [They are] an operator. Operation must be understood as the movement of subtraction, of amputation, one already covered by the other movement that gives birth to and multiplies something unexpected, like a prosthesis. (239)

It seems such an abstract idea, this notion of prosthesis, and indeed it is. Here, there seems almost an admittance of the genuine awkwardness in Deleuze's thinking. As though it were the genuine revolt against being that operates so much in Artaud, and to which we will turn later. This suggested 'operator' then (certainly not surgeon) removes elements to replace them with others: a limb for a prosthesis, words for sounds, space for movement. It is a deliberate act of unbalancing, an unworkable conjunction that 'forges alliances . . . according to the circumstances' (256).

A similar element, the 'movement of subtraction', is in play in Deleuze's thought on disequilibrium in language in the essay 'He Stuttered'. There, discussing Samuel Beckett and Franz Kafka, he writes:

> what they do is invent a *minor use* for the major language within which they express themselves completely: they *minorize* language, as in music, where the minor mode refers to dynamic combinations in a state of perpetual disequilibrium. They are big by virtue of minorization: they cause language to flee, they make it run along a witch's course, they place it endlessly in a state of disequilibrium, they cause it to bifurcate and to vary in each one of its terms, according to a ceaseless modulation. (Deleuze 1994b: 25)

The use of major language as *minorisation* in 'He Stuttered' is, of course, more fully explored (with Guattari) in *Kafka: Towards a Minor Literature*, and we shall go there momentarily. But here, like forest paths, the work of language ceaselessly divides, creating new routes and branches with other connections and lines to follow. To repeat the connection with the work of the operator/director, it seems that the minor use of the major language (French for Beckett, German for Kafka) offers the same sort of 'unexpected prosthetic' that Deleuze finds in Bene. The thinking of the prosthesis, whilst it may impede directional movement, certainly allows us to think of different combinations from which to create a theatre of the future.

How might a literary prosthesis, for example, assist us in thinking theatre, Deleuze and the future? This cannot be thought in terms of a simple 'subtraction', for that would draw us down the route of a reduction of theatre, again, to the text. It is, rather, that the 'minor' of literature can also make us consider the 'major' of theatre. It functions like a bridge that appears at a specific moment in a journey, when you reach a limit. 'On the wooden bridge leading from the main road to the village K. stood for a long time gazing into the illusory emptiness above him' (Kafka 1976: 277).

Pausing a moment, the bridge brings me back to Heidegger. It has a very particular place in his essay 'Building, Dwelling, Thinking', and, by necessity takes the final few steps in this first excursus:

> To be sure, the bridge is a thing of its *own* kind; for it gathers the fourfold in *such* a way that it allows a *site* for it. But only something *that is itself a locale* can make space for a site. The locale is not already there before the bridge is. Before the bridge stands, there are of course many spots along the stream that can be occupied by something. One of them proves to be a locale, and does so *because of the bridge.* Thus the bridge does not first come to a locale to stand in it; rather, a locale comes into existence only by virtue of the bridge. The bridge is a thing; it gathers the fourfold, but in such a way that it allows a site for the fourfold. By this site are determined the places and paths by which a space is provided for.
>
> Only things that are locales in this manner allow for spaces. What the word for space, *Raum*, designates is said by its ancient meaning. *Raum, Rum* means a place that is freed for settlement and lodging. A space is something that has been made room for, something that has been freed, namely, within a boundary, Greek *peras*. A boundary is not that at which something stops but, as the Greeks recognized, the boundary is that from which something *begins its essential unfolding.* That is why the concept is that of *horismos*, that is, the horizon, the boundary. Space is in essence that for which room has been made, that which is let into its bounds. That for which room is made is always granted and hence is joined, that is, gathered, by virtue of a locale, that is, by such a thing as the bridge. *Accordingly, spaces receive their being from locations and not from 'space'.* (Heidegger 1993: 355–6)

It is a curious passage, not for the mystical evocation of the 'fourfold' – which he earlier describes as 'earth and sky, divinities and mortals' (351) – but rather for its concept of space, or *raum* (the essay is from the early 1950s and the echoes of Heidegger's silence are deafening). This spacing is made possible by what Heidegger calls the locale, and that itself is brought into existence by the bridge itself. This is the bridge as an event, as much as an existent structure. The boundary as described here also evokes the kind of philosophical writing Deleuze is so interested in in *Difference and Repetition*, for it is from the boundary that something begins to take shape, not to stop. It is a kind of theatre of space that Heidegger offers here, a sort of future of space which enables events to happen. Strange it should emerge so rooted in the dark territories of a kind of Germany, or a type of poetry, because the more one explores the more the thinking deterritorialises and upsets the very 'boundaries' it constructs. The space being 'freed' here in 'Building, Dwelling, Thinking' is one more perambulatory than static; a movement *between* 'locales' that defines the adjacent 'spaces' as much as the places themselves. Arriving at one locale means moving on to another, already, as further exploration of Heidegger's essay will later reveal.

It would appear that this mountain path has all but petered out; we will have to search for somewhere else.

'Adjacency – that is the schizo-law' (Deleuze and Guattari 1986: 60).

Excursion 1

I did not think that the future would sound like a manifesto but perhaps it does.

'We believe only in one or more Kafka machines that are neither structure nor phantasm' (Deleuze and Guattari 1986: 7). As we examine the curious machine at work in 'In the Penal Colony', with the further operations (subtractions?) of the Kafka-machine operating in the background, it will be worth keeping in mind the processes of movement, performance and the literary space that is enabled by *minor* literature.

In Kafka's short story, a foreign explorer makes a visit to witness an outmoded form of execution on a remote island. The officer, whose duty it is to apply the punishment, is a maniacal adherent to the strict rules of the Old Commandant of the colony who devised and built the machine of execution which administers the sentence by inscribing it upon the skin of the offender. The explorer learns with shock that the legislative procedure of the colony does not inform the prisoner of their crime:

> "He doesn't know the sentence that has been passed on him?" "No," said the officer again, pausing a moment as if to let the explorer elaborate his question, and then said: "There would be no point in telling him. He'll learn it on his body." (Kafka 1992: 145)

It is apparent that texts are culpable in their own disfigurement; machines that enact their own internal law, or generate prostheses. They, like any manifesto, must make a great oration in defence of themselves. They are obliged to be interesting, to have a certain style and wit to be readable; without such qualities they would infringe other boundaries, of genre: from fiction into fact, or even writing into art, literature into theatre. The officer in Kafka's story offers the explorer some texts which show the design of the sentence that is to be inscribed on the prisoner's skin, yet these designs do not obey the conventional structures of readability:

> The explorer would have liked to say something appreciative, but all he could see was a labyrinth of lines crossing and recrossing each other, which covered the paper so thickly that it was difficult to discern the blank spaces between them. "Read it," said the officer. "I can't," said the explorer. (148)

The bizarre nature of this artistic palimpsest leaves the explorer unable to read it. It appears to require some specialist knowledge to interpret it. As with all literature an interpreter is required; a critic, an explorer or officer of the law, or (in Deleuze's reading of Kafka) a mechanic. On the next page of Kafka's story the officer makes apparent that the understanding of the text is dependent on a certain learning:

> It's no calligraphy for schoolchildren. It needs to be studied closely. I'm quite sure that in the end you would understand. Of course the script can't be a simple one; it's not supposed to kill a man straight off, but only after an interval of, on average, twelve hours; the turning point is reckoned to come at the sixth hour. So there have to be lots and lots of flourishes around the actual script; the script itself runs around the body only in a narrow girdle; the rest of the body is reserved for the embellishments. (149)

Such a law makes the understanding of the text into an academic pursuit, of knowledge and meaning. The work of Kafka operates quite differently for Deleuze and Guattari, and it is exactly here that they put their machines into play:

> A Kafka-machine is thus constituted by contents and expressions that have been formalised to diverse degrees by unformed materials that enter into it, and leave by passing through all possible states. To enter or leave the machine, to be in the machine, to walk around it, or approach it – these are still components of the machine itself: these are states of desire, free of all interpretation. The line of escape is part of the machine. Inside or outside, the animal is part of the burrow-machine. The problem is not that of being free but of finding a way out, or even a way in, another side, a hallway, an adjacency. (Deleuze and Guattari 1986: 7–8)

The critic, or reader who interprets, will always be walking around the machine, approaching it from various sides, put simply – only enacting the process of the machine itself, never actually experiencing it. The officer will not understand the script, because it is experienced – and learned – upon the body. Its message is illegible; it is inscribed upon the flesh and must be absorbed through the skin. The law of literature becomes one of pain, of inscription through affective – not knowable – criteria. The Law is seen to be done, that is what is most important. That it uses the skin of another to show this demonstrates the performative action of literature upon the body. It is this performance that the officer finds most instructive, one that begins as the boundary of the skin is overcome:

> When the man lies down on the Bed and it begins to vibrate, the Harrow is lowered onto his body. It regulates itself automatically so that the needles barely touch his skin; once contact is made the steel ribbon stiffens immediately into a rigid band. And then the performance begins. (Kafka 1992: 147)

Yet the real spectacle of the work in progress is only apparent to the prisoner whose knowledge will come from the body. The spectators are there to give testimony that justice has been done, to translate the unreadable words of the law into its ideal of justice. Yet the event of this alteration can only take place through the surface of the body of the prisoner and this is why the torturers strive to keep their victims alive for as long as possible, so that the letter of the Law may become an indelible category of knowledge that is marked upon the body. Those who gather to witness the performance transform the physicality of the spectacle into a transcendental category of justice, as the officer attests: 'Many did not care to watch it but lay with closed eyes in the sand; they all knew: Now Justice is being done' (154). Deleuze and Guattari themselves find the story 'too transcendental' and 'too abstract [a] machine' (Deleuze and Guattari 1986: 39–40).

And finally in Deleuze and Guattari's reading of Kafka, and indeed in their reading of Beckett, there is the question of failure:

> Kafka thus has many reasons to abandon a text, either because it stops short or because it is interminable. But Kafka's criteria are of an entirely new sort and apply only to him; from one genre of text to another, there are interactions, reinvestments, exchanges, and so on. Each failure is a masterpiece, a branch of the rhizome. (38–9)

So again, it appears the trail dissolves into the undergrowth. The means by which minor literature operates is by a sort of exhaustion. This takes Kafka's texts to a point where they operate, painfully, at a performative level, for they resist thought. You have to submit to the situation of just inhabiting them, of allowing their machine process to whirl on, as with the earlier quotation concerning Kierkegaard and Nietzsche. But in giving ourselves up to such theatrical 'dwelling' in the text do we find a home of any kind in Deleuze's thought? It is doubtful, as the urge is always on, ever on, to the next experience, the next impossible event.

I have my doubts if anyone is genuinely capable of this schizo-stroll, the warm hearth of knowledge is always so much more enticing than the psychosis of the woodland *dérive*, alive with manifold rhizomatic possibilities beneath our feet.

Excursus 2

Excursus 1 ended by seeking adjacency, but also by considering the issue of the locale. A certain written locale comes into being by the citation of certain authors, thinkers, actors. It is curious to find in Heidegger a type of connection beyond space, a sort of invisible rhizomatic possibility that connects all potential eventualities of inhabitation:

> To say that mortals *are* is to say that *in dwelling* they persist through spaces by virtue of their stay among things and locales. And only because mortals pervade, persist through, spaces by their very essence are they able to go through spaces. But in going through spaces we do not give up our standing in them. Rather, we always go through spaces in such a way that we already sustain them by staying constantly with near and remote locales and things. When I go towards the door of the lecture hall, I am already there, and I could not go to it at all if I were not such that I am there. I am never here only, as this encapsulated body; rather, I am there, that is, I already pervade the space of the room, and only thus can I go through it.
> (Heidegger 1993: 359)

This seems a particularly Deleuzian concept. It is a fractured entity containing all possible detours. Heidegger seems to go even further by saying that it is actually space in which dwelling occurs, not even 'things' and 'locales'. The space of which he speaks is also one of movement; by going towards one sustains the space as potential for dwelling.

What might a body without organs (BwO) do in such a space? The outward directionality seems already to suggest a body unbordered, released outwards to space itself. As Artaud rants, against the human, in *To have done with the judgement of god*:

> Two roads were open to him:
> that of the infinite outside,
> and that of the infinitesimal inside.
> And he chose the infinitesimal inside.
> (Artaud 1975)

And there is, undoubtedly, always a tension between these two movements. The BwO is torn apart by a competing desire to become a body – 'you are forever attaining it' – and the aspect of movement, already discussed, which Deleuze and Guattari describe as a kind of surface on which you are 'scurrying like a vermin, groping like a blind person, or running like a lunatic: desert traveller and nomad of the steppes' (Deleuze and Guattari 1987: 150).

It is perhaps the infinitesimal homeliness in the concept of 'dwelling' that Deleuze, Guattari and Artaud find abhorrent. It is this infinitesimal that Heidegger finds so appealing:

> The essence of building is letting dwell. Building accomplishes its essential process in the raising of locales by the joining of their spaces. *Only if we are capable of dwelling, only then can we build*. Let us think for a while of a farmhouse in the Black Forest, which was built some two hundred years ago by the dwelling of peasants. Here the self-sufficiency of the power to let earth and heaven, divinities and mortals enter *in simple oneness* into things, ordered the house. It placed the farm on the wind-sheltered mountain slope, looking south, among the meadows close to the spring. It gave it the wide overhanging shingle roof whose proper slope bears up under the burden of snow, and that, reaching deep down, shields the chambers against the storms of the long winter nights. It did not forget the altar corner behind the community table; it made room in its chamber for the hallowed places of childbed and the 'tree of the dead' – for that is what they call a coffin there: the *Totenbaum* – and in this way it designed for the different generations under one roof the character of their journey through time. A craft that, itself sprung from dwelling, still uses its tools and its gear as things, built the farmhouse.
> (Heidegger 1993: 361–2)[1]

It could be the description given by a rambler following a chance invitation to sustenance after becoming lost in the woods. A description added to and 'crafted' after years of retelling. It is rooted in detail and revels in the particulars of history. It makes the house a warm cocoon-like body, birthing its generations and guiding them to the grave. Can such a description, an organ in the body that is 'Building, Dwelling, Thinking', offer any insight into how Deleuze's nomadic theatre of philosophy might function, how the chains of the machine of *minor* literature can give way to a playful environment where thought and words become movement? Yes, but only at the limits of thinking perhaps, and with a sacrifice of the self to the directionality of becoming. And by that I mean where things collapse back into the type of potentiality that Heidegger describes concerning space. For there, despite how hard we may attempt to become the BwO, the world haunts us with our own identity; one constructed by all the histories we carry and multiply as we 'journey through time'. Relinquishing identity becomes a task in itself, but one that cannot be 'thought'; it must become. It is a state that Deleuze himself describes as exhaustion:

> Only the exhausted person is sufficiently disinterested, sufficiently scrupulous. Indeed he is obliged to replace his plans with tables and programs that are devoid of all meaning. For him, what matters is the order in which he does what he has to do, and in what combinations he does two things at the same time – when it is still necessary to do so, for nothing. (Deleuze 1998: 154)

Becoming the BwO demands a certain exhausted resignation to another sequence of meanings and associations, unpremeditated and uncontrolled, but always present in the manifold possible spacings of the movement of the work. In fact we were already going there from the outset. Artaud again:

> When you have given him a body without organs,
> then you will have delivered him from all his automatisms and restored him to his true liberty.

> Then you will reteach him to dance inside out
> as in the delirium of the accordion dances
> and that inside out will be his true side out.
> (Artaud 1975)

The 'true' liberty of the BwO, as with the 'theatre of the future' and the 'machine' of *minor* literature, is, in a sense, that they unhouse being. They make us 'dance inside out' as Artaud puts it. It is that alienated quality that is both disturbing, and familiar, in Deleuze's work. Deleuze's 'equivalent of theatre' is a threat to being. Not a new one necessarily, but one that enfolds a number of movements such as those presented in the work of Bene, Artaud and Kafka. Therefore, while it may be improbable to again attempt to graft Heidegger here, as the unexpected prosthesis, nevertheless I think it possible, for the ambulatory nature of the essay 'Building, Dwelling, Thinking' brings us to a point not far removed from the permanent movement of the schizo-stroll:

> The proper dwelling plight lies in this, that mortals ever search anew for the nature of dwelling, that they *must ever learn to dwell*. What if man's homelessness consisted in this, that man still does not even think of the *proper* plight of dwelling as *the* plight? Yet as soon as man *gives thought* to his homelessness, it is a misery no longer. Rightly considered and kept well in mind, it is the sole summons that *calls* mortals into their dwelling. (Heidegger 1993: 363)

Despite the propriety of thought that comes towards the end of this short quotation, there is an acceptance of the movement of dwelling.

If we called such a movement the BwO, or the 'dances and leaps' of the mind that Deleuze finds in Nietzsche, then the theoretical trajectory of the schizo-stroll becomes one of accepting the homelessness of being, and the revel of perpetual movement. But this situation is less than liberating really, less a theatre of exuberance than a puppet theatre of automata. For when Deleuze, Artaud and all the other dancers in this whirling 'theatre of the future' jettison the mind, they leave behind a senseless being, battered by the elements, performing only to themselves. Rather than reaching for the 'infinitesimal' nostalgia of Heidegger and other 'reterritorialisers', perhaps the impossibility of the BwO suggests only that there is much further to travel than Deleuze when considering the event of the theatre of the future; for schizophrenia, with all of its deranged connectivity and sudden impulses, is not the liberating 'breakthrough' (Deleuze and Guattari 1984: 362) it would appear to be. It breaks bodies apart and leaves them in dark places, far from help, or hope: 'you could lie there for weeks and no one hear you, I often thought of that up in the mountains, no, that is a foolish thing to say, just went on, my body doing its best without me' (Beckett 1958: 22).

Off the Beaten Path or, Notes Towards a Heideggerian Deterritorialisation: A Response to Daniel Watt
Julian Wolfreys

1. Do we know where we're going? Is this true, strictly speaking? Of course there's always death, we are all beings towards death; and in this anticipatory retrospect we are vouchsafed the most uncanny of 'dwellings', an inescapable authenticity in the negation of being as its ownmost inevitability. I can imagine myself, no longer the 'myself', when I am no longer even a body without organs, merely a without. Yet, it is important to acknowledge that in knowing where we are going, nothing in fact could be less certain. For while death is that which is inescapable, that which is the future therefore, and one of the few events to which one can, properly speaking, give the name 'future' as opposed to speaking of that which is to come (that which may one day arrive but which cannot be anticipated or programmed), nevertheless, I cannot experience what I call 'my death'. The Authenticity of futurity is always already haunted therefore by its own inauthenticity, except in the fiction of the *als ob*, the as if; it is haunted by the impossibility of knowing ahead of time, ahead of the absence of all time, all world, and therefore, all consciousness of dwelling. It is haunted by the impossibility of knowing either ahead of time, in time, or on time. When death arrives, it does so in a manner

where time is not, and can never be the issue at stake. Ultimate anach-
rony, all time gone. Dwell on this: untimely death.

2. Spaces of performance, becoming performative. If what haunts
authenticity is inauthenticity, that from which the former cannot escape,
then the felicity of a performance is always troubled, spooked we might
say, by the very possibility, the *eigenartigkeit*, the strangeness and singularity of infelicity, the *Heimlich, Heimisch* as *unheimlich, unheimlisch*.
A Deleuzian troping, the plural-motifs – substitution, mediation, invention, vibration, rotation, whirling, gravitation, dances, leaps (Deleuze
1994a: 8) – all are invested with a performativity and becoming which
can always slip into the merely programmed or mechanical, and thus
into an infelicity that haunts the desire for the truth of a performative
deterritorialisation. Heidegger apprehends as much in those movements
that he traces of the uncanny, the *unheimlich*, as the self flees the self in
the face of own's ownmost authenticity.

3. The Deleuzian desire, the programme if you will for a 'theatre of the
future', immediately apprehends its own impossibility, the inauthenticity
that troubles the proposition of an authentic future. Theatre, as that which
'will surge forward as something representing nothing but what presents
and creates a minority consciousness' (Deleuze 1997: 256), is thus unveiled
through its staged metaphor of the authentic/inauthentic performative as
that in which the particularity of representation gives way from within,
caving in on itself in that modality of its truth where becoming is itself
always the endless motion towards an event which I can never experience,
for which I can never prepare. 'Ceaseless modulation' (Deleuze 1994b: 25)
is that very movement that haunts me, the 'me' in the place I exist, where
dwelling is forgotten, occluded by the quotidian and where I remain on the
road with an illusory assurance of believing I know the map and destina-
tion. Ceaseless modulation *minorises* the cogito, soliciting a recognition
of what becomes unveiled apophatically, and which can be received, if at
all, only through the Kantian *als ob*, through the secret of literature for
example, or through that disquieting force Husserl calls 'analogical apper-
ception', or 'appresentation' (Husserl 1995: 108ff). Thinking (of) prosthesis (the prosthesis of thought), I enact myself as an other, a phantom self
always in the process of becoming between a self and an other, a ghostly
trace of a body, necessarily without organs.

4. So there you have it, suspended for a moment and all time, in no time,
a solitary figure, his back towards you, as if he were about to walk away,

stepping off in meditation through the forest, on no discernible path. We cannot get away from Heidegger, even though he appears to be wanting to get away from us. He's walking off in this photograph, his cane held behind his back, thumbs aligned along its uppermost surface, his hat not a little reminiscent of Buster Keaton. No path, just the leaves, the trees, and a vanishing point into which he will become as nothing. A future forestalled, whereby a locale comes into existence, only by virtue of what lies ahead, but *in which* he will never witness himself, or be capable of retreating from; therein is a space and becoming suspended, an image as the impossible time, representing the inauthenticity of being in the oncoming face of the authenticity of a line of flight, mapping the unmappable becoming of *Dasein*. Thus in the photo, within representation, we attain a glimpse of what we do not see, indirectly we have made known to us, in temporal suspension, 'the boundary [as] that from which something *begins its essential unfolding*' (Heidegger 1993: 355–6). The silence here in the woods may well be deafening, as, despite himself, Heidegger gets off the beaten path; but a performative deterritorialisation of the recuperative ontology of *Dasein* initiates itself, lying in wait.

5. Heidegger walks without path, in the experience of that which cannot be interpreted *as such*. In this gesture, which many attribute to bad writing, obfuscation, a terrorist obscurantism and so forth, he institutes the becoming of what, invisibly, is already underway, on the way, without a map of the way: that is to say an 'inceptual thinking in the other beginning', which 'en-thinks the truth of be-ing'. This necessary gesture, a leap of sorts, will nonetheless fall into the machinic; this is always its risk, thereby forcing an 'opening of the still undecided decision unto the grounding of this truth', even, and especially, when authenticity always retreats before inauthenticity, the felicitous recuperated in the infelicitous, deterritorialisation reterritorialised and so on, all of which result in 'the failure to enact the grounding . . . [as] the necessary destiny of the first beginning' (Heidegger 2006: 55). *Destiny. First. Enact. Grounding.* The transcendentalism of a teleological onto-technics manifests itself in these words, in their reliance on performativity, originarity and eschatological assumption. The false Heidegger, beside the other Heidegger, inseparable these two, don't you think?

6. But where does dwelling remain? Deleuze's tectonic fault, that which opens an abyss mistaken as an ocean and a sky, remains within a misperception, always implicit, that one might dwell, and yet not be territorialised. For dwelling is always *alethic*, a movement, a becoming which

is also, and simultaneously, an unbecoming; in becoming other than myself, as the limit of myself, across that limit, there remains on the way to death as 'my body doing its best without me' (Beckett 1958: 22).

References

Artaud, A. (1975), 'To have done with the judgement of god', trans. Clayton Eshleman and Norman Glass, *Sparrow*, 34 (July 1975).
Artaud, A. (2006), *Pour en finir avec le jugement de dieu* (CD), Sub Rosa: Brussels.
Beckett, S. (1958), *From an Abandoned Work*, Faber and Faber: London.
Beckett, S. (1979), *The Beckett Trilogy: Molloy, Malone Dies, The Unnamable*, Picador: London.
Deleuze, G. (1994a), *Difference and Repetition*, trans. Paul Patton, London: Athlone Press.
Deleuze, G. (1994b), 'He Stuttered', in C. Boundas and D. Olkowski (eds), *Gilles Deleuze and the Theater of Philosophy*, London: Routledge.
Deleuze, G. (1997), 'One Less Manifesto', trans. E. dal Molin and T. Murray, in T. Murray (ed.), *Mimesis, Masochism, and Mime*, Ann Arbor: University of Michigan Press.
Deleuze, G. (1998), 'The Exhausted', in *Essays Critical and Clinical*, trans. D. W. Smith and M. A. Greco, Minneapolis: University of Minnesota Press.
Deleuze, G. and F. Guattari (1984), *Anti-Oedipus: Capitalism and Schizophrenia*, trans. R. Hurley, M. Seem and H. R. Lane, Athlone Press: London.
Deleuze, G. and F. Guattari (1986), *Kafka: Toward a Minor Literature* trans. D. Polan, Minneapolis: University of Minnesota Press.
Deleuze, G. and F. Guattari (1987), *A Thousand Plateaus: Capitalism and Schizophrenia*, trans. B. Massumi, Minneapolis: University of Minnesota Press.
Deleuze, G. and F. Guattari (1994), *What is Philosophy?*, trans. H. Tomlinson and G. Burchell, Columbia University Press: New York.
Heidegger, M. (1993), 'Building, Dwelling, Thinking', in *Basic Writings*, edited by David Farrel Krell, London: Routledge.
Heidegger, M. (1998), *Pathmarks*, edited by William McNeill, Cambridge: Cambridge University Press.
Heidegger, M. (2002), *Off the Beaten Track*, trans. J. Young and K. Haynes, Cambridge: Cambridge University Press.
Heidegger, M. (2006), *Mindfulness*, trans. P. Emad and T. Kalary, London: Athlone Press.
Husserl, E. (1995), *Cartesian Meditations: An Introduction to Phenomenology*, trans. Dorion Cairns, Dordrecht: Kluwer Academic Publishers.
Kafka, F. (1976), *The Castle* in *Collected Works*, London: Secker & Warburg.
Kafka, F. (1992), *The Complete Short Stories*, edited by Nahum N. Glatzer, London: Minerva.
Sharr, A. (2006), *Heidegger's Hut*, London: MIT Press.

Note

1. For a more direct analysis of the essay 'Building, Dwelling, Thinking' in relation to the hut at Todtnauberg, see Sharr (2006: 66–71).

ACT II

Confronting Deleuze and Live Performance

Chapter 6

Becoming a Citizen of the World: Deleuze Between Allan Kaprow and Adrian Piper

Stephen Zepke

Deleuze often remarked on the 'break' between *The Logic of Sense* and *Anti-Oedipus*. It is a break between the rigorous distinction of the virtual and actual realms in Deleuze's earlier work and the beginning, with Félix Guattari, of 'trying to find a single basis for a production that was at once social and desiring in a logic of flows' (Deleuze 1995: 144). This is a move from an 'expressionism' by which the 'actor' actualises, or 'dramatises' the virtual realm, to a 'constructivism' of the virtual in the 'act'. This was, Deleuze says, a shift from the 'theatre' to the 'factory', a shift from the *dramatisation* of becoming *by* the social, to the *production* of becoming *in* the social (144).[1] This transition is similar to that found in Allan Kaprow's Happenings, which gradually rejected the expression of a virtual 'score' in a theatrical performance, in favour of a 'blurring' of the score and its actualisation in a process of composition understood as being 'life'.

In 1961, Kaprow explains: 'A Happening is *generated* in action by a headful of ideas or a flimsily jotted-down score of "root" directions' (Kaprow 2003: 19). The score and its performance are quite distinct, but they nevertheless exist only in their reciprocal presupposition, the former being purely abstract without the particularity of its instantiation, while its instantiation cannot take place without the 'diagram' of its plan. As Kaprow's work develops however, and in this way it prefigures Deleuze's, it tries to find more effective mechanisms by which the score of 'events' can not only be actualised in life, but could directly construct new ways of living. Both Kaprow and Deleuze move towards encompassing the virtual and the actual within a single plan(e) of composition, a plan(e) that overcomes the subjective form of experience in favour of a process that constructs a living plane of immanence.

For Deleuze and Kaprow the 'event' produces something new in our state of affairs, and as such marks a becoming or change in state. But this event is not historically determined – precisely because it is 'new' – and involves a power of invention that Harold Rosenberg, an important influence on both Deleuze and Kaprow, ascribes to a revolutionary actor. In what Deleuze called 'some fine pages' (Deleuze 1994: 91), Rosenberg writes that this actor performs a 'timeless incident', an event of innovation that enters history as another moment in 'an endless series of recurrences' (Rosenberg 1960: 156–7). This is a *tradition of the new* that repeats a kind of 'immaculate conception' (Deleuze 1990: 97) that causes, according to Rosenberg, 'the present to vanish in the eternal' (1960: 166).[2] For Kaprow such events are achieved by a 'truly generative idea' that has the 'capacity to keep on ramifying' (Kaprow 2003: 223). This 'generative idea' was, Kaprow claimed, an 'essential absolute' and formed 'the only human "virtue", the continuous rebirth of the Self'. This, he argued, 'is what a new art is' (Kaprow 1967: 5). Kaprow's Happenings were events that not only sought to introduce something new into life, but were aimed against the normalised subjectivity of human being itself. It is not simply a move from art to life then, a move that would leave the foundational structure of experience untouched; rather, the event transforms the conditions of experience and in so doing constructs a new form of subjectivity, and a new kind of art. Or at least this was the founding ambition of Kaprow's work, one he struggled his whole career to maintain and develop.

Deleuze's most extensive discussion of the event comes in *The Logic of Sense*. There he takes from Stoic philosophy 'two simultaneous readings of time': the passing present, or *Chronos*, and the time of the 'event' that unfolds in an 'instant', in *Aion* as the 'empty form of time' (Deleuze 1990: 5). What happens always occurs within this double dimension. On the one hand, the event is actualised within a state of affairs, within a present whose duration includes a past and future relative to it, while on the other it remains a purely virtual and incorporeal 'idea' expressed in an infinitive verb (e.g. 'to cut'), which is either already over or still to come in relation to its embodiment. Deleuze's description of the incorporeal event is pertinent to Kaprow's score: 'It is always and at the same time something which has just happened and something about to happen; never something which is happening' (63). As such, the event marks a threshold across which a becoming is actualised, and in its virtual existence outside of chronological time it stands, Deleuze claims, as an 'eternal truth' (149). Although a change in a body expresses a virtual event, from which it gains its sense, and the event 'itself' does not exist outside of its expressions, they do not have a direct or causal relation. Instead, they constitute what Deleuze calls, and once more it is a fitting description of the Happening, a 'method of dramatization'.[3]

Let's look more closely at this dramatisation of the Deleuze-Kaprow event. Kaprow's early scores for his Happenings contain two elements: a description of the 'Setting' and a list of the 'Events' that will take place within it. The first lays out an area and the elements that occupy it, as these are relevant to the Happening that will take place there. The 'Events' then describe what will happen.[4] The setting structures the Happening according to the various singularities that constitute its place; 'a patch of woods . . . a road leading to a small wooden bridge . . . a patio table loaded with packages of cheap white bread. . .'. The events describe the various relations between these singularities, as they are acted by the participants: 'Tree women swing hanging furniture, . . . Bread man hawks bread and jam . . . Wall workers taunt tree workers. . .'.[5] The events (to swing, to hawk, to taunt. . .) create differential 'rhythms' of interaction between the elements of the setting, and give the Happening a 'variable' time that is, Kaprow says, 'independent of the convention of continuity' (Kaprow 2003: 63). These rhythmical events – or as Deleuze also calls them 'spatio-temporal' or 'sub-representational dynamisms' – are ontogenetic individuations of a world (Deleuze 2004: 96–7). For Deleuze, the ideal event is entirely determined by the intense and differential rhythms that connect and divide its singularities, these relations forming series that compose an events' 'structure'. Events, in this sense, are 'jets of singularities' (Deleuze 1990: 53), converging and diverging in reciprocally determined differential relations. Kaprow's scores are similarly 'differentiated', their ideal structure/score establishes differential relations between singularities, spatio-temporal dynamisms that are 'rough drafts' dramatised by an actual Happening, where they are 'differenciated' in a performance (Deleuze 2004: 97; 1994: 207).

The 'dramatisation' of the virtual 'event' also requires a further element: what Deleuze calls a 'paradoxical entity', which allows the virtual and actual realms to 'communicate'. This entity has no self-identity inasmuch as of its two sides (virtual and actual) 'one is always absent from the other' (Deleuze 1990: 41). 'It is at this mobile and precise point', Deleuze writes, 'where all events gather together in one that transmutation happens', where the event is dramatised, and where the subjectivity and identity of the 'actor' can become a figure for the 'singular life' of the event. (153). This is a *counter-actualization* (150) achieved by the actor(s) of the Happening embodying the role of the paradoxical entity, a 'structuralist *hero*', as Deleuze elsewhere calls her (2004: 191), who is able to create something new by 'grasping herself as event' (1990:

178). This is the hero's 'resistant and creative force' as she constructs a new future, a 'mutation point [that] defines a praxis, or rather the very site where praxis must take hold' (Deleuze 2004: 191).

Dramatisation is the process by which the artist – at least for Kaprow – creates something new in the world by counter-actualising the event. This is a practical operation that involves, as Deleuze explains,

> producing surfaces and linings in which the event is reflected, finds itself again as incorporeal and manifests in us the neutral splendor which it possesses in itself in its impersonal and pre-individual nature, beyond the general and the particular, the collective and the private. It is a question of becoming a citizen of the world. (Deleuze 1990: 148)

For Deleuze, like Kaprow, in willing the event and so becoming its 'impersonal' and 'pre-individual' 'offspring', we are 'reborn' (151, 149). It is this aspect of the event that Kaprow is most sensitive to: that the 'counter-actualization' of the impersonal and 'neutral' event (151), or in Kaprow's terms the 'neutrality' of the score (Kaprow 2003: 168), 'side-steps' the present (Deleuze 1990: 151) and launches the world into the eternal return of the new. It is this 'moment' that Kaprow is seeking in his Happenings, the moment of the 'essential absolute' where the eternal becoming, or rhythm, of life is not simply revealed, but is actually lived. In this sense, the eternal truth of the event is not Platonic, inasmuch as it does not pre-exist its construction, its counter-actualisation in and as the world. As a result, the essence of the event is not something that could answer the question 'What is X?', because X qua 'new' does not pre-exist its actualisation. In fact, the essence of the event can only be approached through the specificity of its appearance, through the very different questions of *'who? how? how much? where and when? in which case?'* (Deleuze 2004: 96). As we shall see, it is precisely such questions that increasingly come to lay out the coordinates of the Happening as a process of counter-actualisation, and that cause both Kaprow and Deleuze to abandon the process of dramatisation for an event of individuation, in which the score and its actualisation come to occupy a single plan(e) of composition coextensive with 'Life'.

The counter-actualisation of an 'event' or score is, as we have seen, fundamentally and necessarily participatory, and this raised basic questions for Kaprow regarding the relationship of his performances to their audience. The participation of spectators in Kaprow's early Happenings was fairly peripheral, these events being, as Kaprow acknowledges (in 1961), either indoors, and so 'essentially theatre pieces' where the audience 'are commingled in some way with the event, flowing in and among its parts', (Kaprow 2003: 17), or else outdoors, where actors and spectators share a 'habitat' intended to 'melt the surroundings, the artist, the work, and everyone who comes to it into an elusive, changeable configuration' (18). Thus the actor–audience relation ranged from the fairly conventional (in *Chicken* [1962] the audience stood or sat in a large auditorium) to more fluid arrangements (*Mushroom* [1962] called for the 'actors' to exchange roles, to alternate between roles and being part of the audience, and for the members of the audience to become actors themselves). Although the relations between artist, work and audience were more or less interchangeable, they nevertheless retained their structural distinction within the expressive dramatisation of the event-score. Kaprow becomes increasing dissatisfied with this mode of Happening, and especially with the fact that as long as there is an audience of any kind the Happening remains stuck within the realm of 'Art' that reduces it to an avant-garde event, always already in the process of being recuperated as a commodity within the art industry.[6] As early as 1961 Kaprow is seeking to prevent this from happening to his Happenings, by giving them a foundation outside of 'art' and within 'life'. Happenings, he writes, are 'not just another new style. . . . They are a moral act [. . . whose] criterion [is] their certainty as an ultimate existential commitment' (21). As a result, Kaprow became increasingly convinced that the Happening was a counter-actualisation of and in 'life', and as such was a natural (or 'existential') process, rather than 'art'.[7] Consequently, Kaprow's Happenings sought to evade the 'art' experience by becoming ever more indiscernible from life, and by 1964 his scores are explicitly stating: 'There will be no spectators of this event' (for the Happening *Household*: Meyer-Hermann et al. 2008: 174). With the disappearance of the audience comes the disappearance of any description of the 'setting' from the Happening's score, which is now simply a non-specific but everyday location for the event. *Calling* (1965) is an early example: 'In the city, people stand at street corners and wait' (179). Constructing a 'setting' is no longer a part of the Happening, which now takes place entirely within life. 'Life' was, however, a fluid category in Kaprow's work, and appeared in a variety of guises. Beginning with *Fluids* (1967) a series of Happenings focused on natural materials and processes, while at the same time other Happenings began to incorporate electronic feedback loops (for example, *Message Units*, from 1968) to explore the futuristic potentials of new technology, and to utilise the mass media to disperse documentation of the Happening as part of the event (for example, *Six Ordinary Happenings*, or *Course* from 1969). In 1968 Kaprow performed *Runner*, his first solo Happening, which marked a move away from the organisation of social interactions in his earlier work, towards increasingly private and banal events. *Meters*, an 'Activity' from 1972 (as the Happenings are from then on increasingly called), is typical: 'carrying a cube of ice in the mouth . . . swallowing the melting ice till its gone' (227). From 1973, most 'Activities' were performed in domestic settings, sometimes with the isolated participants communicating by telephone (for example, *Basic Thermal Units*).

All of these developments directly concern the relationship between the virtual score and its actualisation within the Happening. As long as this relationship is understood as a theatrical dramatisation – that is, as 'art' – the counter-actualisation it achieves retains an expressive quality that not only guarantees the separation of its virtual and actual dimensions into ideal and material elements, but prevents it from being fully immanent in life. Kaprow's development of the Happening in the face of this problem echoes the change in Deleuze's own thinking regarding the event. Deleuze's 'problem' is that the separation of the virtual event and its actualised 'happening' means their communication – and so counter-actualisation – rests upon the paradoxical instant *as an undetermined principle*. This instant, both heroic and sublime in its revolutionary and ahistorical power of innovation, limits the realm of real transformation to that of virtual events, making dramatisation subsumable to a romantic expressionism in which art took on a necessary and privileged role. Furthermore, the paradoxical instant, being actually undetermined but nevertheless genetic, was a principle that remained outside that which it produced. 'The show is being directed by someone else' (Kaprow 2003: 181). As a result: 'The theatrical model was plainly inadequate; a different genre was necessary' (Kaprow 2003: 185). Deleuze and Guattari attempt to evade the expressionism of dramatisation by turning art into a natural 'living' process, constructing spatio-temporal individuations in and as the world, most famously in their concept of the 'refrain'. Thus they share with Kaprow a move away from an expressive dramatisation qua 'art', towards a counter-actualising construction qua 'life' that abandons both the separation of the virtual (score) and the actual (performance), and the heroic undetermined instant in which they would communicate. For Kaprow, this will mean rejecting the figure of the 'artist' – seen in the trash-messiah 'Neutron Kid' played by Kaprow in *Gas* (1966) – in favour of the anonymous 'worker' of *Runner* (1968) (see Meyer-Hermann et al. 2008: 186, 198). From this point, Kaprow begins to develop what Deleuze and Guattari will call a 'plan(e) of composition' that avoids any dramatisation of the score as an 'organizational principle [that] does not appear in itself, in a direct relation with that which it develops or is organized' (Deleuze and Guattari 1987: 293). The score qua plan(e) of composition is now simultaneously expressed *and* constructed in the Happening in an ongoing, aleatory and autopoietic feedback loop, in which life's virtual and actual dimensions are entirely immanent to each other, and the question of individual subjective expression is subsumed by that of the construction of an individuation of the world.

An important precedent for this form of composition was the work of John Cage. Kaprow attended Cage's 'Experimental Composition' class at the New School for Social Research in New York that ran from 1957 to 1958, and he found three important elements of the Happenings there. The first was Cage's incorporation of chance into the compositional process, the second was his interest in a form of attention inspired by Zen Buddhism, and the third was his understanding of Duchamp's readymade (still almost unknown in America at that time). All three elements were already evident in Cage's composition *4'33'* (1952), where the score acted only to open the 'work' onto the chance and 'readymade' occurrences of life. In this sense, the score did not organise matter into 'art' because its 'idea' did not exist outside of its actualisation. Instead, the score for *4'33'* composes an 'immanent sound plane', as Deleuze and Guattari call it, 'which is always given along with that to which it gives rise' (294). Cage's compositional practice was adopted (and subtly critiqued) by Kaprow, in extending it 'well beyond the boundaries of the art genres themselves' (Kaprow 2003: 224). This was a way of maximising the chance elements that guaranteed the immanence of the plan(e) and the performance, as well as immunising the event against becoming art. As Kaprow explains, 'the sheer magnitude of unforeseeable details and outcomes for any projected event in the real world was so much greater than what a chance score might provide that devising a method to suspend taste or choice became superfluous. A simple plan was enough' (224). A score or 'plan' that contained chance as its autopoietic compositional principle both constructed, *and was constructed by* 'life' rather than 'art'. As Kaprow puts it, 'our newly released art began to perform itself as if following its own natural bent' (225). In fact, Deleuze and Guattari give a description of Cage's work which is highly relevant for our understanding of Kaprow's later Happenings: 'It is undoubtedly John Cage', they write,

> who first and most perfectly deployed this fixed sound plane, which affirms a process against all structure and genesis, a floating time against pulsed time or tempo, experimentation against any kind of interpretation, and in which silence as sonorous rest also marks the absolute state of movement. (Deleuze and Guattari 1987: 294–5)

Cage's sound plan(e) therefore emerges as prior to any determination of its structure or founding act, opening the composition up to, and in fact making it indiscernible from, the aleatory and autopoietic processes of life.

This plan(e) of composition is not defined by its form, by its substance or by a subject. It is, Deleuze and Guattari argue, defined only by the sum total of the material elements that belong to it under given relations of speed and slowness (longitude), and the sum total of the intensive affects or becomings it is capable of (latitude). A Happening, in this sense, is an 'individuation' in which its actual and virtual dimensions, its plan(e) and the happening that occurs through and upon it, is a material composition defined by the differential relations of movement and rest that the plan(e) establishes between its elements, and the affects that express and construct the plan(e)'s becoming. Kaprow's Activities no longer developed *according to* a plan, as its expression, because the plan was inseparable from what happened, making its expression the very mechanism by which the plan(e) qua individuation *was constructed.*

Kaprow's method moves towards constructing a plan(e) of composition from the early 1970s, when the Happenings become largely banal in their actions, and increasingly organised around aleatory events feeding back into the performance (e.g. the Activities *Meters* and *Entr'acte* from 1972). Kaprow's scores did not, perhaps, stick literally to Deleuze and Guattari's formula for the event, '*Indefinite article+proper name+infinitive verb*', (Deleuze and Guattari 1987: 290), but nevertheless there are important similarities. Here is an example from 1976, part of the score for the Activity *7 Kinds of Sympathy*:

A, writing
Occasionally blowing nose

B, watching
Copying A blowing nose

continuing

(later) B reading A's writing
occasionally scratching groin, armpit

A, watching
Copying B scratching

Continuing . . . (Kaprow 2003: 166)

7 Kinds of Sympathy was part of the increasing re-location of the Happening into 'private' spaces, and Kaprow's interest in dis-locating individual subjectivity in the experiences it produced. In *7 Kinds of*

Sympathy, the score constitutes what Deleuze calls 'an abstract drawing, which is like the section of all the various forms, whatever their dimensions' (Deleuze 2002: 69). The virtual events determined by the score (A/B watches, copies, scratches, etc.) are open to an infinite number of potential actualisations, while each actualisation determines the plane of composition on which the subsequent virtual sections will be actualised, and by which the plan(e) itself continues to be (re)constructed. This compositional process is aleatory *and* self-determining; the score and its actualisation are necessarily inseparable and reciprocally determining. The plan(e) of composition is therefore counter-actualised in its individuation, and in being produced through a focusing of attention on very particular actions (rather than the expansive embrace of any-sound-whatever in Cage's 4'33'), this experience is not that of organic bodies or formed subjects, but emerges in an everyday affect producing the vital movement of a non-subjective, but nevertheless entirely material, event (the Happening) qua moving plane of immanence. If this was to extend Cage's plan(e) of composition into a vital experience of and as Life, as Kaprow claimed, it did so, at least in part, through his reading of John Dewey's *Art as Experience*.

Kaprow started reading Dewey's book in 1949 and it remained a seminal influence throughout his career. Dewey saw art as emerging in and as experience, meaning it was always *happening*. The artwork, he wrote, 'is not twice alike for different persons [and . . .] it changes with the same person at different times as he brings something different to a work' (Dewey 1980: 331). The experience of art, like any experience at all, 'is esthetic in the degree in which organism and environment cooperate to institute an experience in which the two are so fully integrated that each disappears' (249). Experience therefore establishes a plan(e) of composition that is always under construction, or as Dewey put it: 'Art is a quality of doing and of what is done' (214). For Dewey, this 'doing' was a quality of experience that 'serves life' (135) – we shall see how in a moment – a statement echoed by Kaprow's claim that the Happening was nothing but 'Doing life' (Kaprow 2003: 195).[8] The disappearance of organism and environment, of subject and object in experience, implied 'an immediate fusion of form and matter' (Dewey 1980: 130) inasmuch as experience was determined by an *'operation of forces'* that was inherent to its material and 'not imposed from without' (136). These forces produce rhythms through their 'opposition of energies' (157) and rhythm constructs an experience that expresses and constructs a plane of composition in 'constant variation' (164). Kaprow often analysed his own work and that of other artists in precisely these terms, whether in the 'continuous and polarized forces' at play in Mondrian's paintings (Kaprow 2003: 30), the differential 'pulsations' composing the 'natural rhythm' of Pollock's work (39–40),[9] or the juxtapositions of elements in the Happening itself. For Dewey, these rhythmic experiences constituted by the intense oppositions of matter-force ramify endlessly, each opposition/experience being itself constituted by another opposition of forces, and so on, encompassing the living plan(e) of Nature. Any experience, therefore, expresses the relations between all forces, inasmuch as they are constructed according to the experience's perspective, and experience reaches its '*integral fulfillment*' (136) in expressing all of life. As a result, an aesthetic experience 'is not a variation in a single feature but a modulation of the entire pervasive and unifying qualitative substratum' (Dewey 1980: 155). This is a beautiful description of univocal being as Deleuze understands it, and which Dewey designates 'Unity in variety' (161). What is 'aesthetic' in experience is precisely our 'intuition' of the rhythmical process that expresses and constructs its background, as the plan(e) of composition connecting things and events in an emergent process of individuation. This is what makes the aesthetic experience an 'individual whole' (215), as the 'unique transcription of the energy of the things of the world' (185). 'We are, as it were,' Dewey writes, 'introduced into a world which is nevertheless the deeper reality of the world in which we live in our ordinary experience. We are carried out beyond ourselves to find ourselves. . . . The whole is then felt as an expansion of ourselves' (195). This world of experience is our world, and in it we have become citizens of a world constantly changing through *and as* our experience. It is this world and its experience that Kaprow's work constantly tries to produce. The aim of art, in this sense, is no longer the production of an object, but the production/consumption of an experience as the construction and expression of life. In Dewey's words: 'In a work of art the proof of the pudding is decidedly in the eating' (94). Or, Kaprow this time, the Happening 'names a method that becomes manifestly unmethodical if one considers the pudding more a proof than a recipe' (Kaprow 2003: 19).

But an important question remains to be answered: why does Kaprow, now deviating from Dewey, wish to place this experience *against* art of any sort? For Dewey and for Kaprow the problem is how to overcome the 'chasm between ordinary and esthetic experience', inasmuch as this has been exacerbated by the rise of museum institutions and capitalist markets, and is now 'embedded in the nature of things' (Dewey 1980: 10). The problem, concisely stated by Dewey, is 'that of recovering the continuity of esthetic experience with normal processes of living' (10).

Although Kaprow begins from Dewey's attempt to 'discover how the work of art develops and accentuates what is characteristically valuable in things of everyday enjoyment' (11), and does this by following Dewey's rejection of the institutional reduction of art to the collection of certain objects in favour of experience, he goes further than Dewey in wishing to escape the recuperation of the rejection of the art institution in avant-garde commodities traded by the art industry. In other words, whereas Dewey and Deleuze and Guattari advocate an aesthetic plan(e) of composition which is at once art and life, Kaprow's absolute fear of recuperation leads him to strategies of counter-actualisation that can no longer be called 'art' or 'aesthetics'. As a result, Kaprow argues that his work is 'nonart', and as such, is a performance practice that 'need not be justified as an artwork' (Kaprow 2003: 176). Instead, Kaprow sees it as closer to 'basic research' or 'inquiry', which he claims would make the Happening like 'performing a job or service and would relieve the artist of inspirational metaphors, such as creativity, that are tacitly associated with making art, and therefore theatre art' (177). From the early 1970s, Kaprow's performances increasingly take on the character of 'work', whether of a physical kind (for example, the hard labour of *Scales* [1971]), or the more immaterial labour involved in documenting physical processes (for example, *Time Pieces* [1973]). In both cases, the 'work' is a means of attaining a meditational awareness that emerges from, but at the same time transforms, the most banal forms of life. Kaprow, inspired by Erving Goffman's study *The Presentation of Self in Everyday Life*, now envisions the Happening, or Activity, as 'Performing Life' (an article from 1979). This is not an aesthetic process, and nor does it produce art. Instead, it is an entirely conceptual decision that turns an everyday action such as shaking hands or speaking on the telephone into a performance, in order to achieve 'displacements of ordinary emphasis [that] increase attentiveness to the peripheral parts of ourselves and our surroundings. Revealed in this way they are strange. Participants could feel momentarily separated from themselves' (198).

Here, Kaprow dissolves the score to its utmost possible point, being simply the minimal selection of an everyday activity as a 'performance'. Mixing Dewey with Goffman, as well as with an interest in the form of Zen Buddhism popularised by D. T. Suzuki that Kaprow shared with Cage, he sees these 'lifelike' performances as a way of 'living attentively', a kind of meditative practice that reveals everyday life's 'hidden features' (188). This awareness is a 'curious' kind of 'self-consciousness that permeates every gesture', allowing one to 'experience directly' the way 'consciousness alters the world' (190). Kaprow's Happenings, as they moved more and more towards 'Performing Life', become exercises in self-observation that were close to Zen Buddhist meditation and its 'enlightenment practices' (218). It is these self-reflective processes that Kaprow claims lead to (Dewey's) feelings of expansion: 'Self-knowledge is where you start on the way to becoming "the whole", whether this process takes the form of social action or personal transformation' (217). Self-knowledge, in this sense, is understood to counter-actualise the rational human subject, giving rise to cosmic awareness through the intense contemplation of banal events (for example, *Taking a Shoe for a Walk* [1989]).

Kaprow had begun practising Zen Buddhism in 1978, and Jeff Kelley has suggested that, after this time, Kaprow's work offers 'secular, operational analogues' to the koan (Kelley 2004: 204). The koan was a study form developed mainly within the Rinzai school of Zen, to which Suzuki belonged, and aimed at intuitive flashes of insight or 'satori': 'cosmic triggers' in which the perspective of the individual ego was overcome and the interconnectedness of the world appeared in its living vitality (200). This mystical style of self-knowledge as self-overcoming, achieved through performance is, Kaprow claims, 'an introduction to right living' (Kaprow 2003: 225), but it is increasingly uncertain that this still bears any resemblance to what Deleuze and Guattari call 'counter-actualization', let alone to what they call art. Despite the fact that, for Deleuze and Guattari, art's production of sensation offers an experience of a vital and univocal plane of Nature that goes well beyond any subjective form, this sensation has two important elements that Kaprow's conception does not. First, it is a form of animal rather than spiritual life, and second, it does not require a level of reflection (or a resulting mystical transcendence) in order for the univocal plane of Nature to be experienced. Kaprow's affirmation of 'awareness' as the aim of the Happening, although giving an interesting Zen twist to Conceptual Art's emphasis on intellectual processes as the essence of art, nevertheless dematerialises the art–life dialectic by dissolving the first in the second through turning it into a state of mind.

Like many of the Conceptual artists, Kaprow dematerialises art and makes it coextensive with life through Duchamp's readymade, which enabled artists, he claimed, to 'carry the art bracket ready-made in their heads for instant application anywhere' (110). As a result, the Happening becomes reduced to a conceptual decision to treat something (anything) as art, and a form of self-reflective attention allowing for a transformative, or at least revealing, experience. Deleuze and Guattari are sceptical of this Conceptual move, because while opening art onto the commercial information circuits that were increasingly coming to control social life, it failed to provide any real resistance to these political transformations. (Deleuze and Guattari 1994: 198–9). Kaprow is symptomatic of this problem, arguing that with the readymade 'the circle closes: as art is bent on imitating life, life imitates art' (Kaprow 2003: 111). In this, life gains the upper hand, because in imitating it, art (qua avant-garde gesture par excellence) is in fact imitating the modern world's constant imitation of itself. This observation, made in 1972, of the emerging importance of communication technologies is nevertheless both utopian and triumphant, because in it Kaprow finds the readymade always already at work, and life has subsumed art in a newly technological nature: 'Art, which copies society copying itself, is not simply the mirror of life. Both are made up. Nature is an echo system' (146).[10] At this point, art has become nature, but nature has become the reproductive technology driving late-capitalist life. In the face of this technological immanence (or perhaps better, interface), Kaprow offers a process of self-reflective meditation on everyday actions and experiences that does not construct new counter-actualisations, but simply promises a mystical transcendence of life. Art can be anything we say it is, just as a performance has become reduced to a conceptual frame placed around anything-at-all. Once more we are reminded of Cage's *4'33'*, and its lack of any constructive intervention within the social realm it opens onto. Indeed, it is this very passivity that risks the collapse of the plane of composition into the banal chaos of the everyday. In other words, anything goes in but nothing comes out. The frame, or score, has simply achieved a conceptual transformation of a part of the everyday into a meditation practice which provides, perhaps, a transcendental awareness or contemplation. From this perspective, the problem with Kaprow's latter performances is one he shares with Cage's 'prepared piano'. As Deleuze and Guattari point out, their process of selection is, on the one hand, too open: 'a machine of reproduction that ends up reproducing nothing but a scribble effacing all lines, a scramble effacing all sounds. The claim is that one is opening music to all events, all irruptions, but one ends up reproducing a scrambling that prevents any event from happening' (Deleuze and Guattari 1987: 379). On the other hand, this process remains 'too "territorialized"' (379) upon the act of selection itself, upon the 'prepared piano' in Cage's case, or upon the meditative self-consciousness that establishes Kaprow's 'performance' and remains the condition of possibility for its mystical evaporation into the One-All.

Given these problems with Kaprow's work, and by way of conclusion, we can turn to some of Adrian Piper's performances from 1970, which also drew on Dewey's *Art and Experience*, to extend the 'event' onto Deleuze and Guattari's plane of composition in a directly political sense.[11] However, it must be pointed out that this work is not especially typical of Piper's practice, which subsequently in fact follows a similar trajectory to Kaprow's, seeking to find a heightened 'self-consciousness' by withdrawing into a private and reflective practice without any sort of spectator. Like Kaprow, this practice was also influenced by Asian 'spiritual' techniques – in Piper's case, yoga. Nevertheless, for a brief moment in 1970, in a series of works Piper calls *Catalysis*, performance becomes indiscernible from a banal and everyday 'life', taking place within public spaces such as the bus, the subway, the department store and the street, while nevertheless aiming to construct new social relations. In these works, the 'score' (such as it exists) is entirely immanent to its actualisation, while its actualisation is a process that constructs new virtual coefficients within the social field, increasing the dimensions of its possible composition. Here, Piper's performances operate as agents of social change, a change that constitutes the work itself. As almost the opposite to Kaprow's search for a private and meditative awareness transcending the conditions of ordinary perception, Piper's work is utterly externalised in its act. Piper, like Kaprow, is inspired by Dewey's interest in recovering the continuity of aesthetic experience with normal processes of living, and by his condemnation of the museum and its capitalist supports. 'To enjoy that discreetness and isolation', she writes, 'is a measure of the artist's integration in and acceptance by the structure – the capitalist structure – of this society' (Piper 1996: 39). In response, Piper recognises herself 'as essentially a social being', and proposes to use this social status to embark on 'specifically political activity' (40). This involves taking her self, qua social being, as the material on which to practice art, meaning that 'the art-making process and end-product has the immediacy of being in the same time-space continuum as the viewer' (42). Art has become life, and nothing but life, but this in no way, at least for Piper, invalidates this work as art, or her activity as an artist. Piper's work introduces an autopoietic impetus to the performance that draws on chance, but in a way different to Cage or Kaprow. Piper keeps the 'score' of her performance as simple as possible, which in the *Catalysis* work consists purely in a simple action or 'event'. This, Piper claims, 'eliminates the separation between original conception and the final form of an idea; the immediacy of conception is retained in the process/product as much as possible. For this reason I have no way of accounting for the final form that an idea takes' (45). As a result, the 'form' of the work, its actualisation, is based upon a chance occurrence. Yet, unlike Cage's *4'33'* or Kaprow's more controlled usage of chance, the aleatory catalysis of an affect by Piper's performance exists immediately on and as a social plane of composition, and operates as a mechanism of its construction.

One work, *Catalysis IV* (1970), involved her travelling on a bus, the subway, and the Empire State building elevator with a white hand towel stuffed into her mouth. Piper argues that the work's 'content' lies entirely within the spectator's 'affective response' (32), and she attempts to project this response against its social programming, as a counter-actualisation aimed against 'racism, racial stereotyping, and xenophobia' (242). In order to do so, the work exists entirely independently of *any* institutional structure, which it must if it is to unleash the full power of its catalytic event. 'I like the idea', she wrote, 'of doing away with all discrete forms and letting art lurk in the midst of things' (37). Similarly to Kaprow, Piper rejects 'an artificial environment or theatrical action' for her performances, but in placing herself, as art, within life she does not wish to transcend their distinction. Indeed, this distinction is crucial to the effective catalysis she wishes to provoke, inasmuch as when her own action is indiscernible from life, or alternatively, when the spectator is aware that they are participating in art, the alterity of Piper's 'performance' cannot construct an affect capable of the 'event' of social transformation (see Piper 1996: 34, 45).

Piper's action of stopping up her mouth is especially significant in this respect, allowing her to inhabit an alterity close to madness, but only in order to create an affect that revitalises 'everyday' sensation through the eruption of an unmediated, and invariably humorous, real. It does so by 'unclasping' (the term is Guattari and Deleuze's) her own body from the social conditioning that has produced it, and from the artistic institutions that might separate her performances from these conditions. In this way, Piper produces an event that appears only in the process of producing new affects, as a process by which performance as an art form is capable of catalysing new social territories in and as life. This, in the end, should be the aim of performance art that seeks to occupy the realm of life, and is one way in which the artist might become a citizen of the world.

References

Alliez, É. (2003), 'The BwO Condition, or, The Politics of Sensation', in É. Alliez and E. von Samsonow (eds), *Biographen des organlosen Körpers*, Vienna: Turia+Kant.
Alliez, É and J.-C.Bonne (2007), 'Matisse with Dewey and Deleuze', *Pli*, 18: 1–19.
Deleuze, G. (1990), *The Logic of Sense*, trans. M. Lester with C. Stivale, edited by C. V. Boundas, New York: Columbia University Press.
Deleuze, G. (1994), *Difference and Repetition*, trans. P. Patton, New York: Columbia University Press.

Deleuze, G. (1995), *Negotiations, 1972–1990*, trans. M. Joughin, New York: Columbia University Press.

Deleuze, G. (2002), *Dialogues II*, trans. H. Tomlinson and B. Habberjam, London: Continuum.

Deleuze, G. (2004), *Desert Islands and Other Texts 1953–1974*, trans. M. Taormina, New York: Semiotext(e).

Deleuze, G. and F. Guattari (1987), *A Thousand Plateaus*, trans. B. Massumi, London: Continuum.

Deleuze, G. and F. Guattari (1994), *What is Philosophy?* trans. H. Tomlinson and G. Burchell, New York: Columbia University Press.

Dewey, J. (1980), *Art as Experience*, New York: Perigree.

Kaprow, A. (1967), *Untitled Essay and Other Works*, New York: A Great Bear Pamphlet. Republished online in 2004 by Ubu classics.

Kaprow, A. (2003), *Essays on the Blurring of Art and Life*, edited by J. Kelley, Berkeley: University of California Press.

Kelley, J. (2004), *Childsplay, the Art of Allan Kaprow*, Berkeley: University of California Press.

Meyer-Hermann, E., A. Perchuk and S. Rosenthal (eds) (2008), *Allan Kaprow – Art as Life*, Los Angeles: The Getty Research Institute.

Piper, A. (1996), *Out of Order, Out of Sight Volume 1: Selected Writings in Meta-Art 1968–1992*, Cambridge, MA: MIT Press.

Rosenberg, H. (1960), *The Tradition of the New*, New York: Da Capo Press.

Notes

1. Both this 'break', and the way it marks a move from expression to construction in Deleuze's philosophy, have been explored by Éric Alliez (2003), and I have drawn on his account here.

2. 'History today', Deleuze and Guattari write, 'still designates only the set of conditions, however recent they may be, from which one turns away in order to become, that is to say, in order to create something new. . . . The event itself needs becoming as an unhistorical element' (Deleuze and Guattari 1994: 96). Kaprow writes something very similar in 1966: 'if something occurred in which the historical references were missing, even for a short time, that situation would be experimental'. The 'essential ingredient' in this 'militant' position was, according to Kaprow, 'newness', which spoke, he argued, 'to questions of being rather than to matters of art' (Kaprow 2003: 69).

3. See, in particular, 'The Method of Dramatization' (Deleuze 2003: 94–116).

4. The first Happening score to formalise this distinction was, to my knowledge, *A Service for the Dead II* (1962) (Meyer-Hermann et al. 2008: 148), but earlier scores also make the distinction implicitly by describing the setting first and the events afterwards. See, for example, the poster for *18 Happenings in 6 Parts* (1959) (Meyer-Hermann et al. 2008: 120).

5. From *Birds* (1964) (Meyer-Hermann et al. 2008: 165).

6. Rosenberg was one of the earliest American art critics to point out this problem. See Rosenberg (1960: 37).

7. In 1966 Kaprow writes: 'Imagine something never before done, by a method never before used, whose outcome is unforeseen. Modern art is not like this; it is always art' (Kaprow 2003: 69).

8. Dewey's understanding of art as experience also has strong echoes in Deleuze and Guattari's work, not least their shared interest in birdsong. Éric Alliez and Jean-Claude Bonne have recently developed the relations of Dewey's and

Deleuze and Guattari's work in relation to the painter Henri Matisse. See Alliez and Bonne (2007).

9. Kaprow lists these, some of which also appear in Deleuze's writing on the visual arts: 'attack/withdrawal, expansion/contraction, tangle/structure, hot/cold, passion/enlightenment' (Kaprow 2003: 40).

10. For an account of art as Nature much closer to Dewey's position, which Kaprow wrote in 1958, see Kaprow (2003: 10).

11. Piper quotes Dewey in her important essay, 'Talking to Myself: The Ongoing Autobiography of an Art Object', written between 1970 and 1973 (Piper 1996: 39).

sub specie durationis

Matthew Goulish and Laura Cull

Latitude has not disappeared, nor is its disappearance imminent. This I propose, respectful of the threat posed by accelerated communication, as theorised by Paul Virilio with a mapmaker's care, to the latitudinal parallel, the imaginary east–west circle measured in degrees along meridians equidistant from the equator on representations of earth. What thought haunts each thinker? In considering latitude I have been haunted by that of Henri Bergson. *The brain does not have thinking as its function but that of hindering the thought from becoming lost in dream; it is the organ of attention to life.*

The Disappearance of Latitudinarianism
Matthew Goulish

Last December I accepted an invitation to a holiday dinner hosted by a student and her family visiting from Oregon. I was touched by their inclusion of me, all the more so because my partner in life was away that week. At a point in the evening, my student's younger brother asked me, 'Have you heard of Spore?' I replied: a one-celled reproductive organism sent through the air by a mushroom. I was after all *the teacher*. It quickly became apparent that brother, father, stepmother, boyfriend and roommate all shared enthusiastic anticipation of a new non-competitive computer game by the engineer who brought us The Sims. The father explained that the player begins life as a spore and evolves to Western civilisation. 'That must take some time', I ventured. We can't know yet, he said, the release date passed two years ago, and the designer is still working. It is expected, however, that when players attain civilisation level, they will network with one another, and trade – cattle, for example, for iron ore – to avoid extinction. My student entered from the kitchen and said, 'It's all about Spore around here.' Later as I took the Damen

Avenue bus home, a digital blare issued from my coat pocket. Nearly every cellular telephone call I receive is a wrong number. Now I read:

Do u want to watch devil wears prada 2nite?

my first wrong number text. Latitude, I realised, was safe.

§

I had received the message 'instantly'. I don't want to reduce or carica-ture the Virilio argument, nor overstate the revelation of the error. Was it not Virilio, however, who observed that new technologies produce new accidents which reveal those technologies' limits, point to their outside? The message's intended and actual recipients were in this case noncoinci-dent. Had the instantness of the messaging caused latitude to disappear, the sender would have known that already.

§

Perhaps philosophers frequently confuse a phenomenon with its inverse. Let us ask: *one or many latitudes?*, a question not of disappearance, but of multiplication. For if we imagine that the acceleration of communications technology compresses distance to the vanishing point, are we not making the fundamental mistake of engaging concepts of space to understand struc-tures of time? Time does not travel from point A to point B; it transforms point A into point AA, not to progress but to evolve. Space involves move-ment; time only change. Duration, a wholeness of an event in time, remains always indivisible, thus unmeasurable, because to measure would be to divide, and division simply proposes other, smaller wholenesses. Intuition is the inhabited method by which we allow the observed parts to coalesce into an indivisible whole, a duration. The introduction of the 'instant' message into the technologies of communication appears as an acceleration if one compares it to, for example, the speed of the same message handwritten onto a postcard and carried in the mail. We then say that the shared latitude has virtually disappeared. Could we not instead say that instant messaging has introduced a different latitude onto the globe; that now we have the postcard latitude and the text message latitude, and we understand speed as a comparative relation between the two? The hare can finish the race many times in the time it takes the tortoise to finish once – a fact so obvious that the hare never bothers to finish at all. Winning the race, as Aesop suggested, was not about speed, but about duration, of which the story concerns two, noncoincident. To race is *to measure one flowing of duration in relation to another*. What if a third contestant had been a spore?

§

I recently travelled to Antwerp. I wrote an email to my host. 'I am leaving Chicago, and will arrive in Antwerp tomorrow.' The next day, I emailed her again. 'I am in Antwerp now.' She replied.

> How wonderful that you can reach me as easily from nearby as from far away!

Yet it was only information that travelled so easily; a series of digitised encoded thoughts, and as such, certainly, a part of me, but only a part, shall we say, not an element. My physical body had to move through a series of segments of intermodal transportation, the financial cost of which had increased in recent years, as well as a series of security checkpoints, the psychic cost of which had also escalated. Nabil El-Aid El-Othmani of Morocco summed up my point when he wrote:

> What is the future of globalization when there is an increasingly greater disproportion between the movements of capital and goods and that of people?

He submitted this question to Nobel economist Joseph Stiglitz in an online discussion, a conversation that instances the disparity, at least if one tries to imagine the difficulties of a face-to-face conversation, and considers information technology in the category of capital and goods. Stiglitz replied.

> This disparity in the liberalization of capital and labor is a major problem. Enormous energy has been focused on facilitating the flows of investment and capital, while movements of labor remain highly restricted. This is so even though the gains to global economic efficiency from liberalizing labor flows are an order of magnitude greater than the gains from liberalizing capital flows.

We can understand this response by way of Chicago's recent big-box ordinance, through which the city government attempted to force an increase in the wages of workers at Wal-Mart and similar stores. The effort failed because of the mayor's aggressive efforts to defeat it, heeding Wal-Mart's threat to leave the city if it passed. Clearly it is easier for Wal-Mart than for a person who works at Wal-Mart to move to the suburbs. The disparity in mobility allowed the store to leverage the government into keeping wages low. Had the mayor called the bluff of Wal-Mart with the argument that an increase in wages increases labour mobility, and contributes more to community economic growth than an increase in profit, which will further increase the mobility of capital and goods, which, Stiglitz goes on to argue, increases economic instability, we can expect that Wal-Mart would have lost the fight and begun to transform from its current state as a cavernous dungeon into that of a store one can shop at with a relatively clear conscience.

§

Latitude has not disappeared for labour, nor has it disappeared for capital. Consider *the disparity*. A bird flies over a prison wall while a prisoner spends his life on one side of it. Yet the prison wall has not disappeared, especially when we consider a part-prisoner-part-bird complex organism; a pigeon with a note tied to its ankle. That complex, increasingly unstable organism, is us.

§

Still, a peculiar thing happened to me the following week. As I stood in the kitchen on a sunny morning waiting for my coffee to brew, my partner in life exited the kitchen door carrying a basket of laundry, and descended the back stairs. A moment later, below the floor, I heard a snap that I identified as the flick of the stiff light switch in the basement on the laundry room's door jamb. I knew that she had turned on the light and stepped into the room to commence the washing, although I could hear no other sounds of her activity. Something in the combination of familiarity and distance gave the moment a tenderness that it would not have had had I followed her downstairs and watched her flick the switch. My pausing to consider this sensation prompted me, a moment later when she re-entered the kitchen, now carrying the empty basket, to tell her, 'I missed you when you were away.' And her to ask, 'When, last week?' And me to say, 'No, just now, when you went downstairs.' The word *missed* only approximated my feelings. The impulse to describe my thoughts and sensations accurately, perhaps gives birth to what we call philosophy, which it seems locates its inception in what we call *the ordinary*. The generative power of the ordinary has everything to do with the increased disparity in mobility between capital (information or the sound of a light switch) and labour (doing laundry, brewing coffee). Only one of these can travel through walls. Whatever the economic result of the disparity, it still prompts us to say: *How wonderful that you can reach me as easily from nearby as from far away!*

§

One enters Lutz's Café from Foster Avenue as into a traditional bakery. A display case runs the room's length. Behind it women bustle filling orders. Before it customers take a number. A corner door at the far end opens into an L-shaped dining area, the door at the crux of the L.

With twelve tables or booths, the dining room wraps the north and east sides of the bakery display. Near the end of the dining room's long side one sees the door marked *rest rooms*, and after passing through it, one encounters the oddity. To the left a darkened coat check counter awaits some large reception. To the right, a door labelled *private* apparently leads to storage areas or an office. Ahead on the right is the Men's room, and straight ahead is the Women's, but before entering these spacious toilets, one may stop, as I did. Once the door has closed to the dining room, one may find oneself momentarily confused as to how to return there, since the wide and undefined tiled area offers several doors on its cornered walls. Its overly complicated plan lends it the appearance of a remainder, a leftover space after all the other rooms had found their appropriate definition. It is the sort of area owners hope visitors will pass through without pausing to notice: the back of the place, but in the middle. As such it casts scepticism not only on its own existence as 'room' but by association on the entirety of architecture. It makes explicit that which remains implicit in most buildings: the gap between concept and reality – a form of failure, an overflow into inefficiency, a gesture that can't be serious. Stopped there by that surprise homecoming, I knew I was standing in the back of my own mind, as behind a stage set, where cobbled together boards prop up scenery, that had not remained out of sight, but insisted itself onto centre stage.

§

Consider my presence in the devil wears prada 2nite dialogue that of unsought x factor. Imagine texter demanding of textee an explanation for nonresponsiveness. Albeit accidentally I lodged myself into their relationship as a provocation. Why else would I have been faced with the ethical responsibility? I may have allowed them to salvage their plans for the evening. My decision to remain silent had to do with not only using my precious last moments on the Damen bus to begin composing this paper, as I wrote in my pocket notebook the word *spore*, but also with my aversion to the film. Allowing them to pass like ships in the night was doing them a favour. More important for us is the question of *one or many multiplicities*. Bergson distinguished between the discrete multiplicity that takes the measure of one of its parts from the number of elements it contains, and the continuous multiplicity that finds its metrical principle in something else – a force unfolding within it or acting upon it. Here we must distinguish between a part and an element. A part is a new smaller wholeness broken off from the original wholeness. An element, while smaller, retains qualities of the original wholeness. One obtains a part by fragmentation and an element by analysis. The artist sketches one of the towers of Notre Dame cathedral and below it writes the caption *Paris*. The tower, for the artist, is not a component part of Paris, but a partial expression of Paris, a partial capture of the Paris duration as the artist inhabited it. One may assemble all the parts or elements, analysed or fragmented, and still never constitute the whole. That accomplishment remains solely the territory of intuition, the method for grasping the continuous multiplicity that belongs to the sphere of duration. *In this way duration is not simply the indivisible, nor the nonmeasurable. Rather, it is that which divides only by changing in kind.* Neither the texter nor the textee understood that the introduction of the x factor of myself had changed the kind of their duration, from linear to triangular, making it susceptible to a new measurability. Within the latitude that instant messaging introduces, there arise two latitudes as the forces that unfold within the continuous multiplicity of the duration of that communication change.

§

Maybe *The Disappearance of Latitudinarianism*, although a title discovered through a compulsive preference for the word in the dictionary immediately following the one I looked up, in the end suggests a kind of sense which I will now attempt to make. Bergson regarded latitude as the freedom to choose between potential actions – a very small, even non-existent spacing for some animals and plants, and a potentially very large one for other beings; including humans. His concern for the loss of this space between excitation and response may lead us to ask how performance figures in the question. Perhaps Bergson's and Virilio's notions of latitude differ without contradiction if we consider the threat not simply a compression of space according to temporal acceleration, but also a subtler phenomenon concerning the freedom to choose between memories. If memory reduces to a one-to-one correspondence with the present, if memory's response is both singular and immediate, can we still call it memory? What are we, if memory is this? Are we minds becoming matter? The endangerment perhaps arises through tendencies of argument, or an element of voice I alluded to earlier as the confusion between disappearance and complexity. Can we link this confusion to an equal desire for speed and conviction? Latitudinarianism favours freedom of thought and behaviour, especially in religion, says my dictionary, sharing latitude's root from the Latin for *width . . . since I am, as finite, threatened with consequences from unforeseeable quarters, I am at any time acting, and speaking, in the absence of what may seem sufficient reason.* The compression of measure between café plan and building, between wholeness reconstructed of parts or elements, and wholeness grasped as duration, between concept and reality, parallels the space between my conviction and my doubt. Let the latitude whose disappearance concerns us be this: the width between answer and question. *What philosophy has lacked most of all is precision. Philosophical systems are not cut to the measure of the reality in which we live; they are too wide . . .* I simply, but hopefully not simplistically, propose that performance figures in our dialogue as a set of practices that enact, or reenact, or articulate duration's multiplicity as live or as lived: *to show us that an extension of the faculties of perception is possible*; possibility, let us say, that allows space of mind, or at the very least, latitude.

Goat Island, Deleuze's Bergsonism and the Experience of Duration
Laura Cull

Let us . . . grasp ourselves afresh as we are, in a present which is thick, and furthermore, elastic, which we can stretch indefinitely backward by pushing the screen which masks us from ourselves farther and farther away; let us grasp afresh the external world as it really is, not superficially, in the present, but in depth, with the immediate past crowding upon it and imprinting upon its impetus; let us in a word become accustomed to see all things *sub specie durationis*: immediately in our galvanized perception what is taut becomes relaxed, what is dormant awakens, what is dead comes to life again. (Bergson 1992: 129)

This fragment of Bergson's *The Creative Mind* reads like a manifesto for a kind of presence. A manifesto that calls upon us to grasp all things from the point of view of duration, and as such to enter into a new found presence – rather than a masked or superficial relation – with ourselves and the world. On the one hand, in this short essay, I want to explore Deleuze's reinvention of this Bergsonian manifesto in *Bergsonism* (1966) and in his two other studies of Bergson from 1956. On the other, I want to explore the extent to which a contemporary Chicago-based company, Goat Island, might be seen to collaboratively construct performances that aim to create just this kind of presence both for themselves, in the creative process, and for their audiences, in the event of performance. Through Bergson, presence might mean the experience of duration that forms the basis of a 'solidarity', reciprocity or sympathy defining the relation between organisms and their environment.

Founded in 1987, Goat Island is a collaborative performance group, directed by Lin Hixson and formed of the core members: Matthew Goulish, Bryan Saner, Karen Christopher, Mark Jeffrey and Litó Walkey. During their twenty years of creating work, the company have earned both respect and fascination in the field of performance for their commitment to (to name but two) the affective potential of intricate choreographies performed by non-expert bodies, and the capacity of a slow, genuinely collaborative research and creation process that, starting from a position of not knowing, goes on to generate new thoughts and unexpected sensations. Disseminating their particular perspective on performance through their carefully conceived Summer Schools as well as through their performances, Goat Island's influence speaks through the work of many in the next generation of practitioners, including the collaboratives – Cupola Bobber, plan b, Uninvited Guests, Deer Park and SpRoUt – each of whom repay their teachers not by remaining pupils, but by 'creatively responding'[1] to the multi-headed, hybrid entity that is Goat Island's body of work.[2]

The connection between Goat Island and Deleuze is already manifest in the writings of founding member, Matthew Goulish, as well as in the work of performance scholars such as Steve Bottoms and David Williams, who have exposed the Deleuzian aspects of Goat Island in a range of helpful observations.[3] Writing about the process of creating 'September roses', for instance, Goulish evokes notions of 'stuttering' in performance and a 'zone of indiscernibility' between human and animal that clearly evidence an engagement with Deleuze's thought. Likewise his earlier monograph, *39 microlectures: in proximity of performance*, draws on the concepts of deterritorialisation, the machinic, and differential repetition.[4]

My goal in this essay is to focus on the relation between Goat Island and the Deleuzo-Bergsonian philosophy of time – as duration, memory, the relation between past and future, and the 'hesitation' between them that is the present. Here I am particularly interested in current debates arising from Deleuze's creative reworking of Bergson's concept of the virtual. In *Matter and Memory*, Bergson makes no apology for asserting the duality of time and space. However, he ultimately emphasises the reality of matter as well as spirit. As Len Lawlor says, for Bergson 'It is not the case that matter is some sort of illusion; rather, matter is real' (Lawlor 2003: xii). The Deleuzo-Bergsonian challenge to think in terms of duration is not an injunction to forget matter. And yet, as my 'partner in life' – John Mullarkey – has noted, there is a tendency in 'Deleuzism' to celebrate the value of the virtual at the expense of the actual, and to neglect to address the connection between them. Drawing from this critique, Matthew Goulish's series of lectures on 'the ordinary', and the 'non-Virtualist' aspects of Deleuze's thought, I'll address a series of examples from Goat Island's performances which foreground the *connection* between space and time, in the intuitive experience of duration, rather than valuing one as more real than the other.

Deleuze's Bergsonism

Goat Island's notion of 'creative response' might also be an apt description of Deleuze's *Bergsonism*. It is not a representation of Bergson, so much as a creative interpretation that aims to generate novelty. Deleuze himself notoriously described the book as exemplary of his style of doing history of philosophy, a history performed as 'a sort of buggery or, no less, . . . an immaculate conception' (Deleuze 1995: 6). And indeed, commentators have since accused Deleuze of, amongst other things, making Bergson 'sound too much like Nietzsche' (Ansell-Pearson 1999: 22). As Alliez suggests, it is Deleuze's emphasis on the question of difference, both in *Bergsonism* and the two shorter studies that preceded it – 'Bergson' and 'The Conception of Difference in Bergson' (both 1956) – that differentiates his Bergsonism from others, such as Merleau-Ponty's, that had come before (Alliez 2001: 394). Written several years before their publication, Deleuze's 1950s studies of Bergson were undertaken in a philosophical climate so hostile to vitalism that, as Keith Ansell-Pearson notes, Bergson's significance had been 'reduced to that of being a philosopher of insects'(Ansell-Pearson 1999: 21)! Contra this, Deleuze's studies reframed Bergson's philosophy as making 'the greatest contribution to a philosophy of difference' (Deleuze 1999: 42), the modernity of which lies in its emphasis on 'the durational character of life' (Ansell-Pearson 1999: 21). We must, Bergson insists, think in terms of duration.

Deleuze's *Bergsonism* reads Bergson's oeuvre through a developmental narrative, suggesting that 'intuition' – the precise empirical method that Bergson evolves – has three 'different moments'. The first is a moment of what Deleuze calls 'pure dualism' in which Bergson criticises 'any vision of the world based on differences of degree . . . [which] lose sight of the essential point; that is, the articulation of the real or qualitative differences, the differences in kind'. In this first phase, intuition is presented as a means to actively challenge what is presented as an almost naturalised intellectual tendency to see things in terms of 'more' or 'less', or to think with 'badly analyzed composites' that cobble together irreducible orders into conceptual generalities. Second, Deleuze argues, Bergson moves towards a 'neutralized, balanced dualism' in which, rather than emphasising a difference in kind *between* the two 'tendencies' of space and duration, Bergson suggests that all differences in kind belong to *one* tendency: to duration. It is the durational aspect of a thing that allows it to differ in kind not just from other things, but more importantly from itself. Finally, in the third moment, in what might seem to be a paradoxical move in relation to the first, Bergson suggests that 'Duration is only the most contracted degree of matter, matter the most expanded degree of duration.' This, Deleuze says, is Bergson's 'moment of monism' in which there is no longer a duality between differences in kind and those of degree (Deleuze 1988: 92–3). But then, in the closing chapter of the book, Deleuze argues that 'a fourth moment must be added – that of dualism recovered' (94). And this turns out to be the controversial dualism of 'virtual' and 'actual': key concepts for Deleuze, but also for current debates within Deleuze Studies.

Borrowing his terms from Bergson's *Matter and Memory* (1896), Deleuze's ontological use of the virtual is proposed as an alternative to the possible/real distinction. The possible, Deleuze argues, prevents us from understanding life's creation of differences because it is retrospectively constructed from the real 'like a sterile double' (98). Whereas the real is understood to be limited to reproducing the image of the possible that it realises, the virtual is actualised in processes of divergence and creativity. The virtual is conceived as a kind of reservoir or source of pure difference that can be called upon to explain the emergence of novelty in actuality. In short, Deleuze says: 'The characteristic of virtuality is to exist in such a way that it is actualized by being differentiated'; the virtual is dependent on the actual to exert its creative force (74). So far, so positive – but then Deleuze later states: 'Life as movement alienates itself in the material form that it creates; by actualizing itself, by differentiating itself, it loses "contact with the rest of itself"' (104). With such references to actualisation as alienation, along with Deleuze's characterisations elsewhere of the virtual as the actual's conditioning ground, it is not difficult to see how a Deleuzian 'Virtualism' has emerged.

Attending to the Ordinary: 'Virtualism' versus 'A modest Americanisation of Deleuze'

If I might analyze what I am attempting, I could call it a modest Americanization of Deleuze; in a sense, trying to align his thinking with a writing approach one might recognize more in the tradition of American than European philosophy, by which I mean *one that springs from the lived, the everyday, the ordinary* (as found in Thoreau, Whitehead and Cavell). (Goulish 2007b, emphasis added)

Perhaps one of the most lively areas of debate in recent Deleuze Studies concerns the nature of the relation between virtual and actual in Deleuze's thought. Does Deleuze place a greater value on the virtual than on the actual, or on 'creation' rather than 'creature' (to translate the question into Peter Hallward's terms[5])? While Ansell-Pearson is comfortable describing Deleuze's thought as 'a materialism of the immaterial', or 'a materialism of the virtual' (Ansell-Pearson 1999: 413), Hallward accuses Deleuze of producing an ascetic philosophy of unworldly, pure creativity with no genuine connection to the actual world of material creativity. As he puts it: Deleuze 'assumes that the most creative medium of our being is a form of abstract, immediate or dematerialised thought' (Hallward 2006: 2). Dematerialised, he says, because Deleuze invokes a separation between thinking and the world. Self-present thinking can only be 'out of this world', since any connection to reality constitutes a distortion of its pure form.

> To claim that purely creative thought becomes abstract or immaterial is not to say that such thought is then simply empty or 'non-extended', so much as *liberated from any constituent relation to anything external to itself* . . . A thinking that proceeds independently of any reference to or mediation through a world or reality external to itself will prove to be our most adequate means of expressing an absolutely creative being or force. (2)

And, certainly, Deleuze's writing on Bergson tends to emphasise the need to go beyond the ordinary – whether in terms of experience or thought. For example, in his essay 'Bergson' he declares that: 'A great philosopher creates new concepts: these concepts simultaneously *surpass the dualities of ordinary thought* and give things a new truth, a new distribution, a new way of dividing up the world' (Deleuze 2004: 22, emphasis added). The 'ordinary' in terms of thought is associated with habit, common sense and the binary oppositions of representations. Likewise in *Bergsonism*, Deleuze argues that: 'All our false problems derive from the fact that we do not know how to go beyond experience towards *the conditions of experience*, towards the articulations of the real, and to rediscover what differs in kind in the composites that are given to us and on which we live' (Deleuze 1988: 26, emphasis added).

This notion of virtual conditions has been taken up and foregrounded by a number of Deleuzian commentators, including Brian Massumi. However, John Mullarkey argues that Massumi et al. represent a larger tendency within Deleuze Studies to denigrate the actual in favour of the virtual.[6] In these readings, he suggests, 'the actual is normally aligned . . . with the merely possible, the molar, the spatial, the phenomenological, and the psychological, while the virtual alone has privileged access to reality, that is, to ontology' (Mullarkey 2004: 470). In contrast, he proposes what he calls Actualism, based on other aspects of Bergson's work in which the virtual is understood, not as *grounding*, but as itself *grounded by* 'a play of actualities' (471). He argues that 'the actual is always already actualised somewhere, to some point of view'; whereas the virtual is but 'a perspectival image seen from . . . an interacting set of actual positions' (469). What may appear 'virtual' from one perspective, is actual from another. Likewise, Actualism suggests that there is not just 'one type of presence everywhere' in relation to which everything else is either past or future, but multiple presents that can be perceived through an enlarged perception (487).

In contrast to Virtualism's emphasis on an other-worldly potential, Goat Island's Matthew Goulish has recently dedicated a series of three lectures to the topic of the ordinary (one of which forms his contribution to this chapter[7]). In the lecture 'The Strain of the Ordinary' (2007a), Goulish associates the ordinary with 'that which can be overlooked' and with a strain of American writing (exemplified by Gertrude Stein amongst others) that refuses to overlook this overlooked. Following an exploration of this writing, Goulish suggests a shift in perception through which 'what we call *the ordinary*' can be seen 'as the object invested with attention that multiplies it'. Here, Goulish does not want 'to value the ordinary over the extraordinary' so much as attend to the extraordinary within the ordinary; to develop a mode of attention, of careful and concentrated sensing, that allows us to encounter the ordinary in all its complexity.

And this complexity includes a 'plurality of presents' or a multiplicity of inhuman as well as human ways of being in time. What I now want to explore is the idea that Goat Island use performance in order to experience their own durations (and other durations), but also offer this experience to their audiences. Each of the processes of making, performing or watching a Goat Island performance, present the opportunity to directly experience this thick present in a performative parallel to what Bergson calls intuition.

Waiting For . . . Something/Nothing's Happening

Goat Island are well known for performances which insist upon slowing down audiences; performances which alter the speed of the audience through the temporality of the performance's unfolding. As company member Karen Christopher explains:

> Slowness is part of our process and is a reaction against speed. Collaboration is a slow process and devising is a slow process for us. On top of this, we are manipulating the viewers' sense of time by going at other than usual paces and using improbable time signatures. A quick understanding of circumstances or ideas often misses depth and complication, so slowness is also away of allowing complexity into the work. (Christopher in Stanier 2004: n.p.)

In part, this embrace of slowness in performance can be attributed to Hixson's earlier experiences of the work of Pina Bausch and Tadeusz Kantor, 'which she read as actively resisting (albeit in very different ways) the contemporary cultural pressure to communicate or entertain quickly' (Bottoms 1998: 442). Unafraid to repeat (differentially), a Goat Island dance sequence will often allow a single minute gesture to take up an unexpectedly extended period of time. For example, in *How Dear to Me The Hour When Daylight Dies*,

> Matthew Goulish spends upwards of 10 minutes standing and rubbing the back of one hand with the fingers of his other hand . . . leaving the audience with time to watch seemingly very little for – in theatrical/performance terms – a long time. (Mitchell in Goat Island 1999)

In this sense, the company are willing to risk boredom, but from the position of conceiving boredom as an affect that can immediately precede an optimum audience state of what we might call a kind of passive alertness; when we have stopped trying so hard to understand *why* what is happening is happening, and concentrate on attending to what is happening – in itself (which is always not itself at the same time).[8] Rather than allowing us to see the gesture as a representation of an existing idea, the slowness of the 'hand-dance' both forces us to look more closely and to listen to our own duration as it is figured by our impatience – an experience which, for Deleuze and Bergson, creates new concepts.

Goat Island are particularly interested in the notion of waiting – a process which I want to address through Bergson's well-known example of the one who waits for sugar to dissolve in water, which Deleuze in turn takes up both in 'Bergson' and *Bergsonism*. In *Creative Evolution*, Bergson writes:

> If I want to mix a glass of sugar and water, I must, willy-nilly, wait until the sugar melts. This little fact is big with meaning. For here the time I have to wait is not that mathematical time which would apply equally well to the entire history of the material world, even if that history were spread out instantaneously in space. It coincides with my impatience, that is to say, with a certain portion of my own duration, which I cannot protract or contract as I like. It is no longer something *thought*, it is something *lived*. It is no longer a relation, it is an absolute. (Bergson 1911: 10)

The sugar can be approached not only in terms of its spatial organisation. The sugar differs from other things in degree, but as Deleuze emphasises:

> it also has a duration, a rhythm of duration, a way of being in time that is at least partially revealed in the process of its dissolving and that shows how this sugar differs in kind not only from other things, but first and foremost from itself. (Deleuze 1988: 32)

Likewise in 'Bergson', Deleuze argues that to ask after the difference of the sugar is not to ask after the difference of the sugar from another thing, which would be to approach it in terms of space. Nor is it to ask after the difference of the sugar from 'everything that it is not' which would be to understand it in terms of 'a dialectic of contradiction'. Rather, Deleuze means to ask after the being of the sugar as defined 'by a duration, by a certain manner of persisting, by a certain relaxation or tension of duration' (Deleuze 2004: 26). In this way, Deleuze conceives this self-alteration of a thing as its essence: 'This alteration, which is one with the essence or the substance of a thing, is what we grasp when we conceive of it in terms of Duration' (Deleuze 1988: 32). Our way of being in time, and the sugar's, are what constitute our individual modes of existence.

But the example of the melting sugar is not just about the sugar, but about the one who waits, and it is in this sense that I think it relates to performance and particularly to the question of audience reception. As Deleuze argues:

> Bergson's famous formulation, 'I must wait until the sugar dissolves' has a still broader meaning than is given to it by its context. It signifies that my own duration, such as I live it in the impatience of waiting, for example, serves to reveal other durations that beat to other rhythms, that differ in kind from mine. . .'. (32)

The affect of impatience is what alerts us not only to our own duration, but to its difference in kind from the many other durations pulsing within the real. There is an inherently performative dimension to all this, in so far as Bergson and Deleuze focus on the act of witnessing as that which triggers the exposure of both my own and other durations. However, as Ansell-Pearson notes, the relationship between the philosopher and the sugar dissolving is not that of spectator to spectacle, but rather 'a special kind of complicity' – a coexistence of multiple durations in the event of attending to life's way of being in time (Ansell-Pearson 1999: 29).

Goat Island approach the notion of multiple co-existing durations with typical lightness and humour in their performance 'The Sea & Poison', in which Matthew Goulish uses the top of his head as a stage, and as a place to attempt to grow a bean in a performance of becoming-earth.

> For example, what is earth? A terrain, not a territory. A place where a bean might grow. Therefore if I become a place where a bean might grow, might I not become the earth? What do I need? Soil, water, light, music, and a bean. He places these ingredients atop his head and waits. A man sits near him and composes a letter. Instead of becoming the earth, he has become a houseplant. An exhausted couple begins dancing to his music, which has generated a dancelike environment. He wants a drink and yells for one. He has forgotten his quest to become the earth. He has discovered the difference between the earth and the human: distractability. The earth remembers; the human forgets. If I did the performance perfectly, would the bean grow? (Goulish in Goat Island 1999)

The power to be distracted is part of the human's way of being in time – distraction affects the character, performer and audience. Even the slowest performance experiments have found it necessary to move faster than the growing bean in order to 'keep' their audience, or indeed, when a performance is allowed to unfold well beyond conventional temporal limits the audience is allowed to come and go according to their own capacity to tolerate its duration.[9] It is all a question of balance: how long is too long (to wait)? How long is long enough for something to happen while seemingly nothing is happening?

John Mullarkey has recently addressed these questions in relation to cinema, admiring the temporal confidence of Hungarian director Béla Tarr. In particular, he writes of 'the necessity of patience' and of a cinema of enforced patience that affectively prompts questions about time. With moments of extra-ordinary duration, films like Tarr's *Sátántangó* force us to ask: Why am I still being made to look at this? Why is this shot taking so long? And these, Mullarkey argues, 'are questions borne of affect, or enforced patience, born from the need to slow down for certain things and speed up for others' (Mullarkey 2009: 166). Likewise, in certain sequences in a Goat Island performance, the audience *feels time* through the 'painful affects' not only of impatience or boredom, but also of confusion. For example, in their early work the company tended to force thought through their performances of strenuous, untrained effort or what Irene Tsatsos calls 'rigorous athletics'.[10] The performance 'It's Shifting, Hank', for instance, involved a sequence in which

> all four performers crawled backwards on their forearms and toes and they did this until they collapsed in puddles of sweat on the floor. One by one they failed to continue and ended up being dragged out of the way by the survivors who then carried on crawling. The crawling went on for a long period of time and the strain it caused on the performers' bodies was both

visible and audible. The rubbing of the bony part of the forearm on the floor caused the skin to peel back and the elbows were bloody by the end of this sequence. (Christopher in Goat Island 1999: n.p.).

In this sense, it is partly the duration of the action that renders it inexplicable, leading the audience to wonder: 'What is making these people on stage do what they are doing? Why do they continue even though it hurts them? What compels them?' The thoughts that this sequence forces register the recalibration of time for the audience by the performance. It reveals a relationship between time and logic – an expectation that things will only last for a 'reasonable' length of time.

While Goat Island's later performances abandon these connections to the tradition of heroic, endurance performance, the notion of 'waiting' remains important. Indeed, it was perhaps of greatest concern to them during their penultimate[11] performance 'When will the September roses bloom? Last night was only a comedy. . .'. Here, it is clear that Goat Island are not only concerned with the waiting of the audience, but with the performers' waiting; and equally, as Christopher explains, they are not interested in *representing* waiting, as much as in occupying a particular mode of embodied attention:

> The tiny hairs on my face are ecstatic. They straighten out from my face and waver in the air around my head. I'm listening. I'm trying not to project a sense of something. My gaze is not direct and my body not in a loud posture that states: I am waiting, I am wanting, I am showing, but merely: I am here. (Christopher in Goat Island 2006)

Fellow performer Bryan Saner equates these frequent moments of stillness and silence in this performance, not with absence, but with a kind of waiting that establishes a connection between that which has been separated or broken apart: 'We have always considered our standing still and silence as repair. It is not nothing. It is a careful, patient listening before action. The stillness is related to the concept of serving people; of waiting' (Saner in Goat Island 2006). Lin Hixson also alludes to this association of waiting and repairing damage:

> It's like you have to be moving in order that your worth as a person is appreciated. You have to be in motion, you have to prove your productivity as a person, and that's very scary for those that are not in motion. For someone who is ill, or doesn't have money, or is not in motion in this capitalistic way: those people are cut off the chart now, in terms of being even considered a part of our culture . . . Repair has to do with stillness . . . People have to stop for a moment . . . and wait. (Hixson in Goat Island 2006)

In these writings, Hixson also intuits a relation between becoming and waiting:

> Becoming someone else feels to me like an active state, but I know that there's something about that that involves waiting as well. And I think it has to do with being able to see the other – by being able to be attentive, and hold the other with yourself, or in yourself . . . These are the things that are circling around in my mind. (Hixson in Goat Island 2006)

As Lawlor discusses, intuition was, for Bergson, first and foremost a 'self-sympathy' rather than some kind of intersubjective experience (Lawlor 2003: 66). However, he does suggest that sympathy with one's self might be the basis for a sympathy with others in a way that seems compatible with the kind of ethical or political value that waiting has for Goat Island.[12] Movement at a speed determined by the needs of capitalism is not the only movement. As the sugar example suggests: seeming immobility is not the absence of movement, but rather movement at a different speed.

Conclusion: Intuitive Practice in Performance and Philosophy

For all kinds of practitioners, discussions of intuition as the experience of duration are more relevant than those of duration 'in itself'. What Bergson and Deleuze show is that this experience – whether undertaken in philosophy or performance – does not involve a flawed representation of duration conceived as alterity or the Other, as Levinas suggests (Lawlor 2003: 62). Rather, this experience is creative – of philosophical concepts or artistic affects, if we follow the mantra of *What is Philosophy?*, that are themselves pure variation. Is it even that performance practices like Goat Island's point to new ways in which philosophy might reconfigure itself as intuitive practice, rather than continuing to prioritise language (Lawlor 2003: 61–3)? In the performance of waiting, I directly experience my own duration, I am immediate to memory, listening to time, a moment of self-sympathy. Performance is no easy solution to philosophy's methodological problem, but it could be a starting point, a directive.

Performance is a privileged space in which we can experiment with a non-utilitarian use of the senses, an education of feeling that enlarges the senses as well as consciousness. This is not about escaping the world, but about constructing a space within the social that turns away from utilitarianism towards intuition; an island where the experience of duration can and does happen. From this description it may sound as if we have failed in our attempt to redeem the actual and matter. But what Bergson calls 'the turn of experience' and what I am aligning with performance is always a double or two-part process in which the break with habit and need only constitutes one part: a turning away that is followed by a return. Perhaps what Matthew Goulish and Goat Island's practice suggests is that this return involves the construction of new habits in which the intuition of duration becomes an ordinary part of life.

References

Matthew Goulish sources:

The brain does not have thinking as its function.
Henri Bergson, *The Creative Mind*, The Wisdom Library, New York, 1946, p. 74.

to measure one flowing of duration in relation to another
Bergson, *The Creative Mind*, p. 180.

What is the future of globalisation?
Daniel Altman, 'Managing Globalization: The High Price of Ignoring Labor Immobility', *International Herald Tribune*, 11 October 2006.

The artist sketches one of the towers of Notre Dame cathedral.
Bergson, *The Creative Mind*, pp. 170–1.

In this way duration is not simply the indivisible.
Gilles Deleuze, *Bergsonism*, Zone Books, New York, 1991, p. 40.

Bergson regarded latitude as the freedom to choose between potential actions.
Laura Cull, correspondence with the author, 29 January 2007.

. . .since I am, as finite, threatened with consequences
Stanley Cavell, *Philosophy the Day After Tomorrow*, The Belknap Press of Harvard University Press, Cambridge, MA, and London, 2005, p. 139.

What philosophy has lacked most of all is precision.
Bergson, *The Creative Mind*, p. 11.

to show us that an extension of the faculties of perception is possible
Bergson, *The Creative Mind*, p. 136.

Laura Cull sources:

Alliez, E. (2001), 'On Deleuze's Bergsonism', in Gary Genosko (ed.), *Deleuze and Guattari: Critical Assessments of Leading Philosophers*, New York and London: Routledge.
Ansell-Pearson, K. (1999), *Germinal Life: The Difference and Repetition of Deleuze*, London and New York: Routledge.
Bergson, H. (1911), *Creative Evolution*, trans. A. Mitchell, London: Macmillan.
Bergson, H. (1992), *The Creative Mind: An Introduction to Metaphysics*, New York: Citadel Press.

Bottoms, S. J. (1998), 'The Tangled Flora of Goat Island: Rhizome, Repetition, Reality', *Theatre Journal*, 50 (4) (December): 421–46.

Cull, L. and M. Goulish (2007), 'A Dialogue on Becoming', in D. Watt and D. Meyer-Dinkgrafe, *Theatres of Thought: Theatre, Performance and Philosophy*, Newcastle: Cambridge Scholars Publishing.

Deleuze, G. (1988), *Bergsonism*, trans. Hugh Tomlinson and Barbara Habberjam, New York: Zone Books.

Deleuze, G. (1995), *Negotiations*, New York: Columbia University Press.

Deleuze, G. (1999) [1956], 'Bergson's Conception of Difference', in John Mullarkey (ed.), *The New Bergson*, Manchester and New York: Angelaki.

Deleuze, G. (2004) [1956], 'Bergson, 1859–1941', in *Desert Islands and Other Texts 1953–1974*, Los Angeles and New York: Semiotext(e).

Goat Island (1999), 'Our Simplest Gestures: 6 short lectures by Goat Island', unpublished.

Goat Island (2006), 'Part 1 – Reflections on the Process: Goat Island's When will the September roses bloom? Last night was only a comedy', *Frakcija*, 32.

Goat Island 'Creative response', available at: www.goatislandperformance.org/creativeResponse.htm

Goulish, M. (2007a), 'The Strain of the Ordinary', unpublished paper, *Performing Literatures* conference, University of Leeds, 1 July.

Goulish, M. (2007b), unpublished correspondence with the author.

Hallward, P. (2006), *Out of This World: Deleuze and the Philosophy of Creation*, London: Verso.

Hixson, L. and M. Goulish (2007), 'A Lasting Provocation', *TDR*, 51 (4): 2–3.

Lawlor, L. (2003), *The Challenge of Bergsonism*, London and New York: Continuum.

Mullarkey, J. (2004), 'Forget the Virtual: Bergson, Actualism and the Refraction of Reality', *Continental Philosophy Review*, 37: 469–93.

Mullarkey, J. (2009), *Refractions of Reality: Philosophy and the Moving Image*, Basingstoke and New York: Palgrave Macmillan.

Stanier, P. and K. Christopher (2004), '7 questions for Goat Island on "When will the September roses bloom/Last night was only a comedy" (with 7 footnotes of varying relevance prompted by the performance and the questions themselves) and 7 answers from Karen Christopher', *Strange Names Collective*, available at: http://www.strangenamescollective.co.uk/writings/Questions%20for%20Goat%20Island.htm

Tsatsos, I. (1991), 'Talking with Goat Island: An Interview with Joan Dickinson, Karen Christopher, Matthew Goulish, Greg McCain, and Tim McCain', *TDR*, 35 (4) (Winter): 66–74.

Williams, D. (2005), 'L'ombre de ton chien: on dogs and goats and meanwhile', available at Art Surgery: http://www.artsurgery.org/contributors.html

Notes

1. 'Creative response' is a central idea for Goat Island that re-thinks conventional notions of authorship. It shapes how the company respond to their sources in preparing a performance, how they respond to one another as they collectively develop performance material in rehearsal and how they encourage audiences and students to respond to the company's work, or to the work of other practitioners. A creative response does not imitate or represent an 'original', nor does it seek to critique it. Rather, Goat Island advise us to 'Think of a creative response as your own work that would not have existed without the work you are responding to.' It combines notions of individual and collective authorship. For more on this idea, see www.goatislandperformance.org/creativeresponse.htm

2. For more information, see: Cupola Bobber's website: http://www.cupolabobber.
com; plan b's website: http://www.planbperformance.net; and Uninvited Guests'
website: http://www.uninvited-guests.net; and for more information on Deer
Park, see: http://www.theatrebristol.co.uk/organisations_details.asp?ID=98. I
have been a member of SpRoUt (www.sproutart.co.uk) since its inception in
2004. Goat Island's influence can perhaps be most directly grasped in *A SpRoUt
Manifesto (in the style of a relay race)* – a collaborative writing project and performance presented as part of Hans Ulrich Obrist's *Manifesto Marathon* at the
Serpentine Gallery, London, in October 2008.
3. Interested readers should see Bottoms (1998) and Williams (2005). I have also
written and presented extensively on the connection between Deleuze and Goat
Island myself. See, for example, Cull and Goulish (2007).
4. There are countless other examples I could have drawn upon here. For instance, I
would argue that it is no coincidence that the company draw on Matheson's *The
Incredible Shrinking Man* for their performance, 'The Sea & Poison'; a resource
central to Deleuze's exposition of the concept of becoming-imperceptible.
5. See Hallward (2006).
6. Amongst the works of Deleuzian Virtualism, Mullarkey also cites Manuel de
Landa's *Intensive Science and Virtual Philosophy* (2002) and Keith Ansell
Pearson's *Philosophy and the Adventure of the Virtual* (2001) (Mullarkey
2004: 488).
7. Ultimately, there will be three works in Goulish's series of talks on the ordinary.
'The Disappearance of Latitudinarianism', his contribution to this chapter, is a
document of the first, originally delivered as a lecture at the Openport Symposium,
*The Disappearance of Latitude – Live Presence & Realtime in Contemporary
Practice*, hosted by Link's Hall, and The School of the Art Institute of Chicago,
23 February 2007. The second work, 'The Strain of the Ordinary', was presented
at the *Performing Literatures* conference at University of Leeds, 1 July 2007. The
final work, entitled 'The Time of the Ordinary' was presented at the *Performance
Studies International #14* conference in Copenhagen in August 2008.
8. While this essay concentrates on slowness and waiting in Goat Island, it is
important to add that the company have also been concerned with performance
at a faster speed. For example, for *How Dear to Me the Hour when Daylight
Dies*, Matthew Goulish created and performed an assemblage, or 'double-
figure', combining traits of Mr Memory from Hitchcock's *The 39 Steps* and the
performer Ron Vawter in his role as Roy Cohn. Here, Goulish was 'delivering
some of Memory's lines from the film using the speed-talking technique Vawter
had used in the Wooster Group's L.S.D' (Bottoms 1998: 438).
9. Here, I am thinking of works like Robert Wilson's *KA Mountain* and of durational performances by Forced Entertainment.
10. In 1991, interviewer Irene Tsatsos asked Goat Island if 'rigorous athletics' were
the company's 'trademark'. Matthew Goulish replied: 'I'm not so sure physicality is a trademark. I think it's a kind of response to dance where you can see the
effort but not the pain. But when an audience sees an untrained effort, it's more
affecting than seeing a trained or hidden effort' (Tsatsos 1991: 67).
11. In 2006, Goat Island announced that their ninth performance, *The Lastmaker*,
would be their last as a company. Director Lin Hixson remarked: 'This decision comes from the challenge that all artists face: How to continue to grow, to
venture into the unknown. We intend this end to present itself as a beginning
. . . We end Goat Island in order to make a space for the unknown that will
follow'(Hixson and Goulish 2007: 3).
12. Of course, performance has also conceived waiting in terms of disempower-
ment, as an enforced stasis which traps minorities in a seeming 'no-time' in

which nothing is perceived to be happening. Faith Wilding's performance-poem *Waiting* (1972) is a case in point:

Waiting for life to begin again Waiting . . .
Waiting for my children to come home from school
Waiting for them to grow up, to leave home
Waiting to be myself
Waiting for excitement
Waiting for him to tell me something interesting, to ask me how I feel
Waiting for him to stop being crabby, reach for my hand, kiss me good
  morning
Waiting for fulfillment
Waiting for the children to marry
Waiting for something to happen Waiting . . .

Chapter 8
Thinking Through Theatre

Maaike Bleeker

Deleuze and Guattari define philosophy, art and science as three modes of thinking, each moving in their own way: art thinks through affects and percepts; science thinks through knowledge; and philosophy thinks through concepts. These three modes of thinking take place on different 'planes' and utilise different 'elements'. The brain is the junction, not the unity, of these three planes.

Deleuze and Guattari introduce these ideas in *What is Philosophy?*, the final book they wrote together. They are not, of course, the first to ask the question 'what is philosophy?', but, they observe, many of the answers that have been given are too abstract and betray the desire to do philosophy, rather than reflect on it. Could it be, they wonder, that one can only ask (and answer) the question of what philosophy is once one is no longer driven by this desire?

> There are times when old age produces not eternal youth but a sovereign freedom, a pure necessity in which one enjoys a moment of grace between life and death, and in which all parts of the machine come together to send into the future a feature that cuts across all ages: Titian, Turner, Monet. In old age, Turner acquired or won the right to take painting down a deserted path of no return that is indistinguishable from a final question. *Vie de Rancé* could be said to mark both Chateaubriand's old age and the start of modern literature. Cinema too sometimes offers us its gifts of the third age, as when Ivens, for example, blends his laughter with the witch's laughter in the howling wind. Likewise in philosophy, Kant's *Critique of Judgement* is an unrestrained work of old age, which his successors have still not caught up with: all the mind's faculties overcome their limits, the very limits that Kant so carefully laid down in the work of his prime. (Deleuze and Guattari 1994: 2)

Of course, Deleuze and Guattari claim that they would not dare to count themselves among these elderly visionaries – 'we cannot claim such a status' (2) – but nevertheless, this is exactly what they do. *What is Philosophy?* is their attempt to gather together all they have been doing in a magnificent final chord with which they present a perspective on their earlier work, whilst at the same time taking a step beyond it. This brings them to an understanding of thinking in terms of three different planes, each with their own elements: 'plane of immanence of philosophy, plane of composition of art, plane of reference or coordination of science; form of concept, force of sensation, function of knowledge; concepts and conceptual personae, sensations and aesthetic figures, figures and partial observers' (216).

Deleuze and Guattari thus invite us to imagine thinking in theatrical terms as an event in which a 'plane' sets the stage for the appearance of a persona, or figure of thought, as the vector of movements of thought taking shape through concepts (in the case of philosophy), compositions (in the case of art), or knowledge (in the case of science). These planes set the stage for the movements of thought. Unlike the material stage of the theatre building, these planes on which the movements of thought take place do not precede the movements taking place on them. Rather, movement and plane are both elements of how Deleuze and Guattari invite us to imagine the unfolding of thought. They are 'the image thought gives itself of what it means to think' and of what it means 'to find one's bearings in thought' (37).

Deleuze and Guattari themselves do not mention the theatre. Nevertheless, I will argue, the theatre as cultural practice may illuminate what it means, or could mean, to 'find one's bearings in thought'. Furthermore, Deleuze and Guattari's account of thinking suggests the possibility of conceiving of theatre in terms of thinking, where the theatre is not understood as a representation of thoughts, or processes of thinking, originating from subjects expressing their ideas through theatrical representations, but rather as a practice of thinking in which we, as audience, participate. In what follows, I will explore this relationship between theatre and thinking through a confrontation of Deleuze and Guattari's philosophical staging of thinking with Ivana Müller's theatrical staging of thinking in *How Heavy Are My Thoughts?* (2004).[1]

Thinkers and Idiots

How Heavy Are My Thoughts? is a lecture performance that reports on Müller's attempts to find an answer to the question: 'If my thoughts are heavier than usual, is my head heavier than usual too?' Her question touches the core of the Cartesian mind/body dualism in that what she wants to know problematises the distinction between the material body (res extensa) as part of the natural world and governed by physical laws,

Figure 8.1 Ivana Müller in *How Heavy are my Thoughts?* Photograph by Nils de Coster.

and the mind as a thinking entity (res cogitans) supposedly outside, or distinct from, the natural and material world. Cartesian dualism places the mind in a position of hierarchical superiority over and above nature and materiality, including the nature and materiality of the body. This exclusion of the mind from nature, this evacuation of consciousness from the world, is linked to the foundations of knowledge itself, in so far as it is the prerequisite for founding a science which is indifferent to considerations of the subject. This is a science in which the correlation of our ideas with the world or reality they represent is a secondary function, supposedly independent from the existence of consciousness.[2]

With her performative attempts at answering the witty question ('If my thoughts are heavier than usual, is my head heavier than usual too?'), Müller not only questions the separation of the mind as thinking entity from the materiality of the body but also the implications of such a dualism for how we might find an answer to this question, and to what will count as an answer. In *How Heavy Are My Thoughts?* we see Müller (on video) talking to scientists and a philosopher and we witness a series of specially designed experiments. Like a true Cartesian, Müller sets out to doubt everything, yet instead of solid knowledge, her quest only brings more questions that lead to more doubt until she loses herself in an experiment. She gets stuck, literally, in the experiment and therefore cannot be present at her own performance. On stage, the audience does not get to see her; instead, someone else – Bill Aitchison – reports on her quest. When the audience enters the theatre space, Aitchison is already on stage, sitting behind a desk. He apologises for Ivana Müller's absence and sets out to reconstruct her line of thought on the basis of a series of documents he finds on her computer. He shows material from her research which has taken many months and resulted in the experiment in which she got stuck. In his report, Aitchison constantly refers to Ivana Müller as I.M.

How Heavy Are My Thoughts? invites the audience to go along with 'his' reconstruction of Müller's train of thought. In this, I.M. functions as what Deleuze and Guattari have termed a conceptual persona. The conceptual persona is the 'I' that speaks through the philosophical speech act. This is in some ways comparable to the speech act as theorised by Austin and Searle in what has become known as speech act theory, but with an important difference: 'In philosophical enunciations, we do not do something by saying it but produce movement by thinking it, through the intermediary of a conceptual persona' (Deleuze and Guattari 1994: 65). This conceptual persona is the 'I' that says 'I think therefore I am' and, in this way, founds the Cartesian cogito, with all the subjective assumptions constitutive of a science which is supposedly indifferent to considerations of the subject.

This 'I' that speaks in and through the philosophical speech act, therefore, is not the author. It is not the same as the philosopher as a person. The philosopher is the container or 'envelope', as Deleuze and Guattari put it, of his or her conceptual persona. The philosopher is the one who speaks the thoughts of the conceptual persona or, the other way round, the conceptual persona is the one who speaks through the thoughts of the philosopher. The conceptual persona speaking through Descartes' words is not Descartes the person, on his quest for true and solid knowledge, but the 'I' implied within a conception of thinking in which doubting everything but thinking itself is understood to bring such knowledge; a conception of thinking in which thinking is something private done by an autonomous thinker. Deleuze and Guattari call this conceptual persona of Cartesianism, 'The Idiot':

> The Idiot is the private thinker, in contrast to the public teacher (the school-man): the teacher refers constantly to taught concepts, whereas the private thinker forms a concept with innate forces that everyone possesses on their own account by right ('I think'). Here is a very strange type of persona who wants to think and who thinks for himself, by the 'natural light'. (62)

This is what Müller does too. As a true Cartesian, she sets out to doubt everything in the hope that this will bring her knowledge that is no longer based on concepts she has been taught, but on something that will emerge from the depth of her soul. She ends up upside down with a dunce's cap on her head: the familiar conical hat that, as Aitchison explains, goes back to John Duns – a famous Scottish philosopher of the late Middle Ages. Duns, Aitchison tells us, had a theory about this hat, namely that knowledge becomes centralised in the apex of the cone and is then funnelled down into the person wearing the hat. For this reason, he made all his pupils wear such hats during his lectures. Duns died in 1308. Fashions in the world of philosophy changed, his theories became regarded as too complex, and the hat he designed was given to stupid and misbehaving children to wear in school, to clowns and to people at parties or a carnival. From a learning aid and symbol of intelligence, the conical hat became a hat suitable for idiots, given to them by those who have, or think they have, the correct answers.

Staging Thinking

One might read the transformation of Ivana Müller into I.M. as the shift from Ivana Müller (as thinker/researcher aiming for true knowledge) to the Cartesian conceptual persona that speaks through her experiments and the kinds of conclusions she draws from them. The meaning of I.M. cannot be understood from the psycho-social characteristics of Ivana Müller as person or character, but is the result of how I.M. functions as what Deleuze and Guattari term a 'philosophical shifter' (64) mediating in the thought events represented on stage. By taking up the position of I.M. in our imaginations, we, the audience, are carried along with the movements of her thinking, the borders of which are the effect of the characteristics that define I.M as a thinker.

Conceptual personae 'must always be reconstituted by the reader' write Deleuze and Guattari (63), and in *How Heavy Are My Thoughts?* this happens quite literally. I.M. emerges from Aitchison's reconstruction of the absent Ivana Müller's experiments on the basis of her notes. This reconstruction produces I.M. as the subject of Ivana Müller's thinking. This reconstruction happens (if we believe Aitchison) 'on the spot'; he has been asked to replace Ivana Müller only at the very last moment. Unprepared as he is, he will do his best to explain to us the events that have resulted in the condition in which Ivana Müller finds herself.

The improvised character of his performance is, of course, carefully staged to engage with presuppositions concerning sincerity and the truth of direct, improvised responses. His supposed unpreparedness suggests a connection between Aitchison and the audience, as if he shares with us the experience of suddenly being confronted with the unexpected absence of Ivana Müller. The audience is invited to take his unpreparedness for real (and, by extension, to believe his observations on Ivana) while at the same time his remarks are obviously filled with self-reflexive commentary on his kind of performance, our expectations, and Müller's experiment. As a result, his reconstruction of Ivana Müller's quest for true knowledge highlights the theatrical character of his own behaviour, as well as that of Müller and the various experts interviewed by her. Theatrical, not because this behaviour is shown to be make-believe, but because Aitchison's performance draws attention to the way in which the transformation of Ivana Müller into the Cartesian cogito I.M. involves an operation that, to speak with William Egginton, turns the world into a stage.

How the World Became a Stage

Descartes' formulation of *cogito ergo sum* as the foundation for all knowledge is generally acknowledged as the initiation point for modern thought as well as for the birth of the modern subject. But what exactly is this subjectivity, Egginton wonders; is it 'grammatical'?

> Do Modern people refer to themselves with personal subject pronouns while medieval people had the primitive tendency to talk about themselves in the third person, or to use the personal pronoun in writing exclusively as an abstract universal, displaying no subjective insight or emotion? (Egginton 2003: 123)

Or does it suggest a philosophical distinction referring to the fact that modern individuals experience themselves as autonomous agents acting upon a material world, much like a grammatical subject acting upon a material world? Or is 'subjectivity' a term from political theory, referring to the subject of a state, or to an individual whose self-consciousness is formed through a socio-cultural process of subjection? (123). The use of the same word in several fields of study, Egginton observes, has created the illusion of some kind of 'thing' that 'emerged' in the sixteenth century to change the course of modern history, something to which all the different uses of the word 'subjectivity' refer, and of which the different discourses provide partial descriptions. But was it the appearance of modern subjectivity that caused people to experience their world in new ways? Or, is what has come to be known as 'the modern subject' actually an effect of changed practices of sense-making with which people responded to a world in transformation? What would happen if we consider this 'thing' called 'the subject' to be not that which inspires the discourses characteristic of modernity, but rather itself part and parcel of new discourses emerging from the sixteenth century onwards; discourses that responded to changes in the skills and practices which constitute human existence? This would involve a shift from an epistemological approach to a phenomenological approach or, as Egginton puts it:

> [I]f the discourse of subjectivity is concerned with describing the appearance in the world of a new or different form of self-consciousness, and with showing how the relation between this self and the 'world out there' is exhibited in philosophy, political organization, and art and literature, then the phenomenology I am proposing attempts to describe what Heidegger would call the 'worlding' of the world, that is, how ideas of selfhood are found alongside the various skills and practices that constitute human existence. (4)

Crucial to Heidegger's account of the worlding of the world in Modernity is his notion of spatiality. Heidegger moves the notions of space and time from 'inside' the perceiving being – where they had been since Kant, as forms of intuition in which all perceiving occurred – to the 'outside', to make them the most fundamental of phenomena. Individuals, Heidegger's argument implies, do not order their world within the confines of a pre-given, neutral space; rather, this pre-given, neutral space is but one historical manifestation of the individuals' spatiality: the experience of space that underlies their interactions in the world and that is specific to their own (culturally and historically specific) world. This supposedly pre-given, neutral space, that sets the stage for the appearance of the modern subject, is inherently theatrical in that it involves an *image* of space as existing independently from ourselves, while at the same time informing an *experience* of this space, through identification with a position within it. Indeed, it is through this identification that our experience of space comes into being as the experience of a subject on the world stage.[3]

Egginton traces these changes in the experience of space through a description of the practices and conventions of spectacle. Spectacle, he argues, is that medium of interaction whose conventions structure and reveal to us our sense of space or spatiality, and he sets out to demonstrate how the practices and conventions of spectacle changed from the Middle Ages to the early modern period. He describes how, during the sixteenth century, conventions changed to produce a theatre based on meta-theatrical staging practices: practices that assume, and help to construct, viewers capable of navigating an often bewildering edifice of imaginary spaces that open onto further interior spaces. This telescoping of separable spaces requires audiences to negotiate different levels of reality, which they do by means of characters or avatars, virtual selves that become conditioned to a new, fundamentally scopic organisation of space, in which they watch and are watched watching; they become bodies saturated by the gaze (Egginton 2003: 121).

Double Consciousness

The implication of Egginton's account of how the world became a stage is that modern subjectivity should be understood as the effect – or what Deleuze and Guattari (following Whitehead) term 'the eject' – of processes of worlding typical of modern times. Deleuze and Guattari describe the brain as 'a state of survey without distance' and subjectivity as its effect. It is the brain that thinks, and not man – the latter being only a cerebral crystallisation emerging from the movement of thought (Deleuze and Guattari 1994: 210–11). What Egginton adds to Deleuze and Guattari's account of thinking is the idea that the cogito, as the image of modern subjectivity, emerges from culturally and historically specific practices of human beings engaging with the world as they find it. Typical of modern times, according to Egginton, is a new sense of spatiality that allows people to navigate between a variety of real and imaginary spaces into which they imaginarily project themselves. This produces the kind of double consciousness typical of the psychoanalytic account of subjectivity: the account of modern subjectivity *par excellence*.

There are, as many have pointed out, remarkable similarities between this model of selfhood and the tradition of Western dramatic theatre. Great works of drama play a crucial role in Freud's work, which has led some commentators to criticise Freud's theories for generalising not only from a historically and culturally specific series of observations, but from a specific form of cultural expression as well. Dramatic theatre, as the expression of a culturally and historically specific (modern Western) subject, becomes the model for understanding human subjectivity in general. This is, indeed, problematic. However, taken as a culturally and historically specific account of selfhood – that is, as an attempt at making sense of what within Western modernity is experienced as self, as subject – the theatricality of psychoanalysis might actually present a perspective on the structural characteristics of modern Western thinking: the kind of thinking from which, to speak with Deleuze and Guattari, the Cartesian cogito emerges as 'eject'.

Understood as eject, the Cartesian cogito does not describe the modern subject as the origin of the kind of thinking typical of Western modernity, but refers to a position in the discourse within which modern Western thinking finds its expression. This is quite literally the case in *How Heavy Are My Thoughts?*, where I.M. appears as a discursive position within Aitchison's attempts at making sense of Ivana Müller's thinking. As audience, we are invited to identify I.M. with Ivana Müller, i.e. to ascribe the process of thinking represented by Aitchison to Ivana Müller, as the origin of the thoughts represented on stage. At the same time, however, Ivana Müller's emphatic absence from the theatrical representation of her thinking highlights the distance between the movement of her thought and the expression this thinking finds in discourse. In *How Heavy Are My Thoughts?* Ivana Müller only features as absence. The entire performance reads as an attempt at making her present through a reconstruction of her attempts at grounding her being in her own thinking.

In the theatrical representation within which this attempt finds its expression, the conceptual persona I.M. functions as a deictic marker or 'shifter'. This shifter does not refer to fixed reference points with spatio-temporal coordinates. As Deleuze and Guattari put it: '"To orientate oneself in thought" implies neither objective reference point nor moving object that experiences itself as subject and that, as such, strives for or needs the infinite' (37). Yet, the materialisation of Müller's thinking in Aitchison's (fictional) attempts at reconstructing her train of thought does point to the way in which our understanding (or attempts at understanding) what it means to 'find one's bearing in thought' involves a particular spatiality. His reconstruction of Ivana Müller's thinking consists, to a large extent, of his pointing out what happened when and where, starting from the beginning of her quest a couple of months ago and ending with the final experiment in which Ivana is (supposedly) now involved, and of which we are offered a glimpse through a (supposedly) live video stream. I.M. thus emerges from the way in which the staging of her thinking process locates the movements of her thought in time and space in a way that allows us to imagine where and when her thinking took place in the actual and material world. The theatre sets the stage on which Müller's thinking becomes located in the material world as a supposedly neutral and pre-given space. From this staging, I.M. emerges as a position within Aitchison's representation of the unfolding of Ivana Müller's thoughts. That is, the staging invites a conflation of the spaces opened up by Aitchison's representation of the unfolding of Ivana Müller's thinking with the space in which Ivana Müller finds herself; and it is the theatre that sets the stage for this conflation.

Getting Lost

'Beginning with Descartes, and then with Kant and Husserl, the cogito makes it possible to treat the plane of immanence as a field of consciousness' (Deleuze and Guattari 1994: 46). The Cartesian cogito that says 'I think, therefore I am' is a conceptual persona for whom the truth of his being lies in his ability to become the 'I' that speaks through his thinking, that is, to identify with a position in the discourse within which thinking finds its expression. As a result, the field of immanence becomes the field of consciousness of an 'I' separated from itself, which is the always alienated ego of psychoanalysis.

This alienation is also addressed in *How Heavy Are My Thoughts?* Whereas Aitchison's representation of the unfolding of Ivana Müller's thought stages I.M. as the origin of her thinking on a stage that represents her field of consciousness, the impossibility of locating thinking is precisely what frustrates Müller in her attempts at answering her question 'If my thoughts are heavier than usual, is my head heavier than usual too?' In trying to answer this question, weight – an indicator of materiality – is taken as proof of the location where thinking takes place. When several experiments using scales in an attempt to determine the weight of thought fail, Müller opts for an MRI scan at the Goethe Universität, Frankfurt, taking her cue from Einstein's famous formula $E = MC^2$. MRI presents the promise of visually locating thinking. And if thought is energy, if energy equals mass multiplied by C^2, and if the scanner presents a visualisation of this energy, then it should be possible to deduct the weight of her thoughts from the MRI visualisations. The answers given by the scan, however, appear unsatisfactory. Locating Müller's thoughts appears to be more difficult than expected (her thoughts are scattered all over the place, the expert concludes), which inspires a new series of experiments with various ways of locating and visualising thinking – without much success. It appears to be impossible to locate her thinking, in the sense of pinpointing its coordinates, at any particular place in her body. Furthermore, Müller's attempts at pinpointing where her thinking takes place only seem to increase the awareness of the impossibility of controlling her thoughts. Rather than being their source and origin – the author of her own thoughts – she seems to be taken along by them.

I Think Therefore I.M.

In line with Deleuze and Guattari's critique of representational thinking, *How Heavy Are My Thoughts?* presents an image of what it means to think in which thinking does not proceed through representations of thought-content, but as a performative act that sets the stage for the appearance of conceptual personae as vectors of the movement of thinking. In such thinking, we never coincide with the 'I' that is the subject of our thoughts. Thinking, Deleuze and Guattari observe (11), is a self-positing, and it is from this positing that we, as subjects, emerge. However, the 'I' that emerges as the subject of our thoughts is not the self that does the positing. The conflation of these two is what turned Descartes into an idiot. We are being thought rather than thinking. This is nicely illustrated in *How Heavy Are My Thoughts?*, since I.M. emerges from how Aitchison thinks through Ivana Müller's thoughts, and 'therefore I.M.' With his reconstruction of Ivana Müller's thinking, he sets the stage for I.M. to appear as a position for us to take up; as a position from which to imaginarily enter Ivana Müller's field of consciousness. 'I think therefore I am', 'I think therefore I.M.': like Derrida's *différance*, this difference touches the core of what is at stake here.[4]

How Heavy Are My Thoughts? shows thinking in Deleuzian terms as something that happens 'in between': between people, and between people and the things they find themselves confronted with. It is precisely the attempt at excluding the rest of the world that result in Ivana Müller's increasing madness. Deleuze and Guattari's conception of thinking as happening 'in between' opens towards an understanding of thinking as a movement proceeding through cultural forms (concepts, compositions, knowledge) in which we participate and from which we emerge as subjects.[5]

With this account of how thinking proceeds and how we as thinkers find our bearings in thought, Deleuze and Guattari shift attention from an understanding of thinking focused on thought-content, towards a focus on the constellation of elements *through which* thinking proceeds, and *from which* what is thought emerges in relation to an 'I' as the subject of this thought. This brings them to their explanation of thinking in theatrical terms, as an event in which a 'plane' sets the stage for the appearance of a persona, or figure of thought, as the vector of movements of thought taking shape through concepts (in the case of philosophy), compositions (in the case of art), or knowledge (in the case of science). At this point, Egginton's account of how the world became a stage presents a perspective on the cultural and historical specificity of this constellation of elements, a specificity that is not explicitly addressed by Deleuze and Guattari, yet is implicitly indicated in their account. Crucial here is the plane of immanence (of philosophy), of composition (of art), and of reference or coordination (of science) as that which sets the stage for the different movements of thought typical of each of these three modes of thinking.

Shared Shadow

The differences between the three planes are a recurring motif throughout *What is Philosophy?* However, Deleuze and Guattari observe, there are also cases in which art, science and philosophy cannot be understood as distinct in relation to the chaos into which the brain plunges. Having stressed the differences between the planes throughout their book, they conclude at the very end that what seems to be more important today are the problems of interference between the planes that meet in the brain. They distinguish between three types of interferences. The first type appears when, for example, the beauty of a philosophical concept is grasped within a sensation that gives it percepts and affects characteristic of art. These are what they call 'extrinsic interferences', since each discipline remains on its own plane and utilises its own elements (217). A second type of interference is called 'intrinsic interference'. This happens when conceptual personae slip in among the functions and partial observers, or among the sensations and aesthetic figures, on another plane, or when partial observers introduce into science sensibilia that are sometimes closer to aesthetic figures (217). Apart from these two, a third type exists that cannot be localised on one particular plane, but has to be understood in relation to the 'No' that is to be found where the planes confronts chaos.

> Now, if the three No's are still distinct in relation to the cerebral plane, they are no longer distinct in relation to the chaos into which the brain plunges. In this submersion it seems that there is extracted from chaos the shadow of the 'people to come' in the form that art, but also philosophy and science, summon forth: mass-people, world-people, brain-people, chaos-people – non-thinking thought that lodges in the three, like Klee's non-conceptual concept of Kandinsky's internal silence. It is there that concepts, sensations, and functions become undecidable, at the same time as philosophy, art and science become indiscernible, as if they shared the same shadow that extends itself across their different nature and constantly accompanies them. (Deleuze and Guattari 1994: 218)

With this remark, which concludes their book, Deleuze and Guattari historicise the concept of thinking they have unfolded, whilst leaving it to the reader to conceptualise its historicity from the promise of the possibility of a situation of radical interferences of the third kind, in which 'concepts, sensations, and functions become undecidable' and 'philosophy, art and science become indiscernible'. This 'shared shadow' that extends itself across the different natures of philosophy, art and science has to be understood from how each need their own 'No': art needs non-art, science needs non-science, and philosophy needs non-philosophy as that against which they come into being. These three No's are distinct in relation to the planes of art, science and philosophy but not in relation to the chaos into which the brain plunges. It is within their relation to this chaos that the three No's (from which the three modes of thinking – art, science and philosophy – distinguish themselves) become indistinguishable 'as if they shared the same shadow'.

This shadow they share is not the chaos through which each mode of thinking cuts its plane. This shadow is to be found in how that from which they distinguish themselves (as 'that which they are not') relates to this chaos through which they cut their planes. This 'that which they are not' (non-philosophy, non-art, non-science) is not chaos, but already part of making sense of chaos; it is the 'No' these modes of thinking need at every moment of their becoming. And this 'that which they are not', I propose, is *theatricality*: as constitutive of modern thinking, but also that which has to go unnoticed in order for the cogito to appear as the origin of his own thoughts.

References

Damisch, H. (1995), *The Origin of Perspective*, Cambridge, MA: The MIT Press.
Deleuze, G. and F. Guattari (1994), *What is Philosophy?* trans. H. Tomlinson and G. Burchell, New York: Columbia University Press.
Derrida, J. (1978), *Writing and Difference*. London: Routledge & Kegan Paul.
Egginton, W. (2003), *How the World Became a Stage: Presence, Theatricality, and the Question of Modernity*, Albany, NY: State University of New York Press.
Grosz, E. (1994), *Volatile Bodies: Towards a Corporeal Feminism*, Bloomington and Indianapolis: Indiana University Press.
Müller, I. (2004), *How Heavy Are My Thoughts?*, in collaboration with Bill Aitchison and Nils de Coster, Mousonturm Frankfurt and Gasthuis Theatre, Amsterdam.

Notes

1. Ivana Müller is an example of a maker who moves gracefully between theory and practice, as well as between a lot of other places and practices. Born in Croatia and now living and working in Paris and Amsterdam, her works have been produced through production houses and performed extensively throughout Europe, as well as in the USA and Asia. Informed by a background that encompasses (among others) comparative literature and contemporary dance, her work does not fit the usual categories. In December 2007, Müller's performance *While We Were Holding It Together* won two out of three prizes that were granted at Festival

Impulse. Müller is one of the founding members of Association Lisa (Amsterdam). For more information, see: http://www.associationlisa.com/ivana

2. For an illuminating critique of the implications of Cartesian dualism and its consequences for our understanding of knowledge, see Grosz (1994).

3. See Damisch (1995) for a similar argument starting from perspective as what he terms the paradigm underlying modern thinking. Perspective turns the world into an empty stage on which the modern subject appears.

4. The term *différance* is central to Derrida's critique of theories of language. At the phonetic level, there is nothing to distinguish the more standard notion of difference from Derrida's concept of *différance*. The anomalous spelling is designed to signal the primacy of writing over speech. See Derrida (1978).

5. Here too there is an interesting comparison with Damisch (1995) and his account of perspective as a paradigm through which Western modern thinking proceeds.

Chapter 9

Becoming–Dinosaur: Collective Process and Movement Aesthetics

Anna Hickey-Moody

This chapter puts forward two arguments. First, I contend that bodies with intellectual disability are constructed through specific systems of knowledge; namely, schemes of thought that are grounded in medical models. These medically based knowledges generate particular systems of affect – where affect is understood as taking something on, as changing in relation to an experience or encounter. Deleuze employs this term in differing ways, but for the purposes of this chapter I am primarily interested in the notion of 'affectus', understood as a kind of movement or subjective modulation. In *Spinoza: Practical Philosophy* Deleuze describes 'affectus' as 'an increase or decrease of the power of acting, for the body and the mind alike' (Deleuze 1988: 49).[1] So, to be affected is to be able think or act differently; although, as responses, affects can easily become habitual. Familiar responses are learnt in relation to bodies and subjects and it is only by challenging the 'truth' that is acknowledged in the known response or habitual behaviour that we can learn a new way of responding and of being affected.

Second, I argue that performance spaces can offer radically new ways of being affected by people with disabilities. It is my contention that people who are known as 'intellectually disabled' are primarily understood in relation to systems of affect, or kinaesthetic economies of relation, established through medical discourses. As I have argued elsewhere (Hickey-Moody 2006), kinaesthetic economies of relation established via medical discourses of intellectual disability are based upon understandings of bodily limits, rather than bodily capacities. As a system of knowledge, medical discourses of intellectual disability teach us about the things that bodies with intellectual disability can't do and establish economies of relation based on this approach. Sociological discourses of disability tend to replicate and extend this focus on corporeal limits and, as such, activism based on 'the social model' of disability tends to assume certain 'truths' inherited from the medical model that I would like to temporarily bracket or disregard.[2] As I have established this argument elsewhere (see Hickey-Moody 2008), it will not be explored in great detail here. However, this contention forms the template for the second argument advanced in this chapter: namely, that performance texts can offer unique spaces in which economies of relation that differ from those established within medical and sociological knowledges of intellectual disability are developed.

In exploring these contentions in detail, I take up the work of Deleuze and Guattari as a conceptual lens. I do so for three reasons. First, certain concepts from Deleuze and Guattari's thought – such as affect, faciality[3] and the assemblage – offer ways of understanding 'intellectual disability' as a product of a system of knowledge and material belief, rather than as a singular 'truth'. Such an understanding allows alternative stories and knowledges of bodies with intellectual disability to be developed alongside dominant systems of knowledge. Second, the concepts of corporeal and artistic affect developed in Deleuze's work, and in Deleuze and Guattari's joint projects, offer a useful theoretical framework through which to explicate the ways in which artworks (including dance theatre texts) emanate force and impact on bodies. Third, Deleuze and Guattari's work offers models for understanding 'minor' or politically marginalised knowledge systems, such as the kinaesthetic economy of relations that I argue is created within integrated dance-theatre.[4] I begin by explaining my first contention, that bodies with intellectual disability are constructed through schemes of thought grounded in medical models.

'Truths' to Disregard

In 1999, the World Health Organisation published definitions of impairment, disability and handicap that established worldwide models for disability service provision. For the WHO, impairment is 'any loss or abnormality of psychological, physiological, anatomical structure or function'; disability is a 'restriction or lack (resulting from an impairment) of ability to perform an activity in the manner or within the range considered normal for a human being';[5] and a handicap is a 'disadvantage for a given individual, resulting from an impairment or disability, that limits or prevents the fulfilment of a role that is normal (depending on age, sex, and social and cultural factors)'. The term is also a classification of 'circumstances in which disabled people are likely to find themselves' (Healy 2000: 1).

There isn't any mention of particular skills in these definitions. No mention of the fact that someone with autism can often pay exceptional attention to detail. No mention of the fact that a person with Down Syndrome can have the capacity to laugh in an uninhibited fashion. No consideration of what people with disabilities might offer contemporary cultural formations. Rather, interconnected ways of thinking about disability, impairment and handicap have been constructed in order to facilitate cultural awareness of, and practical support(s) for, a wide range of embodied limits that differ from a majoritarian norm.[6] In November 2001, the WHO remodelled this three-part definition of disability, impairment and handicap as the International Classification of Functioning, Disability and Health, or ICF. The ICF guidelines for assessing health and disability were designed to reconfigure existing ways of thinking about disability, a goal that is transparently acknowledged by the WHO. This conceptual focus is illustrated in statements such as:

> ICF changes our understanding of disability which is presented not as a problem of a minority group, nor just of people with a visible impairment or in a wheelchair. For example, a person living with HIV/AIDS could be disabled in terms of his/her ability to participate actively in a profession. In that case, the ICF provides different perspectives as to how measures can be targeted to optimize that person's ability to remain in the workforce and live a full life in the community. . . . The ICF takes into account the social aspects of disability and provides a mechanism to document the impact of the social and physical environment on a person's functioning. (World Health Organisation 2001)

As this quote suggests, the ICF classification guidelines are notably broad in so far as they are skill based, rather than defined in relation to people's specific medical conditions. As such, people with a range of quite different conditions might be conceptually brought together via a shared focus on their competencies and inabilities. Yet this approach remains a far cry from the concept of grouping people around their particular capacities, such as the capacity to draw, or extra sensitivity to light, or synaesthesia. That said, the WHO ICF classification guidelines are implemented in 191 countries around the world as the international standard for assessing and conceptualising health and disability.

As a discursive system, the ICF does not solely inscribe the identities of people with intellectual disabilities by connecting each body's identity to a singular trajectory of medical thought. Identities are also produced through association and affiliation, through considering what bodies do and do not do. The WHO ICF offers a model for thinking about intellectual disability which – at a pinch – can be read as a technical translation of Deleuze and Guattari's (Spinozist) suggestion that '[w]e know nothing about a body until we know what it can do' (Deleuze and Guattari

1987: 257). In the ICF, the WHO has moved away from its original discussion of impairment, disability and handicap, and endeavoured to think
about bodies in terms of what they do, rather than in terms that suggest
what bodies 'are'. However, in the realm of the social, medical discourses
of intellectual disability can also act as what Deleuze and Guattari call a
system of facialisation. Faciality is a system of attributing cultural meaning
to material bodies, within which a 'single substance of expression' (181) is
produced, as opposed to a dichotomy of matter and its possible meanings.
Deleuze and Guattari's theorisation of faciality mobilises a 'white wall/
black hole' dialectic, as it is in relation to a white wall and a black hole that
social visibility and group identity are produced (167–91). The white wall
is a wall of signification: a collection of signs upon which identifying features are inscribed. Black holes are loci of subjectivity. In order to become
a subject, to be consolidated and socially coded, one must also limit one's
capabilities and desires. The subject is captured in a black hole. While the
name 'black hole' sounds ominous and the 'white wall' virtually conjures
the image of a prison line-up, subjectification is an essential part of life.
The individual's face is constructed in relation to the social, mediated faces
of cultural groups. Relations between social and cultural groups are processes of (re)construction in which faces (of both individuals and collective
social bodies) are remade, re-visioned, and through which some collectives
are defaced. In order to have a social identity, a configuration of bodies
must have a face. The face both allows social visibility and delimits some
possible actions of those it holds in a black hole.

The face is expressed as social identity but also as capacity, possibility,
action, thought and desire. The face is a social and political economy.
Acculturated reading practices or visual codings are part of a more comprehensive value system that organises bodies and practices in hierarchies
of power. Here, external signifiers, such as actions or visible features, are
given a comprehensive meaning that stretches beyond their physicality.
For example, the human face as a vector of significance is privileged
over other parts of the body. According to Deleuze and Guattari, visual
economies of the developed world are connected to performative and
institutionalised economies. In a manner comparable to the white wall/
black hole of the face referred to by Deleuze and Guattari, medical
knowledges are grounded in semiotic systems that are performances of a
libidinal economy, or a structured flow of desire (Bateson 1972; Deleuze
and Guattari 1987: 167–91). Here, visual or genetically inherited signs
are read as signifiers of a particular medical condition or disease. These
signifiers are captured in the black hole of 'intellectual disability' as a
system of subjectification. Semiotic methods of medical identification

fold into a more comprehensive social value system and kinaesthetic economy that organises bodies in hierarchies of power.

The classification of a body as intellectually disabled in medical terms can be read as a specific socio-cultural positioning and it often inserts bodies into certain affective registers. People are taught how to respond to, or be affected by, the 'intellectually disabled' body in specific ways: paternalistic care, fear, pity. From visual features which identify people as being intellectually disabled through to contextualised performances of 'intellectual disability' within institutionalised systems established to support people with intellectual disability, medical discourses are connected to wide-ranging, performative and institutionalised economies of affect. In order to unpack the affective economies arising from medical knowledges of intellectual disability, I now turn my gaze to examine some specific categories for defining intellectual disability. Categories of definition, such as those explored below, constitute a white wall upon which the face of intellectual disability is signified; they articulate the signs and significance(s) captured in black holes of the intellectually disabled subject.

Employing a different approach from that of the WHO, the first major local source mobilised as a point of comparison to the WHO's ICF is the South Australian Disability Information Resource Centre (DIRC 2001). DIRC is the primary resource for information about intellectual disability in South Australia,[7] the place in which the majority of research was undertaken for this chapter. As such, the initial site of referral when looking for information about intellectual disabilities in South Australia is usually the DIRC library. A local government funded community resource, the DIRC library consists of a wide range of materials which document medical and social facets of various disabilities. DIRC employs fairly exacting medical categories to define intellectual disability. As a meta-statement on a range of specific conditions, intellectual disability is defined by DIRC, albeit very generally, as a connection between specific medical conditions (DIRC 2001). The following discussion explores some of DIRC's categories of definition contained within the meta-heading of intellectual disability. As local, detailed medical definitions of intellectual disabilities listed by DIRC, I discuss the implications of these specific medical trajectories for conceptualising and relating to people with intellectual disability, especially in terms of affect, identity, capacity and possibility.

Black Holes of Medical Subjectivity

The medical disorders around which DIRC has developed its definition of intellectual disability include, but are not limited to, the conditions of Angelman Syndrome, CHARGE Syndrome, Cardio Facio Cutaneous Syndrome, Coffin-Lowry and Coffin-Siris Syndrome, Cri Du Chat Syndrome, Down Syndrome, Edward's Syndrome, Joubert Syndrome, Kabuki Syndrome and Lowe Syndrome. Each of these medical conditions constitutes a unique set of physical attributes and, perhaps more importantly, engenders a particular experience of corporeality and sensory awareness. While it is important to give space to the different experiences of reality that accompany medical syndromes that produce intellectual disability, the names of these conditions have a somewhat dehumanising affect. The medical conditions in relation to which DIRC has developed its definition of intellectual disability begin with Angelman Syndrome (in that this is the first condition listed alphabetically). Within medical discourses, Angelman Syndrome is characterised by developmental delay and intellectual disability, an attitude described as a happy or excited demeanour, frequent bursts of laughter, bodily tremor, balance difficulties and speech impairments. Those with Angelman experience hyperactivity, seizures and jerky or agitated movement referred to as 'hyperkinetic movement' (ASF 2004).

The Angelman Syndrome Foundation (ASF) also contends that children with Angelman Syndrome (AS) can be somewhat emotionally isolated as a result of their short attention spans. The ensuing logical proposition – that people with AS are therefore unable to connect with others – is discursively constructed in relation to the virtual body of AS as a medical condition. The reader is presented with a capacity to identify material or physical referents, located in the body of the person with AS, which are attributed specific functions in the discursive construction of the medical condition. Before one has even met a person with AS, one is encouraged to affectively read the body in light of the brief attention spans and hyperactive demeanours associated with AS by medical discourse. Subjectivity begins to be constituted in medical terms.

In contrast to the embodied characteristics of AS, people with CHARGE Syndrome, the second disability which DIRC refers to in categorising intellectual disability as a condition, have very different states of embodiment. Medical discourses of intellectual disability contend that people with CHARGE usually have atypical fields of vision, obscured or difficult respiratory functions, and hearing impairments. CHARGE is an acronym that stands for choanal atresia[8] (blocked nose), posterior coloboma[9] (an eye condition), heart defect, choanal atresia (restated), retardation, and genital and ear anomalies. Vision and hearing loss, breathing difficulties, developmental delay and genital abnormalities are also present in this disability. Nearsightedness, farsightedness and extreme sensitivity to light are other common features of CHARGE Syndrome (CSF 2004). These examples illustrate some of the ways in which medical discourses read bodies within certain physical parameters and through visual and performance-based codes. The way a person looks, the things they do, become taken up as indicative of what they 'are'.

Understandings of people with intellectual disabilities that are not grounded in medical discourses are rare, because even if the topic of intellectual disability is approached from a non-medical background, information relating to, and experiences of, people with intellectual disability tend to be grounded in existing medical knowledges. My experience as a dance workshop facilitator working with people with disabilities supports this contention, in that I have been introduced to participants in light of medical readings of their disabilities. As the DIRC (2001) definition suggests, 'intellectually disabled' is a name that is applied to a diverse array of bodies. This point is further illustrated by the fact that facilitating workshops for people with CHARGE Syndrome is experientially very different from facilitating workshops for those with Angelman's Syndrome. In both instances, in order to offer constructive directions and develop enjoyable, appropriate movement tasks, I need to imagine what will and will not be possible for these participants, working from an imagined sensory template which is markedly different from my own.[10] The diagnostic criteria and characteristics of a particular intellectual disability translate into a range of very different people. While medical perspectives on intellectual disability offer certain kinds of insights into the life worlds of people with intellectual disabilities, medical definitions need to be understood as having affective force, which can both engender specific responses and position bodies in particular kinaesthetic economies of relation.

(An)other Story

I argue that medical discourses construct social faces for people with intellectual disability through attributing particular significances to their physical features and suggesting that these are signs of a specific kind of subjectivity. For example, taken together, an elongated tongue, short stature, webbed toes, a cleft palette and folds of skin over the upper eyelid (epicanthal folds) signify Down Syndrome: a kind of intellectual disability. No space is provided for the proliferation of alternative, relational and sense-based knowledges of bodies with these features. I want to counteract such relationships of power/knowledge by offering an alternative

Figure 9.1 Fin Carries Dan, from *The Laminex Man*, features Finnegan Krukemyer and Daniel Daw. Photograph by David Wilson, courtesy of Restless Dance Company.

way in which thinking about intellectual disability can be re-designed through integrated dance theatre.

I use the term 'integrated dance theatre' to refer to dance theatre devised and performed by both people who identify as being with, and those who identify as being without, intellectual disability. Here I will explore enmeshments of subjectivity and aesthetics via the process of devising and performing dance theatre. Specifically, I discuss the work of a former member of Restless Dance Company, Angus Goldie-Bilkens,[11] during the process of devising and performing a work entitled 'Sex Juggling' (1997). Restless Dance is Australia's leading youth dance company inspired by cultures of disability. Many Restless dancers have Down Syndrome, autism, general developmental disabilities or Cerebral Palsy. Others don't have an intellectual disability. Restless is one of a select number of companies operating in this field of integrated dance in Australia. Following Goldie-Bilkens' work, and focusing on his negotiations of gendered identity across the process of devising and performing 'Sex Juggling', I investigate ways in which this dance text effected subjective changes for Goldie-Bilkens and for other members of the ensemble. His work negotiating masculinity is taken from a movement piece entitled 'dinosaur dance'. Goldie-Bilkens' 'dinosaur dance' is of interest because it illustrates one way in which the work of integrated dance theatre can be a 'turning away' from individuals' personal constructions of intellectual disability – a minor becoming-other – while simultaneously constituting an artistic affect in the dance theatre text.

Deleuze and Guattari describe artistic affect as the Antarctica of civilisation; an unprecedentedly different cultural and physiological landscape that performs an inimitable, singular difference (or haecceity) amidst established traditions of sameness. Deleuze and Guattari qualify this by arguing as follows:

> The affect certainly does not undertake a return to origins, as if beneath civilisation we would rediscover, in terms of resemblance, the persistence of a bestial or primitive humanity. It is within our civilisation's temperate surroundings that equatorial or glacial zones, which avoid the differentiation of genus, sex, orders, and kingdoms, currently function and prosper. It is a question only of ourselves, here and now. But what is animal, vegetable, mineral, or human in us is now indistinct. (Deleuze and Guattari 1994: 174)

This quote elucidates subjective systems of reference as constructions; constructions which can be reconfigured or augmented through affect. Indeed the idea of sameness, the very thought of 'our civilization's temperate surroundings', is a cultural or discursive construction. Affect reminds bodies that, within a culture that adores sameness, zones of infinite differences live on. Artistic affects dissolve the systemic construction of opinion – our automatic 'differentiation of genus, sex, orders, and kingdoms'. Affects also offer new distinctions, internal atmospheres or landscapes that allow us to dissolve inflexible ideas of the way things 'are'. An affect is a kind of 'rhizome' in that it changes an individual's relationship with a socialised structure (Deleuze and Guattari 1987: 3–25). Like a rhizome, an affect has transformative capacity; it is a singular difference.

Within group discussions and during the conceptual development of performance material, dancers often name 'Restless' as a space where they are able to become other than their 'daily selves'. Dancers within the Company who identify as being with intellectual disability have often performed and vocalised 'Restless' as a space in which they turn away from their own ideas of intellectual disability and from that which they are – and are not – capable. That said, power structures which serve to differentiate between people 'with' and people 'without' disabilities can often remain part of dancers' styles of relation, whether on or off the dance floor. For example, the dancers often sustain a social hierarchy that is contingent upon ideas of intellectual disability. This social hierarchy is partly maintained for practical reasons. Friendship groups within the Company are maintained during break times and are often primarily established between women 'with' intellectual disability, men 'with' intellectual disability, and men and women 'without' disabilities.

The dynamics that are produced by these social situations tend to influence the Company's processes of devising and performing. At the beginning of every process of devising a new work, or at the beginning of a performance period, all Company members participate in a group discussion that focuses on 'leaving special friendships outside rehearsals'.[12] These discussions are a very important part of maintaining a productive work ethic and encouraging dancers to stay focused on the task at hand.

As a dancer in Restless, one of the most significant, ongoing processes of turning away from static constructions of self and disability was one that I constantly enacted by trying to explain to dancers with intellectual disabilities that I was no more of an 'expert' than them. I was perpetually surprised when a person from whom I would take cues within a dance piece would then turn around and look back at me to 'check' they were doing the right thing. These situations rarely had anything to do with the dancer in question not knowing what they were doing. They were predominantly a performance of parts of the 'history' of the dancer's life: a history of being told to watch people 'without'. For example, most settings that bring together people with and without intellectual disability involve people 'without' disability role-modelling the 'right' thing to do. Indeed, Australian television recently featured a documentary about a dance company in which people without a disability 'helped' people with intellectual disability learn dance steps, like the foxtrot or the waltz.

When the steps have been learnt to a particular standard, the dances are performed in public. By contrast, in the work of Restless Dance, dancers with intellectual disability are invited to explore their own movement styles and dancers without a disability are asked to support this process. Moments of watching the people 'without' disabilities still tend to haunt people with a disability in these explorations, yet there can also be powerful moments of resistance to the dancer's own ideas of their disabled selves. These moments of resistance are most often required in producing 'works of art . . . [that] contain their sum of unimaginable sufferings that forewarn the advent of a people . . . [they] have resistance in common – their resistance to death, servitude, to the intolerable, to shame, to the present' (Deleuze and Guattari 1994: 110).

It is not always the dancers 'with' disabilities who catalyse the construction of affect or sensation. However, the nature of the sensations produced within Restless do necessarily embody the work of dancers with disabilities. Sensation often encompasses a process of 'turning away from intellectual disability', but this is not to say that the dancer in question sheds the characteristic features that make them who they are (Hickey-Moody 2003). Nor do I mean to imply that intellectual disability is a static and negative aspect of a body, something that a person would always want to turn away from. I am referring here to patterns of personal history, patterns that everyone owns, and to static constructions of the self which can be tied to such lived habits. The atmosphere of a performance in which a dancer executes a beautifully choreographed work and in so doing turns away from what they believe they can, or cannot do, is often what Deleuze and Guattari describe as:

> the pure lived experience of double becoming. . . . [For example] the tarantella is a strange dance that magically cures or exorcises the supposed victims of a tarantella bite. But when the victim does this dance, can he or she be said to be imitating the spider, to be identifying with it, even in an identification through an 'archetypal' or 'agonistic' struggle? No, because the victim, the patient, the person who is sick, becomes a dancing spider only to the extent that the spider itself is supposed to become a pure silhouette, pure colour and pure sound to which the person dances. One does not imitate; one constitutes a block of becoming. (Deleuze and Guattari 1987: 305).

Becoming is constituted in the movement beyond category, in the critical enmeshment of states of newness. The spider becomes a set of shadows, a movement aesthetic, and a novel incarnation of what an arachnid might be. The dancer becomes with the dance. No longer a body on stage, the dancer of the tarantella becomes-spider. Not a familiar spider from children's songs, or a garden spider, rather, the *becoming-spider of the*

Figure 9.2 Lachlan and James, from *Rebel Rebel*, shows Lachlan Tetlow-Stuart (left) and James Bull. Photograph by David Wilson, courtesy of Restless Dance Company.

dance. The shadow, the colour, the aesthetic that is the spider-becoming. A critical enmeshment of newness: a zone of indiscernibility.

In Restless, sensation is constituted through the style in which a dancer performs, the choreography they perform, the dancers' personal becomings, and the actualisation of the previous becoming-others that are an immanent part of the process of devising and performing dance theatre. For example, while intellectual disability cannot be regarded as a singular personal deficit, during a performance, intellectual disability can be a fear, a turning away from fear, and an immanent strength that emanates from a dancer. A turning away can be an atmosphere of revolution.

The process of turning away that I describe cannot be understood if intellectual disability is seen as a limit placed upon an otherwise 'competent' body. Dancers within Restless who identify as being 'with intellectual disability' do so for political and practical reasons. The assumptions about ability, disability and intelligence that are carried within the term 'intellectual disability' need to be moved beyond in order to think the specific nature of both corporeal and artistic becomings. All bodies are different. There are specific types of difference, yet again; the nature of embodied difference becomes specific to the body in question. New ways of relating to embodied difference are opened up in dance theatre.

Goldie-Bilkens Becomes-Dinosaur: A Haecceity and a Bloc of Sensation

> There is a mode of individuation very different from that of a person, subject, thing, or substance. We reserve the name haecceity for it. A season, a winter, a summer, an hour, a date, have a perfect individuality lacking nothing, even though this individuality is different from that of a thing or a subject. They are haecceities in the sense that they consist entirely of relations of movement and rest between molecules and particles, capacities to affect and be affected. (Deleuze and Guattari 1987: 261)

> By means of the material, the aim of art is to wrest the percept from perceptions of objects and the states of a perceiving subject, to wrest the affect from affections as the transition of one state to another: to extract a bloc of sensations, a pure being of sensations. A method is needed, and this varies with every artist and forms part of the work. (Deleuze and Guattari 1994: 167)

The first of these quotes describes the haecceity, a word derived from the Latin *haecceitas*, or 'thisness'. The term refers to the properties, qualities, or characteristics of a thing that make it identifiable. Haecceity is a person's or object's specificity. The second of the quotes explains a way of making haecceities, or characteristic things. A bloc of sensations, a being of sensation, is a kind of heccaeity, fashioned from the palette of the artist. Or, in this case, from the body of the dancer, the sensibility of the choreographer and the score of the composer. Artists make up the perceptions of the universe inside their artwork; they speak in a language of affects specific to the world of their work. In doing so, they create haecceities, events that have a 'thisness' specific to the time and place of the artwork.

In theorising the construction of sensation within Restless, this chapter takes as a foundation the re-definition of a dancer's performance style and quality, and the creation of an atmosphere of change. The re-definition of ideas of 'intellectual disability' and 'dance' are always already a part of this foundation, as Restless dancers embody a history of challenging ways of thinking about 'intellectual disability' and 'dance'. By the time an affective sensation is constructed, the history a person turns away from in becoming sensation has already been detailed into their movement. As such, various transformations of this movement have metamorphosed through the entire ensemble and have been explored via a range of different methods of creative development. Any one gesture folds hours and hours of rehearsal on the dance floor into a performance piece.

Restless' 'Sex Juggling' looked at gender dynamics within the Company and drew upon 'gender' as experienced in the broader personal and family lives of Company members. Dancers experimented with the idea that gender is a performance; it's what you *do* at particular times, rather than a universal *who you are*. That is, as Judith Butler asserts, '[t]here is no gender identity behind the expressions of gender; . . . identity is performatively constituted by the very "expressions" that are said to be its results' (Butler 1990: 25). Building upon such a performative understanding, relationships within families were seen as complex and powerful gendering forces in dancers' lives and work. This was especially the case for dancers with intellectual disabilities, who often have to negotiate conservative family ideas surrounding their gendered identities. For example, during the devising and performing process of 'Sex Juggling', dancers explored ideas of 'man' and 'woman', the ways in which they related to and performed these ideas, and the ways in which these styles of relation were manifested in Company dynamics. The notion of 'being a man' or 'being a woman' was seen as inherently controversial by many dancers' families. Parents were not able to reconcile themselves to the fact that their post-pubescent child was not only a person 'with' an intellectual disability, but one with a gendered subjectivity they chose willingly, and a separate (yet related) sexual subjectivity. Indeed, two dancers – both over the age of 21 – were removed from the production by their parents, who deemed the subject matter inappropriate for people 'with' intellectual disability.

The majority of performance material was devised in gender groups, which was then combined and structured into the choreographed piece that became 'Sex Juggling'. The work was structured in five sections: moving from men's and women's dances into a conclusion which emerged after a gradual integration of the two. During the early stages of working, the dynamics of both gender groups became highly competitive; indeed, the men's group became quite anarchic. Up until this point in the rehearsal process, the men's group had focused on performing what it meant to be 'masculine', what being masculine could look like, how 'masculinity' might move and so on. The process which had facilitated this examination included dancers sourcing lived experiences of constructing their identity around the ideas of masculinity, disability, different ways of expressing feeling like a 'man', and explorations of discrepancies between their own conceptions of masculinity and their families' and friends' notions of masculinity. Engaged in a creative and consistently redefined process of testing the limits and possible morphologies of masculinity, the male half of the Restless ensemble had been working to challenge their own perceptions and practices of masculinity. This process was both difficult and stimulating for the dancers and their director, who worked through questions of whether or not being a man is an 'essential' quality, a material state, or a way of acting that is both socialised and chosen. In undertaking this process of sourcing performance material, the male members of the Company had interrogated and (re)positioned the ways in which they came to know themselves as gendered.

It was during this process of challenging norms that the male dancers with intellectual disabilities became uncontrollable. I was invited to work with them, as it was hoped that having a woman join the group might calm the situation. Of course, I was keen to be as constructive as possible, although in this context not being unruly was deemed disciplinary. One of the most experienced company members, Goldie-Bilkens, was full of verve and energy on the day we devised some material together. He was fluctuating between abandoning the rehearsal process altogether and performing a sharp, playful dance that he had developed, and which he called the 'dinosaur dance'. The dinosaur dance was Angus-becoming-'masculine'-becoming-dinosaur – and surely a raptor or pack-hunting dinosaur at that.

To revisit Deleuze and Guattari's account of becoming animal:

> Becoming produces nothing other than itself . . . What is real is the becoming itself, the block of becoming, not the supposedly fixed terms through which that which becomes passes. Becoming can and should be qualified as becoming-animal even in the absence of a term that would be the animal become. *The becoming-animal of the human being is real, even if the animal the human being becomes is not*; and the becoming-other of the animal is real, even if that something other it becomes is not. (Deleuze and Guattari 1987: 238, emphasis added)

Indeed, Goldie-Bilkens' dance was a literal construction of otherness, an active re-creation of the self as an animal, which simultaneously redefined the terms upon which the other ensemble members understood the notion of 'dinosaur' and the way Goldie-Bilkens performed his assemblage of subjectivity. His becoming-dinosaur combined a carnivorous energy with a speedy playfulness. The dinosaur dance is gentle and graceful as well as cutting, surprising and strong. The director of the male members of the ensemble, and the other Company members present, were amazed at the detail and specificity of the idiosyncratic movements that constituted Goldie-Bilkens' becoming-dinosaur. He taught the dance to me and another performer, Alex Bickford, as both of us had a long-standing collegial relationship with him. A description of the dance taken from my ethnographic research journals follows:

> The dance was performed in unison, and in a uniform pattern. Alex and I were positioned diagonally behind Angus, who is downstage centre: the focal point of a triangle pattern. All cues were taken from Angus, who had an immanent feeling for the dance that neither Alex nor I possessed with

such certainty. The perfect synchronicity of the dance made it an amazing moment for me to perform and for many of those who watched it during our rehearsal period and preview performances.

On our opening night, Goldie-Bilkens began the dance as usual. Not half way through the movement phrase, he looked directly over his shoulder to watch Bickford, and completed the remaining two-thirds of the dance with his head craning over his left shoulder, keenly observing Bickford's every move. I was privately amazed, as was Bickford, and we both continued to work through the piece, which by this stage was known as 'Angus' dance', since this was the dance that Angus devised and he especially had a masterful sense of its rhythm and detail. The looking back was clearly an example of the habit of looking to someone 'without' disability for direction.

Turning back to look at Alex Bickford became a feature of the dance and, as it was Goldie-Bilkens' dance, he remained in command of the way that it was performed. However, what I would describe as the crafting of pure sensation and a profound moment of turning away occurred when Goldie-Bilkens performed the piece at the Australian Youth Dance Festival. Upon commencing the dance, Goldie-Bilkens threw himself forward, his chest in a high release, his body in a lunge and with a sense of wild eccentricity and indulgence, he powered through the work without a look anywhere other than directly at the audience in front of him. The particular strength and character of this performance was noted by many. In the moment, Goldie-Bilkens emanated a feeling of breakthrough, of multi-dimensional movement, which his dance, alongside Bickford, I and the work of the ensemble, compressed into sensation.

This was, perhaps, an event (Deleuze and Guattari 1996: 110–11). Not Goldie-Bilkens' performance quality becoming-strong, although this was a catalyst for the event, but Goldie-Bilkens becoming-man-becoming-dinosaur-becoming-teacher-becoming-woman-becoming-friend-becoming-afraid-becoming-supported-becoming-strong. As Goldie-Bilkens changes, all that he becomes changes with him. Critically, his sense of 'man' became the idea of a dinosaur, which became a style of movement, a choreographed work and then an affect experienced by the spectator.

The dinosaur was reincarnated as a bodily extension, a flick of the hand, a mechanical, rigid turn from side to side. The dance moved on from earlier, ensemble-based, gendered performances. Movements had affective force outside any teleological or language-based context that might have identified Goldie-Bilkens' dinosaur as an imagined prehistoric animal. In other words: meaning stopped being about Goldie-Bilkens, or the dinosaur, and became about the materiality of the dance.

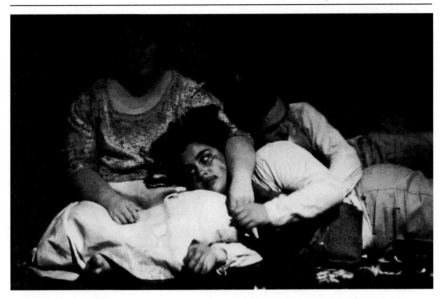

Figure 9.3 The Flight, from *The Flight*, shows (from left to right) Rachel High, Lauren Smeaton (behind), Sasha Zahra (front) and Angus Goldie. Photograph by David Wilson, courtesy of Restless Dance Company.

Goldie-Bilkens' reconfiguration of his experiences of being a man with an intellectual disability can be read as a pathway into re-thinking bodies with intellectual disability through affect. These processes of identity re-negotiation are facilitated by ensemble process and are inextricably linked to the production of movement aesthetics. As such, part of the subjective labour of dancers creating original performance material is the enmeshment of self with a movement aesthetic developed in relation to the ensemble. Here becomings of the self, through which performers extend or decrease their capacities for connection and experience, are linked to the production of affect. This production of affect is a becoming in art; a sensory transformation of matter into the media of an affective force.

Conclusion

The event in its becoming, in its specific consistency . . . escapes History . . . To think is to experiment, but experimentation is always that which is in the process of coming about – the new, the remarkable, and interesting that replace the appearance of truth and are more demanding than it is . . . History is not experimentation, it is only the set of almost negative conditions that make possible the experimentation of something that escapes history. (Deleuze and Guattari 1994: 110–11)

In this passage, Deleuze and Guattari describe history as a section within thought that becomes de-territorialised through creative experimentation. One of the ways I have engaged with the deterritorialisation of 'intellectual disability' in this chapter is through focusing on lived, kinaesthetic knowledges of 'intellectual disability' as the local terrain that the dance work of Restless reconfigures or reterritorialises.

My experiences of dancers 'with' intellectual disability challenging staid psychological limits, which are often imposed upon them, are local instances of 'turning away' from history. Such limits are generally constructed through majoritarian or popular cultural understandings of intellectual disability. In order to reterritorialise intellectual disability, to effect a becoming-other within thought, I emphasise the ways in which dance theatre facilitates bodies with intellectual disability disrupting and existing outside of medical discourses. These practices of becoming speak to Deleuze and Guattari's micro-ethics and their argument that creativity is always a becoming, a reterritorialisation and an establishment of new affective systems of relation. One cannot become-other unless there is something from which one turns away.

Whatever has become familiar to the 'self', one's own indigenous territory, becomes the ground for the new. Legacies of medical knowledges passed on through socialisation are a kinaesthetic ground reterritorialised by the work of Restless Dance Company. In sensory terms, they make the argument that 'intellectual disability' must be seen as, among other things, a construction of thought that can be temporarily disregarded.

References

Allan, J. (2005), 'Disability Arts and the Performance of Ideology' in S. Gabel (ed.), *Disability Studies in Education: Readings in Theory and Method*, New York: Peter Lang.

ASF (2004), Angelman Syndrome Foundation, 'Facts about Angelman Syndrome: Information for Families': http://www.angelman.org/factsofas.htm

Bateson G. (1972), *Steps to an Ecology of Mind*, New York: Ballantine.

Bateson, G. and M. Mead (1942) (reprinted 1995), *The Balinese Character: A Photographic Analysis*, New York: New York Academy of Sciences.

Butler, J. (1990), *Gender Trouble: Feminism and the Subversion of Identity*, New York: Routledge.

CSF (2004), CHARGE Syndrome Foundation Inc, CHARGE Syndrome-Related terms online: http://www.chargesyndrome.org

Deleuze, G. (1988), *Spinoza: Practical Philosophy*, trans. R. Hurley, San Francisco: City Lights Books.

Deleuze, G. and F. Guattari (1983), *Anti-Oedipus: Capitalism and Schizophrenia*, trans. R. Hurley, M. Seem and H. R. Lane, Minneapolis: University of Minnesota Press.

Deleuze, G. and Guattari, F. (1987), *A Thousand Plateaus: Capitalism and Schizophrenia*, trans. Brian Massumi, Minneapolis: University of Minnesota Press.

Deleuze, G. and F. Guattari (1994), *What is Philosophy?* trans. H. Tomlinson and G. Burchell, New York: Columbia University Press.

DIRC (2001), South Australian Disability Information and Resource Centre: http://www.dircsa.org.au

Healy, J. (2000), *Disability and Discrimination*, Balmaine: Spinney Press.

Hickey-Moody, A. C. (2003), 'Turning Away From Intellectual Disability: Methods of Practice, Methods of Thought', *Melbourne Studies in Education* 44 (1): 1–22.

Hickey-Moody, A. C. (2006), 'Folding the Flesh into Thought', *Angelaki: Journal of the Theoretical Humanities* 11 (1): 189–97.

Hickey-Moody, A.C. (2008), 'Deleuze, Guattari and the Boundaries of Intellectual Disability', in S. Gabel and S. Danforth (eds), *Disability and the Politics of Education: An International Reader*, New York: Peter Lang Publishers.

Kuppers, P. (2007), *The Scar of Visibility: Medical Performances and Contemporary Art*, Minneapolis: University of Minnesota Press.

McHenry, L. (1999), 'Thinking Through the Body: Moving Beyond the Social Construction of Disability', Masters Thesis, School of Information and Communication Studies, University of South Australia, Adelaide.

World Health Organization (2001), 'WHO Publishes New Guidelines to Measure Health': http://www.who.int/inf-pr-2001/en/pr2001-48.html

Notes

1. Deleuze expands this definition by arguing that 'affectus' is different from emotion. 'Affectus' is the virtuality and materiality of the increase or decrease effected in a body's power of acting.
2. This point is also made by Petra Kuppers (2007), Lalita McHenry (1999) and Julie Allan (2005).
3. 'Faciality' is a system of attributing cultural meaning to material bodies, within which a 'single substance of expression' (Deleuze and Guattari 1987: 181) is produced, as opposed to a dichotomy of matter and its possible meanings.
4. In other contexts, the term 'integrated dance theatre' is employed to refer to dance theatre performed by people who identify more broadly as being with and without disabilities, not specifically intellectual disabilities.
5. This definition of disability continues to include 'functional limitation or activity restriction caused by an impairment. Disabilities are descriptions of disturbances in function at the level of the person. Examples of disabilities include difficulty seeing, speaking or hearing; difficulty moving or climbing stairs; difficulty grasping, reaching, bathing, eating, toileting' (WHO 1999, quoted in Healy 2000: 1).
6. Deleuze and Guattari argue that social investments occur between two poles, the 'molar pole' (social consolidation) and the 'molecular pole' (dispersion/minoritarian becomings), and that different types of libidinal investment pass between the two poles (Deleuze and Guattari 1983: 340). In creating a unity, libidinal investments move from the molecular to the molar through a process of sedimentation or aggregation. Molar entities are bodies such as nation states, people or cities.
7. Major disability organisations in South Australia other than DIRC include the Down Syndrome Society of SA (DSSSA), Minda Incorporated and the Intellectual Disability Services Council (IDSC). These organisations offer relatively distinct services, ranging from information provision to services provision, housing and medical care.
8. The choanae are the passages that connect the back of the nose to the throat. Atresia is a blockage and people with CHARGE often have completely blocked or severely narrowed choanae, or nasal passages.

9. Posterior coloboma is a gap between eyelids or failure to close the eye. Posterior coloboma can result in an unusual pupil shape and atypical development of the retina or optic nerve.

10. For example, inverted yoga positions are not possible for people with CHARGE due to their breathing difficulties, as the participant's airways are further restricted or blocked by the inversion. The participants I have taught with CHARGE needed to be positioned in the darkest areas of a workshop space, a consideration which means re-orientating rehearsals in relation to the position of the sun. At times, verbal communication needed to be given in close proximity to the participants in question, as broad group directives might not be heard.

11. Angus Goldie-Bilkens died in a road accident in 1999. Much loved by colleagues, family, friends and housemates, he is greatly missed.

12. These discussions were initially designed to identify rehearsals as a space in which it was not appropriate to express sentiments relating to or arising from romantic or sexual relationships with other Company members. These discussions have evolved into a more comprehensive means of maintaining a productive Company culture.

Interval

Chapter 10

. . . of butterflies, bodies and biograms . . . Affective Spaces in Performativities in the Performance of *Madama Butterfly*

Barbara Kennedy

Through the process of movement, the 'beautiful' can be newly discerned as a notion of duration and brain formations. How is the beautiful accommodated through movement and motion? Various forms of motion are more appealing, more alluring, more beautiful to the eye-brain. For example, the pathways of the flight of the butterfly will produce the most invigorating, beautiful and captivating pathways of motion, a cartography of visionary dance across the eye-brain, but also an amorphous fragility within the tactility of the image. The highly variable trajectory of the butterfly will make the brain continually break and form, break and form, breaking any symmetry, thus engaging all three fields of view of the eye. The eternal return of the eye-brain activity (and the butterfly) creates a kinaesthetics, wherein the brain's activities are beyond the merely visual, but become tactile, fluid, in process. (Kennedy 2000: 116)

Within the green fields of Deleuzian grasses the white butterfly's movement captures: aparalletic evolution – the wasp and the orchid. (Kennedy 2000: 115)

The Event/Affect: From Complexity to the Edge of Chaos

For too long the arts and humanities have been haunted by a theoretical impasse which has prioritised the liberal humanist subject, projecting theories of subjectivity, identity, the affective and the aesthetic through recourse to a range of critical theory, such as psychoanalysis, with which to explore the exigencies of the human subjective response to the arts. All that is fresh, passional, scintillating and inspirational about the pleasures of performance has been lost in a theoretical diatribe from semiotics, structuralism, post-structuralism, active audience theory, reception theories, postmodernism, psychoanalysis and social constructionist theories, all of which prioritise ideological and political foci to the detriment of affectivity and art. Where was the body and feeling in such debates? Why did none of this theory explain the vital, visceral and electric pulsations of my 'autonomic' response to the arts? In an attempt to let my body speak (a dancer, not an academic), to find those autopoietic breaths pulsating the rhythms of artworks, I was seduced by the lines of flight of Deleuze. As a result, my own work on cinema and in visual practice has embraced an *aesthetics of sensation* and philosophy as a theoretical paradigm through which to distanciate much critical theory in favour of a return to the materiality of art, material poiesis and the event of material capture. Hence it began to mobilise a critique of the cinematic through an understanding of the *neo-aesthetic* as that which emerges from a machinic, intervallic space of duration and process (Kennedy 2000). Elsewhere, I explored ideas through concepts of duration and intuition in practice and choreography, taking Deleuze's *Bergsonism* as a text for inspiration (Kennedy 2007: 773). In academia more generally, media and film theory have widely embraced the Deleuzian realm of the 'sensible' and the Deleuzian 'event' (Pisters 2002; O'Sullivan 2006; Powell 2006).

More recently however, the humanities and new media theory[1] have become fascinated with chaos theory, complexity theory, neuroscience and ontologies of emergence and kinaesthetics in resonance with Deleuzian-Bergsonian affect and autopoiesis. Systems theory has been inflecting the multivalencies and microidentities of all disciplines across the arts and sciences. Ontologies of emergence in dynamic systems and from continental philosophy are nurturing innovative and transversal knowledges for the arts and humanities. In a book collection concerned with Performance Studies, then, I was intrigued to consider how it might be possible to meld together some transversal processes of thought initiated by my engagement with Deleuze to offer a posthuman theory of *emergent aesthetics* which embraces the scintillation, the electricity and the passion of much performative art, in this case of a filmed operatic performance. This chapter is, however, neither a piece of musicology nor performance theory, but a collision of knowledges brought together by a Deleuzian concern with production, participation and process rather than text, signification or ideology. The latter are still nonetheless mediated within the other molecular spaces and never truly separated from them. It seems that in the twenty-first century such a posthuman discourse is one infected with contagious outpourings of interconnecting rhythms and vectors across a variety of disciplines. Katherine Hayles, in *How We Became Posthuman*, argues that

> distributed cognition replaces autonomous will, embodiment replaces a body seen as a support system for the mind, and a dynamic partnership between humans and intelligent machines replaces the liberal humanist

subject's manifest destiny to dominate and control nature . . . the distributed cognition of the emergent human subject becomes a metaphor for the distributed cognitive system as a whole, in which 'thinking' is done by both human and non-human actors. (Hayles 1999: 288)

An interest in chaos, complexity theory and open systems theory in contrast to the structurally closed systems of linguistics, has begun to impact upon all the disciplines across the academy. All the arts are now influenced by the development of a field of study in emergent and dynamic systems, recursive systems and complexity theory. Complexity prevents reductive and simplistic conceptions of process by forwarding co-emergent processes of movement premised on mathematical/differential and algorithmic configurations. Therefore, ideas premised on concepts like flow and process are used in collusion with Deleuzian concepts of affect, autopoiesis, interval, rhythm, intuition and haecceity as productive of the creative act (Kennedy 2000). Concepts arising in such thinking find aparalletic evolution with those of process philosophy, in the context of discussions of virtuality, intuition, relationality and individuation (Mullarkey 2006; Protevi 2006). Performance Studies is now presciently aware of such theoretical paradigms emanating from philosophy, emergence theory and computer (AI) theory. It seems that a discourse of dissonant but convergent cognitions has provided us with a rich palette of modulations through which to explore the concept of the 'performative'. An *emergent aesthetics* mobilises our performative spaces, whether in installation art, dance, film, video, computer web jamming, or theatrical, musical and operatic events. This emergent aesthetics has a fundamental recourse to processuality, participation and an understanding of the intuitive space of the topographical and biogrammatic. The focus of this *aesthetics of emergence* lies beyond any conception of a 'subjective' understanding of the performance as a connective, diagrammatic, topological and biogrammatic, incorporeal dimension of the body of the spectator/observer/experiencer.

The work of Deleuze and Guattari, and indeed Bergson, forms a fundamental central intensity within such discourses and I find myself filtering, faltering and fragmenting across this array of discourses on emergence. Assuming some knowledge of the concepts by the reader, this chapter will unapologetically dance its way across the intervallic spaces of such discourses in its differently inflected explorations of *Madama Butterfly* as directed by the filmmaker Zeffirelli. It must be acknowledged, however, that this is a filmed version of an operatic event in Verona, filmed by Zeffirelli in 2004, not a live operatic performance. Rather than a concern with any 'subjective' encounter with the performance on screen, this chapter argues for a production of the 'codes' of subjectivity premised upon the processuality and participatory nature of affect, the aesthetic and the emergent. It is an argument for an *emergent aesthetics*.

In *What is Philosophy?* Deleuze argues that the mind/brain provides the interstice for the codes of subjectivity. This interstice is felt at a level of the proto-subjective: an involvement of the brain in connection with both mind and the body as molecular coagulation. In their final collaborative text Deleuze and Guattari write that science, art and philosophy as forms of thought or creativity have the brain as the junction of all three. I want to take up some of their ideas in a strategic encounter with scientific discourse which moves beyond phenomenological parameters into thinking through *affect* within what I shall refer to as the biogrammatic (see Massumi 2002).

Current debates within Deleuzian-Bergsonian film studies are taking some new directions in an imbrication of the technoscientific and bio-aesthetic through philosophic engagement with brain/bodyworld relationals (Pisters 2002; Manning 2006; Powell 2006; Kennedy 2007, 2009). Dance and performance, whether live or filmic, effectuate a wide range of physical, emotional and aesthetic traces. Where do these sensations reside? How can we explore the temporalities of moving bodies (sonic, visual, haptic) both in real time and in recorded time beyond the more formal debates of aesthetics? What and how we *know*, what and how we *feel* are part of a mobile, multi-directional, distributed and indeterminate interrelation between non-human and human actants in an emergent dynamic set of ecologies. This chapter then argues for an interdisciplinary transversal approach to theory by using debates on cognitive/proprioceptive states which assemble discourses from psychology, philosophy and science. In so doing it explores the *working* of movements in/through and beyond the texts/bodies/vectors of the operatic performance of *Madama Butterfly* through resource to the concept of the biogram. The biogram is that which advances us from the diagram, through synaesthesia, in a cyborgian collusion with bio-aesthetics and theories of proprioceptivity and viscerality. Sounds, movements, bodies and brains are affective 'modulators' through which we experience the *moves of the butterfly . . . the entraining of the brain*.

Complex systems theory provides a model for considering non-linear relations at work in arts processes. Thus *products* are not prioritised, but the *relations of process* of engagement across the artwork. In computer systems theory and chaos theory, a methodology allows for explaining a range of subjects, whether biological, social or scientific, in non-linear, dynamic thought patterns of relationality, For example, in the field of

cyberculture, relationality has become a significant element for understanding new patterns of thinking. Discussing the work of Lenoir and
Alt in *Cybercultures*, I argue that

> Lenoir and Alt begin with an analysis of how biology has been affected by
> discourses which shift towards open and disunified systems, rather than
> structural, mechanistic models of science: fixed subjectivity is distanciated,
> planning and simulation directed at an individual, independent 'actant'
> rather than a consensual homogeneous subject. (Kennedy 2007: 654)

Similarly, I write here of architects and their use of computer algorithms
to focus on their innovative strategies of design. Complexity prevents any
reductive conceptions of process and facilitates the precedence of a range
of multiple, co-emergent systems. Thus concepts like flow, process, fold
and movement are framed and become processed in aparalletic evolution
with Deleuzian concepts of affect, autopoiesis, interval, rhythm, intuition and haecceity as being productive of the 'creative' act.[2] Emergence
thus bridges all three areas of art, science and philosophy, as *What is
Philosophy?* articulates. However, the use of the concept of 'emergence',
in Deleuze and Guattari, needs to be positioned very clearly in relation
to what John Protevi calls 'diachronic emergence': a production of 'new
patterns of behaviour in what Deleuze will call an "event", which is not
to be confused with a mere switch between already established patterns
or with a trigger of an "external event". The Deleuzian event *repatterns*
a system' (Protevi 2006: 6). Diachronic emergence is premised on unpre-
dictability and novelty; a creative production of new patterns. According
to Protevi, this type of emergence 'leaps' and 'evolves'. Emergence then
is like a 'two-sided coin': one side in the virtual, the other in the actual
(Massumi, 2002: 35).

In *Bergsonism*, Deleuze addresses the virtual/actual relational in his
exploration of the two types of multiplicity functioning within the pre-
personal. One is represented by space – quantitative differentiation,
difference in degree and numerical difference: it equates with the *actual*.
The other is pure duration, and is an internal multiplicity, fusion, heterogeneity, difference in kind: it is *virtual*. The affective is the hinge/blend/
co-existence of the virtual and actual and as such explains a process of
'becoming'. The virtual is that which is

> maximally abstract, yet real, whose reality is that of potential – pure relation-
> ality, the interval of change, the in itself of transformation . . . it is nonlinear,
> moving in two directions at once: out from the actual (as past) into the actual
> (as future). The actuality it leaves as past is the same actuality to which it no
> sooner comes as future: from being to becoming. (Massumi 2002: 58)

This is however, in contrast with synchronic emergence which merely develops. The repatterning of the system mobilises through material *functions*, not textual signifiers. Like Guattari, Deleuze posits the existence of what he refers to as proto-subjectivities, as a realm of autoconsistency, before or beyond any 'subject', before the social and cultural world of language structures and before an emergent sense of a psychic self.

The term *autopoiesis* is used to define a state of 'self-enjoyment', and comes out of Deleuze's ideas of the pre-personal where there exists what he refers to as absolute interiorities. This pre-personal state exists as a kind of field of different forces of intensities, wills to power, 'that resonate with one another, that interact in ways that produce effects on one another' (Kennedy 2000: 91). The pre-personal is that which contracts a habit and is therefore a form of repetition. These pre-personal states are not *had* by a self, but are constitutive of the self. It is, as such, an impersonal state and a non-subjective space. This impersonal and cellular space is the space of affect, according to Deleuze, an intensity which has its rhizomatic roots in the bifurcation points of chaos theory. It is the 'body without organs' of *A Thousand Plateaus*. Varela writes:

> autopoiesis attempts to define the uniqueness of the emergence that produces life in its fundamental *cellular* form. It's specific to the cellular level. There is a circular or network process that engenders a paradox: a self-organising network of bio-chemical reactions produces molecules which do something specific and unique. (Varela 1995, quoted in Doruff 2006).

To trace the move from a humanities' critique based on text, signification, semiotics and ideology, and indeed the liberal-humanist subject, this chapter will now follow the development of the chaotic concept of the *diagram* in relation to the work of Deleuze, and hence its progression into the vocabularies of production, participation, affect, process and what has been called mesoperception (Massumi 2002: 62), or what I have referred to as sensation (Kennedy 2000: 108).

In a comparable line of flight to the ideas proffered by N.K. Hayles on 'distributed cognition', Deleuze's project on schizoanalysis and the diagram provides a good starting point to explore this 'new' language for explaining the performative in art, science and indeed philosophy. In philosophy the concept of the diagram has a rich texture which we can draw upon to take a step into the biogrammatic. In consilience with theories of diachronic emergence, 'the meaning of diagram . . . is movement that constantly redraws itself' (Knoepsel 2000: xvi). In his recent exploration of post-continental philosophy, John Mullarkey writes that 'the diagram is a purity, and as pure, it must be virtual. The diagram is what "retains the most deterritorialised content and the most deterritorialised expression, in order to conjugate them". Diagramming raises a trait to its highest power, it "carries it off"' (Deleuze and Guattari 1987: 141–2; Mullarkey 2006: 174). He refers to Deleuze's diagrams in *The Fold* as further examples of an 'in between state': 'In *The Fold*, diagrams are not representations, or icons of Baroque architecture, but they enable us to understand what is the *function* of the architecture, what it *does*, not what it means' (174). Deleuze's texts refer to the diagram as a germ of order or a rhythm. It is what modulates or subtracts from the virtual (Deleuze 2003: 102, 110).

Deleuze's concept of virtualism develops from a general theory of the diagram. His texts such as *A Thousand Plateaus* and *Logic of Sensation* explore the notion of the diagram. For Deleuze, thinking is a kind of topological process, an enfolding process where outside and inside meld in continual 'mobius strip' relations. Deleuze's ideas on the complexity of thought are useful in helping us to rethink some basic beliefs about language and its possibilities. In *A Thousand Plateaus*, he advocates the concept of the 'abstract machine' which he sets up as different from the closed structures of structural linguistics. He argues that thought is an effect or process which participates and collides or colludes with other processes to make up what he refers to as a 'machinic assemblage'. These processes function with other components such as time, space, bodies and matter. Artistic performances such as opera, then, it might be argued, function by means of a range of different components, constituting a machinic assemblage in part-icipation. However, this 'abstract machine' is not physical or corporeal in nature, existing rather in what he refers to as 'aparallel evolution'[3] with other materials. An 'abstract machine', then, is really a condition of experience or a condition of existence, of being in the world, that exceeds what is perceived and recognised through language. It acts, as participation, as modulation. It rejects semiotic formats and conventions, and does not exist to 'represent' our realities, but rather to produce a different reality.

As in cinematic theory, verbal, literary, structured and organic languages remain too static and immobile, too sedimented and frozen to explain the intensities and pulsations of dramatic or operatic performance. Bodies are not objects but perform as actants of the abstract machine. Here gesture, mimesis, rhythm, aleatory and pathic tendencies across a wide range of different 'bodies' – technological, biological, sonic, visual, theoretical or material – constitute a different reality premised on flows, as an open system, in a way similar to how Kathryn Hayles explains the concept of 'distributed cognitions'. There is no formal structure to the utilisation of distributed cognitions as they grow and evolve as emergent ecologies. Similarly, the abstract machine has no formal structure or design, unlike language. Content and expression are not distinguished. The abstract machine functions through open systems (as in systems theory) in which systems oppose structures. It works as a kind of 'amorphous' matter or material, not as a substance with structures. It functions as a *diagrammatic* system, and as a material for exploring the experiential. The abstract machine connects, collides and works as a 'body' of matter which connects with other bodies of matter. Machinic systems work through a series of syntheses and multiplicities premised in mathematical algorithms rather than binary thought patterns, as we find in the axiomatics of structuralist linguistics. The abstract machine is diagrammatic, 'the diagram is indeed a chaos, a catastrophe, but it is also a germ or order of rhythm' (Deleuze 2003: 102).

The virtuality of the diagram is also explored in *Logic of Sensation*, where the approach, in John Mullarkey's description, 'is taken up with prolonged reflections on rhythm, in art – the co-existence of all movements on canvas. Subtending the concrete machines of each canvas, the abstract machine is a diagram of spots, lines and zones . . . haptic, rather than optical, tactile, rather than visual'. 'The diagram is not just an outline, but involves the fullness of colour – as sensation . . . [the haptic] is a part-icipation rather than a representation, a material belonging and becoming of one part in another rather than by one specular whole of another' (Mullarkey 2006: 176, 159). As I explore in Deleuze and Cinema, 'this hapticity is simultaneously optic and tactile. The visual becomes "felt". The felt connection between eye and hand is felt, in coagulation, an evolution of hand into eye' (Kennedy 2000: 117). It is this focus on the chaos of rhythm and the role this plays in performing the sonic and visual patterns of sensation/mesoperception in operatic performance which has provoked my foray into exploring the operatic event. In a move to mobilise this model of the diagram and the haptic into the topologies of the biogrammatic I want to posit a model to inflect it further with a fuller rendition of bodily productions which potentially involves the rhythmicities of aurality as part of the mix. This will enable us to theorise the sonic, haptic and biorhythms of the operatic performance. Neither musicologist[4] nor philosopher, I write as an artist/dancer in exploration of feeling and love of the performance – a kinaesthetics, wherein the brain's activities are beyond the merely visual, but become tactile, fluid, in process (Kennedy 2000: 116).

What steps take us from the diagram to the biogram? The 'biogrammatic . . . is a synaesthetic extension of a diagram' (Doruff 2006: 6;

see Deleuze and Guattari 1987: 43–5). Processual affectivity resides in the durational and volatile contingencies of the body/mind relational (Kennedy 2007: 773), an *incorporeal* dimension of the body which Brian Massumi refers to as the biogram. The biogram is neither form nor matter but a contingent potentiality of form/matter through duration and process. The biogrammatic is 'a space that does not exist IN the world but in the intersticial realm of vision-object; a peri-personal world and liminal space'. Synaesthetic forms are formulated from 'experience that has already been lived: habit, memories, a pastness within the present, enfolding in a co-existence to mobilise futurity' (see Massumi 2002: 187). Our existences are neither purely physical, emotional nor psychological but constitute a non-Euclidean topology, in a similar vein to those of computer algorithms. Our intuitive movements in collusion with space, time, sound and bodies incur/concur with topological dimensions which orient our affective responses through fibrous and cellular networks. Affectivities incorporate participatory synaesthetic dimensions such as seeing/tasting a sound or hearing a colour. Synaesthesia recombines as elements of proprioceptive (an enfolding of tactility into the body) memory – a recursivity projected through the muscles, ligaments, fibrous tissue and cells of a body's physical receptors. Muscular proprioceptors provide information for different upper spinal structures involved in the programming and in the control both of staticity and of movements. This involves contortions and rhythms, actions and passions, not images. We might say speeds and intensities.

Massumi refers to synaesthetic forms as 'diagrammatic' in the Deleuzian sense explored above, but there is an added hinge-dimension – already lived experience orients further receptivities. This is more than a diagram – this is the biogram: a 'liminal non-place characterised as peri-personal' in the same way as Deleuze explains the pre-individual singularities of affectivity. This faculty of proprioception is nonetheless 'of' the body, of the flesh, involving visceral sensations or excitations such as the enteric nervous system – a fleshy gut reaction felt outside and before thought. Taking a lead from the work of Massumi, who explains the biogram as the 'mode of being of the intersensory hinge-dimension' (Massumi 2002: 188), Erin Manning writes:

> The emergence of the biogram is not a creation of a static body, but a virtual node out of which a body-ness can be felt. The feltness of the body is an affective experience. It is a tendency of the body to become that the biogram makes palpable. What is felt is the affective tone of the event. For the becoming body has no form as such – it is an exfoliating body. (Manning 2009)

The hinge-dimension of proprioception and viscerality produces what I have referred to as sensation (Kennedy 2000), or as Massumi has it, mesoperception. The biogram, then, is a conjunctive mode of becoming which is multi- and inter-sensory. It is no longer sufficient to explore ourselves and our worlds (including artistic worlds) through representation or reflection. What we must consider is our *participation* in experience – our creative potential in the event. In consilience with Protevi's description of diachronic emergence as new 'thresholds of behaviour' (Protevi 2006: 23), the biogrammatic is rhythmically meshed to 'bring something new' to create, to leap, to mutate, to transform, to conjugate a series into the unexpected and unplanned – the event.

The Event of the Operatic: *Madama Butterfly*

> . . . the intervallic, between-space of affect as a Lorenz-like butterfly effect.
> (Doruff 2006: 58; see Massumi 2002: 227)

What follows is an exploration of how the opera *Madama Butterfly* *works* to effectuate the 'event' of an abstract machine. *Madama Butterfly* as directed by Zeffirelli in 2004 is a masterpiece in operatic staging and performance. Puccini's adaptation at the turn of the century (eighteenth to nineteenth), from a stage performance by David Belasco, had already mutated from a short story by John Luther Long. Even prior to that it had initially emerged as an earlier literary source, *Madame Chrysantheme*, which became an operatta by Andre Messager in 1893. Set entirely in Japan, unlike previous versions, Puccini's opera has a time-scale of 24 hours. Giacosa and Illica began to assist him in construction of the libretto with dialogue written by Illicia and the rhythms of the verse composed by Giacosa. Japonaiserie and folk song, which became an integral part of the composition, were studied intensely, as they were by many European artists at the turn of the century. The narrative holds together a romantic tragedy of unfaltering, unconditional love and melancholy as a result of innocent naivety and cultural divisions. The narrative has undoubtedly drawn a variety of socio-political critiques, especially in relation to Western perceptions of the Orient, and is still considered by many to present a problematic rendition of Japanese culture, and a misogynist treatment of women (although the irony here is that Pinkerton's outrageous behaviour stands in moral subservience to the honour, strength and resilience of Cho Cho San). Japanese honour and integrity have the final moment of splendour, albeit metaphorically through the final sequence. The cultural and aesthetic aspects distanciate the gendered text. With all critiques of Japanese sexual politics what is lacking in textual deconstruction is an awareness of the biogrammatic, affective and sensual proclivities of Japonaiserie, the very *calligraphic*, not representative, beauty of linearity, space, grace, line and ethereality that inspired the art of Impressionism, nowhere more so than in the work of Van Gogh. Hiroshige's work permeates the scenic backdrops of this performance. Nonetheless, on a molar ideological plane, the entire opera produces a critique of Western socio/sexual politics through the abhorrent character of B. F. Pinkerton.

But we need to move beyond the representational into the *participatory* of the biogrammatic. The biogram operates as a conjunctive: rather than being a representing image, the biogram carries a movement across or between series so that the music itself becomes visual. This has particular resonance in opera. The relational event of theatrical and operatic performance brings together philosophy, art and science. An operatic performance – like any performative compositional work – implicates, involves and inheres *as* intuitive practice (Kennedy 2007: 773). Operatic dialogue, voice, music, tone, motif and intermezzo inhere as intuitive, sensational and affective durations, but they also meld in a machinic assemblage with the space/time in which they perform. The arts, (particularly poetry, literature, music and opera) as modulators of experience, *produce* the creative 'event' and the affective, by the contingent synthesis of intuitive processes which involve heterogeneous qualitative multiplicities. These qualitative multiplicities make up the intuitive duration of these tiny events unfolding. Through the process of intuition, the actual and the virtual are consistently looped back recursively, and this reciprocal action mobilises 'affect'. The abstract machinism of the performance is mobilised through complex visual and aural rhythms, haptic and sonic bodies which conduct and participate as differential operatic codes. Sound, silence, movement, colour, shape and textures inflect as a complex series of actants which participate or conjugate biogrammatically for the audience.

An orchestral prelude introduces what will be two themes in the course of Act I. Rhythm provides the 'body' of the operatic event. As Dalcroze has written, 'it is impossible to conceive of rhythm without thinking of a body in motion' (Dalcroze 1921: 82). Rhythm performs as an act of transmutation rather than representation. The music provides a 'body without organs' which functions as part of the overall abstract machine of the work. The first of these themes is rhythmical, energetic, vibrant, resonant and animated; it functions in *allegro* (fast) creating a dynamic tempo and rhythm. It takes the form of a fugue (Latin: fuga = flight), which is a contrapuntal *flow* of sounds evocative of energy, intensity, noise and confusions. The fugue is a four part expositional piece and is premised on an opening figure that will constantly recur throughout.[5] As a stream of flowing sounds which act in variance and duration with the next, the fugue 'proceeds': it is processual, not formative. It provides a textured set of sounds which are identifiable throughout in relation to other identifiers and creates a biogrammatic wave across the text. This presents a virtual wave of voices/sounds with different inflections and dialogues. Counterpoint creates a wave of vibration across the characters' voices in contrast with the orchestral background. Fugues are premised upon melodic themes and mobilise the 'speeds' of the different characters in the narrative.

The second of the themes is a four chord figure, which is a 'becoming-Nagasaki' of the opera. The sound and inflection of voice in Na-ga-SA-ki is mobilised aurally. The tone is set as one of contempt and amusement (from Pinkerton), indicated by the tempo and pulse of the music. The tempo is balanced in consilience with the performative actions of Goro and hence biogrammatically with the audience. We feel ourselves *hear* the movements as well as act them out. The performance begins with a vast set, designed as a monument to Buddha, as an ornamental moving sculpture which acts to display both interior and exterior locations. The bustling Japanese landscape is mobilised through sound/vision in a variety of methods. The fugue of the musical score will resonate durationally throughout the entire script with Japanese miniaturisation mobilised in material capture through percussive and orchestral string movements. Goro presents the servants to Pinkerton, accompanied by a change in the instrumental music to more delicate flutes and a graceful, endearing, lighter heartfelt tone modulating the grace and demeanour of Japanese style and honour. Suzuki expresses these elements, while Goro himself is evoked as a clown-like figure, both in costume (yellow and blue spotted trousers) and in musical form, the tones of the deep resonant bassoon indicating the humour. A variety of parallel visionary gazes is instigated by the camera work which crosses from right to left and left to right indicating the bustling worklife of the Japanese town, sailors linking the arms of decorative geishas. Colours – pinks, lilac, lavenders – vibrate against the drab and dour costume of more local Japanese workers and the Americans. Beautiful textures of silks and brocades of flirtatious geishas clash with the simplicity of American uniforms, and the formidable and masculine white uniform of Pinkerton. A haptic and diagrammatic event. The small delicate footsteps of geisha movements resonate with the musical score in contrast with the lack of grace and beauty of Goro and Pinkerton who, in comparison, bound across the set. A recurring musical motif and a change in tempo and instrumentation (now lyrical violin music) announce the arrival of Sharpless, which follows through the entire opera to denote the clash of cultures. A close up of a child's face mobilises a theme of sincerity, love and emotion. A toast to America follows in the first duet of 'Amore o grillo' in *allegretto moderato* (fairly fast to moderate speeds); Pinkerton's discussion of Butterfly as 'light and delicate', 'a figure on a screen', 'she flutters like a butterfly', is followed by a 'whisky toast' to the future and an American wife.

We hear the approach of Butterfly before seeing her, the haunting music visually answering in vibration to the beautiful camera work of geishas in cross movements, parasols producing encircling, calligraphic motions with faces, colours and textures processed through dissolves, 'becoming-geisha', until we see the entrance of Butterfly. This viscerality and synaesthesia are felt through the proprioceptive intensity of the biogram. The biogrammatic is the virtual at the hinge-dimension with the actual. We feel ourselves in motion, in duration with this sequence. Dressed in sumptuous turquoise/red and yellow silks and satins, her movements are slow, graceful and endearing. The music answers to the visuals with delicate Japanese bells, oboe and piccolo, harps and flutes. Japanese folk music inheres in the piece with a delicate cadence which balances the texture of the visuals. Butterfly's dialogue with Pinkerton conveys a voice composed in dissonant tones and chords, creating an Oriental feel to her admissions of poverty, childhood and history; her father's death is denoted by the sombre woodwind and brass. The flow of the camera movements follows young girls taking the Japanese dolls (Ottoke) to the altar whilst Butterfly joins in a commitment to Christian belief. An understated wedding ceremony proceeds, but is quickly distanciated by the entrance of Bonze cursing the abominable match as betrayal. The cacophonous discordant theme of the music, here in *allegro*, is brutal, harsh and formidable, its sounds conjugating fear and loathing. Pinkerton's comforting of Butterfly then precedes their first love duet together. Close up shots of facial expressions, lips, eyes, mouths in tender accord, whisper back to the plangent chords from violins and violas. The graceful hand movements and gestures are aleatory and mimetically poetic in a becoming-butterfly of their embrace: a biogrammatic convergence of cultures and sexes: a thousand tiny sexes. The early part of their love duet intuits durationally some of the earlier Japanese themes/motifs from the fugue compositions transversing and modulating the process of the opera. The main part of their love duet 'Viene la sera' acts as a triptychal melody in synchronisation with the colours which modulate the rhythms of the piece, Butterfly in her white flowing robes and orb, with purple and blue fan dancing in cameratic dissolves. The butterfly movements of the fan biogrammatically entrain the participatory actants in this 'machinic opera'; flowing and falling in harmonious accord: a different fate of course to be awaited in enclosure, imprisonment, entrapment and death. The butterfly concedes to innocence, naivety, vulnerability and pain in the trauma of this devotion to unconditional love. Her words 'love me just a little', whilst wrapped in childish composure on the ground, encapsulate such destructive masochism, whilst in ironic contrast Pinkerton sings 'Love does not kill, it gives life!' A blue haze dissolve mobilises their union in love with the lighting effects creating a contrasting resonance with the earlier bustling colours and vibrant activities. The camera pulls back to give a long shot, dissolved in aqueous, liquid blue tones in a crescendo of musical notation: a conjunctive mode of becoming, *multi-* and inter-sensory.

Act II, part one, opens to a prelude with gentle Japanese orchestral sounds, bird song, violins. The resonances of the earlier fugal exposition underlies the sounds. The statuesque sculptured structure opens up to reveal Butterfly asleep whilst Suzuki keeps close by in prayer. The lighting in this scene has changed to a darker, more sombre atmosphere and conveys the poverty of Butterfly three years on from marriage. The Hiroshige prints of her household maintain the Japanese intensities of her living, and the moving screens motivate our brain/bodies into an evocation of change and fearful anticipation. It is here that the famous melodic aria 'One Fine Day' begins. The rhythms and pitch here move from calm to anxiety, agitation and ultimately to despair, with a final maternal repose of Suzuki and Butterfly in embrace. Its conclusion in *fortissimo* (very loud) motivates her longing and desire in a mix of trumpets, woodwind and horns. Sharpless returns with suggestions of a new suitor in Yamadori (introduced with motifs from *The Mikado*, tremolando[6] violins and woodwind arpeggios[7]) for Butterfly. A ritornello of earlier themes is evoked through the Japanese folk tunes. Persistent fanning across her countenance indicates her lack of desire to follow this suggestion, proclaiming her determination and stubborn love for Pinkerton. Sharpless reveals the letter he has received from Pinkerton, whilst soft melodic tones of strings and brass, bassoon and *pizzicato*[8] strings, provide what is to become the haunting, sweeping dance of the Humming Chorus. The close up of Butterfly with her child (to the sound of the 'Pathetic Melody') is a moving finale to the scene, the darkly lit blue lighting introducing the motivation of later moods of 'blueness', melancholy and tragedy. Music and vision work as intensive states in a process of conjugation. They mobilise as an 'event' of the tragic, not as a representation of the tragic, involving us in the participation of the action, as actants in the machinism. Distant cannon shots in the harbour end the scene with the repetition of riffs from 'One Fine Day'.

Butterfly remains optimistic, looking out to the harbour and detecting Pinkerton's ship, the *Abraham Lincoln*. Contrasting types of choreographed movement occur simultaneously as the child moves gently to pray at the Buddha following an eloquent Madonna and Child pose with Butterfly; Suzuki chases Goro in horror at his rumours. Butterfly's dance around the stage is vibrant and exhilarating as she swings the child to the floor, falling with him in delight and anticipation of perceived pleasures to come. She sings of flowers – lilies, roses, jasmine, violets, verbena, tuberoses, peaches – conjoining different bodies, different *sensual series*, whilst the blue light of the set bathes her in an evanescent mist: the poetic, assonantal and alliterative intonations of the Italian vocalisation of such words making a fitting series from which 'The Flower Duet' ensues. There is a synaesthetic becoming-nature of art: the sounds fluidly become-colour, become-perfume in a becoming-flower. Two soprano female voices blend in ecstatic harmony with a wide range of different tonalities. They sing 'their Flower Duet, whose closing section in euphonius thirds has something of the voluptousness of Viennese operatta, a la Lehair' (Osborne 1981: 169). Dressing in her marital orb and white diaphanous robes, together with a red poppy in her hair, Butterfly prepares for her vigil. We hear the famous 'Humming Chorus', a haunting flow of female voices, in poignant melodic harmony, a 50 bar *cantilena*,[9] with only a touch of orchestral intonations from delicate *pizzicato* strings. The light fades to a cadence of stillness; darkness fades to black.

To the 'Edge of Chaos': Death of the Butterfly

The haunting harmonies of the Humming Chorus meld in intensive states with the diaphanous flowing dance of the spirit of Butterfly, one of the most beautiful and tender scenes in the opera. Lighting is in monochrome blue modulating the mystery and spirituality of Butterfly's spiritual self. Geisha veils, twists, flows and swirling gestures pan in circular movements to delicate *pizzicato* strings. She waves her fan in harmony with the music, enhancing the regularity of the rhythmical dance. Her facial/mask expression transmutes as a haunting mix of pleasure and death. Zeffirelli invokes a series of earlier sequences and flows, close ups of the Japanese dolls, Butterfly's smiling face as she remembers Pinkerton, dissolves of the earlier geisha dance with swirling synaesthetic tones/fragrances of oranges, pinks, lavenders and blues, carrying us back to the intensities of Act I. A recursivity which coexistently melds the *before* in to the present and anticipates the future. Cuts and edits to earlier sequences are interspersed with the haunting melancholy of the spirit-Butterfly. Act II, part two, follows a long intermezzo and a dawn chorus evokes intonations from *Tristan und Isolde*, sounding the potential tragic denouement. Butterfly takes vigil with the child whilst a lullaby is played with violins to a moving cadence, accompanying Suzuki's singing.

Pinkerton and Sharpless return accompanied by the serious and daunting tones of a *largo* (broadly) theme. An harmonic and intersecting trio ensues from the baritone and tenor of their voices with Suzuki, in a *terzetto* (three-part piece), which modulates as a beautiful lyrical calligraphic intensity. The interweaving of this series transmutes into Pinkerton's remorseful solo aria, '*Addio, Fiorito Asil*' (Farewell, Flowery Refuge). Gesture and dialogue answer in contrast to the drama of Pinkerton's contritional farewell. The drama escalates as Butterfly returns and encounters Kate Pinkerton. Fast camera shots follow her as she floats around in anticipation of exhilaration, the speeds of the scenic actions vibrating against the stillness of Pinkerton's farewell gravitas. Cellos create an intensity of emotional resonance at her recognition of events. Harsh trumpets in dissonance mobilise the pain. She thus creeps, craves and crawls around the set in despair at her understanding. In her solo, '*Sotto il gran ponte del cielo*' (Under the great arc of the sky), Butterfly 'achieves the status of a tragic heroine' (Osborne 1981: 170). What ensues is the tragic and beautiful acknowledgement of the betrayal and the relinquishing of her being – her child. Her death solo is a lyrical poignant soprano piece. This final aria is excruciatingly and painfully ecstatic in its intense tones and rhythms. Her death knell is sounded with a haunting chorus as she dresses in majestic red/gold and green brocaded orb for her final act of honour as she takes the sword into her hands and ends her life.

A terrible beauty is thus born – a tragic death premised on innocence and naivety, but most of all on unfaltering love and honour. What can we conclude then from such an exploration of an operatic performance? It seems that in the humanities it is now time to turn to a new aesthetic awareness which embraces a complex understanding of the concept of movement; not what movement is, but what movement can *do*, what it mobilises and processes, and how it performs as an intersticial and intervallic realm of conjugation and participation. In Performance Studies, which includes the operatic as I have shown here, movement captures the pleasures of the visceral, the proprioceptive, the synaesthetic, but it also mobilises bodies in biogrammatic and machinic ways. We can then begin to move away from textual deconstruction premised upon antiquated concepts of ideology and representation, beyond an aesthetics of 'becoming' and 'the event' to an aesthetics of 'emergence'.

References

Budden, J. (2002), *Puccini: His Life and Works*, New York and Oxford: Oxford University Press.

Dalcroze, E. (1921), *Rhythm, Music and Education*, trans. H. F. Rubinstein, New York: G. P. Putnam and Sons.

Deleuze, G. (1988), *Bergsonism*, trans. H. Tomlinson and B. Habberjam, New York: Zone Books.

Deleuze, G. (2003), *Francis Bacon: The Logic of Sensation*, trans. D. W. Smith, London: Continuum.

Deleuze, G. and C. Parnet (1987), *Dialogues*, trans. H. Tomlinson and B. Habberjam, London: Athlone.

Deleuze, G. and F. Guattari (1987), *A Thousand Plateaus: Capitalism and Schizophrenia*, trans. B. Massumi, London: Athlone.

Deleuze, G. and F. Guattari (1994), *What is Philosophy?*, trans. H. Tomlinson and G. Burchell, London: Verso.

Doruff, S. (2006), *The Translocal Event and Polyrhythmic Diagram*, PhD thesis, University of London.

Hayles, K. (1999), *How We Became Posthuman*, Chicago: University of Chicago Press.

Kennedy, B. M. (2000), *Deleuze and Cinema: The Aesthetics of Sensation*, Edinburgh: Edinburgh University Press.

Kennedy, B. M. (2007), 'Thinking Ontologies of the Mind/Body Relational: Fragile Faces and Fugitive Graces in the Processuality of Creativity and Performativity', in B. M. Kennedy and D. Bell (eds) *The Cybercultures Reader*, Second Edition, London: Routledge.

Knoepsel, K. J. (2000), 'Digrammatic Writing and the Configuration of Space', Introduction to Gilles Châtelet, *Figuring Space: Philosophy, Mathematics and Physics*, trans. R. Shore and M. Zagha, Dordrecht, The Netherlands: Kluwer Academic Publishers.

Manning, E. (2009), 'From Biopolitics to the Biogram, or How Leni Riefenstahl Moves Through Fascism', in *Relationscapes: Movement, Art and Philosophy*, Cambridge, MA: MIT Press, forthcoming.

Massumi, B. (2002), *Parables for the Virtual*, Durham and London: Duke University Press.

Mullarkey, J. (2006), *Post-Continental Philosophy: An Outline*, London and New York: Continuum.

Osborne, P. (1981), *The Complete Operas of Puccini*, New York: Di Capo Press.

O'Sullivan, S. (2006), *Art Encounters Deleuze and Guattari*, London: Palgrave Macmillan.

Pisters, P. (2002), *The Matrix of Visual Culture: Working with Deleuze in Film Theory*, Stanford: Stanford University Press.

Powell, A. (2006), *Deleuze and Horror*, Edinburgh: Edinburgh University Press.

Protevi, J. (2006), 'Deleuze, Guattari and Emergence', in *Paragraph: A Journal of Modern Critical Theory*, 29 (2): 10–39.

Varela, F. (1995), 'The Emergent Self', in J. Brockman, *The Third Culture: Beyond the Scientific Revolution*, New York: Touchstone.

Zeffirelli, F. (2004), Giacomo Puccini's *Madama Butterfly*, directed for stage. Set Design: Franco Zeffirelli; Costume Design: Emi Wada; Choreography: Michiko Taguchi. Director of Stage Design: Huiseppe De Filippi Venezia; Lighting Design: Paolo Mazzon. Orchestra dell'Arena di Verona. Chorus Master: Marco Faelli.

Notes

1. Sher Doruff's work in new media and emergence theory shows a consilience with my own current work, and I respectfully wish to acknowledge material from her October 2006 PhD thesis as having informed this piece.
2. See the section entitled 'Beyond Cybercultures', in B. M. Kennedy and D. Bell (eds), *The Cybercultures Reader*, Second Edition, London: Routledge.
3. Deleuze and Guattari define the concept of 'aparalletic evolution' as the 'becoming' that exists between contrasting matters. As an example: 'There are no longer binary machines: question/answer, masculine/feminine, man/animal, etc. This could be what a conversation is, simply the outline of a becoming. The wasp and the orchid provide the example. The orchid seems to form a wasp image, an orchid-becoming of the wasp, a double capture, since "what" each becomes changes no less than that which "becomes". The wasp becomes part of the orchid's reproductive organs at the same time as the orchid becomes the sexual organ of the wasp. One and the same becoming, a single block of becoming, "aparallel evolution" of two beings which have nothing whatsoever to do with one another' (Deleuze and Parnet 1987: 2).
4. I wish to acknowledge the texts of both Budden (2002) and Osborne (1991) in help with musical terms and concepts, and biographical details on Puccini.
5. With thanks to Osborne and Budden for discussion of this.
6. *Tremolando*: very rapid repetitions of one or two notes.
7. *Arpeggio*: the playing of the notes of a chord in succession instead of simultaneously.
8. *Pizzicato*: achieved by plucking instead of bowing the string.
9. *Cantilena*: a sustained, smooth-flowing melodic line.

ACT III

A Digital Deleuze:
Performance and New Media

Chapter 11

Like a Prosthesis:
Critical Performance à Digital Deleuze

Timothy Murray

> It is not surprising that, among the many of the authors who promote it, *structuralism* is so often accompanied by calls for a new theatre or a new (non-Aristotelian) interpretation of the theatre: a theatre of multiplicities opposed in every respect to a theatre of representation, which leaves intact neither the identity of the thing represented, nor author, nor spectator, nor character, nor representation which, through the vicissitudes of the play, can become the object of a production of knowledge or final recognition. Instead, a theatre of problems and always open questions which draws spectator, setting and characters into the real movement of an apprenticeship of the entire unconscious, the final elements of which remain the problems themselves. (Deleuze 1994: 192)

While the work of Gilles Deleuze might not always resemble a theatre of problems, it consistently grounds its readings of philosophy and its musings on cinema and art in the always open question of representation. Indeed, Deleuze opens the philosophical text framing his lifelong project, *Difference and Repetition*, by contrasting the theatre of representation with the more dynamic theatres of movement and repetition. The theatre of representation, whether on the classical stage or the philosophical page, is said to subscribe to a naturalised reliance on the presentation of 'sameness'. This sameness of representation revolves around the quadripartite structure of representation that neatly aligns and contains text, perception, and subjectivity: the identity of concepts, the opposition of predicates, the analogy of judgement, and the resemblance of perception. The power and force of difference itself is rendered numb within this nexus when difference becomes a mere object in relation to reason, given that reason constitutes the medium of representation vis-à-vis conceived identity, judged analogy, imagined opposition and perceived similitude (Deleuze 1994: 29). It is the philosophical aim of the theatre of representation to leave identity intact, whether of character, author, actor or spectator.

From the outset of his philosophical career, Deleuze adopted the guise of something of a revolutionary street performer by urging lively resistance to the numbing circularity of theatrical analogy and resemblance. He wished to mess up representation's sameness with the intensities, movements and repetitions of a theatre whose end is to problematise the final object of knowledge, or the final recognition of anything traditionally understood as identity. Drawing on the dynamic theatrical assertions of Nietzsche and Artaud, what he calls the theatres of movement and repetition enliven the process by immersing it in the nomadic distributions of the phantasms and simulacra constitutive of the work of art as experimentation. The underappreciated key to Deleuze's theatre of movement is how its shift away from the sameness of identity opens the path to the revolutionary imperatives of sociability and community that take place within the framework of interrogation (157).

Like a Prosthesis

While Deleuze's affection for conceptual revolution could provide one path of approach for an analysis of Deleuze and performance, his passion for cinematics, if not his distrust of photography, has led me to pursue a variant framework of investigation. While significant issues of sociability and community will continue to inform the remarks that follow, I will be situating them within the interrogative context of something like a Digital Deleuze. How might we understand the theatres of movement and repetition within the context of theatre's contemporary openness to, if not its elision with, broad structures and practices of mediality, new media and representational fields of simulacra?

The second volume of the cinema books, *Cinema 2: The Time-Image*, is where Deleuze elaborates most eloquently on the theatrical body and the vicissitudes of performance in the medial age. Here Deleuze suggests that cinema adds to the performative potential of theatre through its capacity 'to *give* a body'. In *giving* a body, what he calls the 'theatre–cinema relationship' brings about the body's birth and disappearance while also marking the point where the visible body disappears through aphasia, or through the complicating timbres of music and speech (Deleuze 1989: 189–203). In being-given, the body is particularly theatricalised as it also bears the track of movement and motion, whether through its everyday postures and attitudes, through its theatricalised motions and gestures, or through its performative utterings and mutterings. But what happens, what is given, when this body is constituted not so much by veins, muscles, tongue and skin, as by data, digits, networks and pixels

– as something of a literal/digital body without organs? In order to stage the theatre of problems from within the new media context, we need to question what is given, what is understood, by the body when it is enveloped in the electronic fabrics of digital performance. Does the body become mere prosthesis in so far as, following the position of Stelarc, it is rendered obsolete by the force of digital supplementation?[1] Or might the body's medialisation and datalisation return us to a renewed framework of the theatrical interrogation with which we began? Could it even be possible that digital performance might return us, paradoxically, to dwell on the very logics of signification from which we departed, even when inscribed in the economy of difference? In coming to appreciate the radical shifts of critical performance when put into digital motion, we could end up appreciating how the creative approach to mediality given by Deleuze's writings on performance returns us not only to consideration of the problematic force of the signifier itself – one from which Deleuze ambivalently profits – but also to an articulation of electronic forms of sociability which Deleuze almost could not have foreseen.

My approach to a networked performance depends on the critical ground articulated by the philosopher in his approach to the theatre–cinema relationship. As models for his interrogation of the theatre of problems, Deleuze not only returns throughout his work to the rather predictable sources of Nietzsche and Artaud, but also frequently references the likes of James Joyce, Francis Bacon, Jean-Luc Godard and Alain Resnais, while less loudly evoking the emergent practices of Marguerite Duras, Agnès Varda and Chantal Akerman. His texts challenge his readers to place pressure on the very stuff of resemblance and analogy that fuel literary and artistic production, at the same time as rendering them thoughtless. Aesthetics is revolutionary, in the Deleuzian sense, when the certainty of thought gives rise to the accident, the multiplicity, and the event of works of art that are 'developed around or on the basis of a fracture that they never succeed in fulfilling' (Deleuze 1994: 195). Inscribed in movement, the theatre of repetition amounts to the most fundamental element of theatricality in which the fractured event itself consists of the representational matter:

> Critical theater is constitutive theater. Critique is a constitution. The theatre maker is no longer an author, an actor, or a director. S/he is an operator. Operation must be understood as the movement of subtraction, of amputation, one already covered by the other movement that gives birth to and multiplies something unexpected, like a prosthesis. (Deleuze 1997: 239)

Critique as constitutive theatre here gives birth to and multiplies not the body, that stable apparatus of theatrical performance, but something unexpected. For what is birthed by critical theatre is the multiplication of subtraction as the supplementation of corporeality, like a prosthesis.[2] It's in this sense that the theatre of movement could be epitomised by the spectacle of Stelarc whose body moves in sync with the electronic, robotic prostheses to which it is attached and to which it responds. Consider his performances of the *Third Hand* (1992–99), that provided the performer with a prosthesis resembling a third arm that extended the physical limitations of the body. Ironically, the body itself, rather than becoming merely obsolete, itself provided impulses, via skin sensors, orienting the seemingly independent motions of the *Third Hand*. What was unexpected in Stelarc's early robotic performances was the resultant accident of something of a corporeal Döppelganger through which the movement of the body itself performed literally . . . like a prosthesis.[3] It was in this sense that the performance gave birth to and multiplied the unexpected; an extended network of pulsing corporeality fused with the wired complexity of technics.

Stelarc's performances, then, enable us to image a practice of theatricality the end of which is a response to fracture by the subtraction or paring down of script, character and actor for the exposure of form, whether of electronic impulse, of power, of force, of desire, of belief or even of performativity itself. In this theatrical space, the gesture or the cry constitutes the performative thing in itself. Moreover, it goes without saying that the range of examples informing Deleuze take us far beyond the site-specific realms of theatre and performance. For Francis Bacon, the performative thing is the sensible force of the cry and the insensible force of what gives rise to the cry, '*crier à*' (Deleuze 2003: 61). For Lewis Carroll, this would amount to 'the form of the smile without a cat' (Deleuze 1994: 156). For Flaubert, it would be the pure ground of individuation 'staring at us, but without eyes' (152). And for Artaud, it would amount to 'the terrible revelation of a thought without image' (Deleuze 1997: 147). As the driver, the operator, of the performance event, 'the subtraction of the stable elements of power [would] release a new potentiality of theatre, an always unbalanced, non-representative force' (242). Here the emotive itself, perhaps in the form of a tear, would literally tear or peel away from the representational surface of faciality, script or projection surface to give rise to an unexpected, non-representative force. This is something that cannot be achieved by the relegation of emotion to the Aristotelian goals of theatrical representation in which action – the performative event – always stands in as a part for the whole, as the representant of something else. Here, the tear stains the fabric of resemblance at the same time as it signals the socket without its vile jelly.

Note Bene

Gilles Deleuze not only imagined such an unbalanced theatre but appreciated its articulation in the analog works of the Italian director and filmmaker Carmelo Bene, about whom Deleuze wrote his sole manifesto on the theatre of subtraction, 'One Less Manifesto'. This dense text reflects on the performative power of Bene's films and adaptations of Shakespeare that receive similar adulation in *Cinema 2: The Time-Image*. In praising the fundamental criticality of Bene's theatre pieces, *Romeo and Juliet*, *S.A.D.E*, *Hamlet*, and *Richard III*, Deleuze stresses their revolutionary drive away from the standards of mimesis and representation and towards the relationship between theatre and its critique.

Deleuze's articulation of this move depends on his fascinating censure of Brecht for not pushing the critique of representation far enough. While Deleuze acknowledges Brecht's commitment to pushing contradictions and oppositions beyond the scale of normalised representations, he remains critical of Brecht's commitment to a hermeneutics of understanding. 'Brecht himself only wants [contradictions] to be "understood" and for the spectator to have the elements of possible "solution". This is not to leave the domain of representation but only to pass from one dramatic pole of bourgeois representation to an epic pole of popular representation' (252). It is important to emphasise that Deleuze means to problematise only Brecht's investment in understanding as the ground of representation, not his commitment to the popular itself, which could be understood to bleed into Deleuze's dedication to the 'minority discourse' with which he identifies Carmelo Bene. Concerned, then, that Brecht does not 'push the "critique" far enough', Deleuze turns to Bene for a strategy of breaking free of official and institutional representations that in themselves may nevertheless assume the guise of conflict or opposition.

This is where Bene's minority performances enter the picture. They catch Deleuze's eye by substituting the representation of conflicts with the more aggressive movements of 'continuous variation' that are characteristic of the brute politics of minority discourse, on which Deleuze dwells in more detail with Félix Guattari in *Kafka* and *A Thousand Plateaus*.

Might not continuous variation be just such an amplitude that always overflows, by excess or lack, the representative threshold of majority measure? Might not continuous variation be the minority becoming of everybody in contrast to the majority rule of Nobody? Might not theatre, thus, discover a sufficiently modest, but nevertheless effective function? This anti-representational function would be to trace, to construct in some way, a figure of the minority consciousness as each one's potential. To render a potentiality present and actual is a completely different matter from representing a conflict. It could no longer be said that art has power, that it is still a matter of power, even when it criticizes Power. For, by shaping the form of a minority consciousness, art speaks to the strengths of becoming that are of another domain than that of Power and measured representation. (Deleuze 1997: 253–4)

Although Deleuze argues that continuous variation manifests itself with particular effectiveness in the abstract fluctuations of language and speech, made evident in his passion for the stutterings and mutterings that transform hermeneutic understandings into performative variations, he appreciates how Bene inserts the various flavours of his particular southern Italian district into the rhythm and tone of his French, English and American hybrid performances. 'What he takes from Puglia is a line of variation, air, earth, sun, colors, lights, and sounds that he himself will vary in a completely different manner, along other lines' (255). To thus 'give' a body within the context of Deleuze's minority lines of flight would be to make manifest the intensity of variations in performative language, speech, gesture, light and sound, here as a distinct marker of the force of minor variation.

In praising Bene's 'theatre of non-representation', Deleuze aligns his performance work with that of Artaud, Robert Wilson, Jerzy Grotowski, and the Living Theater. He argues that the new potentiality of such a theatrical alliance deeply disturbs the comfort of contemporary theatre. Yet Deleuze is quick to differentiate Bene, not to mention the theatre of repetition, from anything close to the movement of a theatrical avant-garde. Bene is said to be less interested in points of origin or termination, the future results of a theatrical past, than in what's happening in the temporal middle where becoming is the stuff of performance, 'becoming-revolutionary, and not the future or the past of the revolution' (242).[4] And it is in *Cinema 2* that Deleuze elaborates on the paradoxical commonplace of such a theatrical-cinematic time. Time's crystal, or the crystallisation of time, constitutes the structural paradox of temporality, its activation of passing presents, in which one moment goes while another comes to shape the future, all the while preventing the past from falling into the inaccessible depths of the totally obscure.

Deleuze consistently attributes his celebration of the paradoxical commonplace of passing presents to the project of Henri Bergson, by building his notion of the time crystal around Bergson's belief that time itself is subjectivity. Rather than arguing that the subject creates time through thought or action, Deleuze joins with Bergson in maintaining that the subject is *in* time (as *in* fantasy). Deleuze's approach to cinema is guided by his rather simple formula of cinematic time, or time's subjectivity: 'it is in the present that we make a memory, in order to make use of it in the future when the present will be past' (Deleuze 1989: 52). The body or shape of time, the event within which we find ourselves, is itself something of a phantom oscillating between the not yet and the no longer, virtual but graspable in the actual. Deleuze insists that this phantom has been fundamental to both theatre and cinema, haunting them and their spectators, until the arrival, that is, of 'modern cinema' (where he locates the filmwork of Bene) which has given form to the virtual image of time. The time of cinema always already awaits its passing actualisation in the future present of modern cinema.

It is similarly in the middle, insists Deleuze, that Bene 'experiences the becoming, the movement, the speed, the vortex. The middle is not a means but, on the contrary, an excess' (Deleuze 1997: 242). In *Cinema 2*, Deleuze compares Bene with Jean-Luc Godard, one of the champions of modern cinema, while elaborating on the political praxis of the 'in between', one turning aside from oppositional dialectics towards confrontational, even revolutionary, co-habitations and incompossibilities. It is neither the historical nor the eternal but the untimely for which Deleuze praises the politics of Bene's mixture of theatre and cinema. The result is a rearticulation of political aesthetics away from the future, utopian vision of the avant-gardes into the current temporal swirl of untimely action by which different times and world views communicate incompossibly. In *Cinema 2*, Deleuze understands these untimely variations to contribute to modern cinema's fabulations of and by peoples not yet falling within the register of representation. Bene's cinematic productions, from *Notre-Dame de Turcs* to *Don Juan* and *Capricci*, are said to mark 'the failure of fusions and unifications' underlying the reality of minority cinema that there is no 'people', 'but always several peoples, an infinity of peoples, who remained to be united, or should not be united' (Deleuze 1989: 220). It is crucial to note that what Deleuze gleans from Bene's cinema is not its literal representation of a newly found people, an epic folk of Puglia, but rather a more revolutionary notion of struggle in the name of form. 'Instead of replacing a negative image . . . with a positive one', Bene

> multiplies types and 'characters', and each time creates or re-creates only a small part of the image which no longer corresponds to a linkage of actions, but to shattered states of emotions or drives, expressible in pure images and sounds: the specificity of [minority] cinema is now defined by a new form, 'the struggle that must bear on the medium itself'. (220)

Bene's performative operations thus give birth to and multiply something unexpected: like a filmic prosthesis.

Giving Virtual Body to Performance

It is something of the struggle within the medium that both opens performance to a variation of participants and peoples, and also extends the parameters of performance: from an emphasis on corporeal presence and avant-garde futurism, to the struggles that bear on performative media themselves. These struggles are currently nowhere more evident than in the intersections between performance and digital technology. Here, the theatrical adaptation of spectacular forms of technological interface promises to expand the fractal space of passing presents while linking separate peoples within provocative webs of vital criticality. Although Deleuze expressed enthusiasm in *Cinema 2* for the potential of the electronic and digital screen arts, whose artistic possibilities remained emergent at the time of his death, his fervour for new media remained deeply tempered by his sentimental attachment to the vigour of the theatre–cinema trajectory. He spoke most explicitly to this ambivalence at the conclusion of *Cinema 2*: 'The electronic image, that is, the tele and video image, the numerical image coming into being, either had to transform cinema or to replace it, to mark its death' (265). The ontological threat seems to turn around the possibility that performance could become only 'like a prosthesis'. For the electronic future carries for Deleuze a certain threat of deadening violence against his most cherished aspects of cinematic thought. 'It is the time-image which calls on an original regime of images and signs, before electronics spoils it or, in contrast, relaunches it' (267).[5]

Had Deleuze been able to benefit from dialogue with the range of new media performance over the past decade, I suspect he would have embraced its relaunching of an energetic regime of images and signs that directly and indirectly 'give a body' to digital forms of sociability and critical theatre. He would be fascinated, no doubt, by the struggle of new media's form, which bears on philosophical assumptions regarding the medium itself and its structural embodiment of simulation. Although the dissolution of his own mortality deprived Deleuze of the opportunity to dwell on new media form with the intensity that he brought to the theatre–cinema trajectory, he certainly articulated its basic precepts as early as *The Logic of Sense* (1990; originally published in 1969), when he promoted the event of simulation over the aesthetics of representation. Deleuze goes to great lengths in the appendix, 'The Simulacrum and Ancient Philosophy', to recount Plato's differentiations in *The Sophist* between copies and simulacra. In valorising copies over simulacra, Plato distinguishes between good or bad copies (the degree of resemblance to Idea) and simulacra which are always mired in the phantasmatic confusion of dissemblance, the latter being an image lacking resemblance. Deeply suspicious of the ideology of resemblance based on the models of sameness and similitude, Deleuze passionately embraces the promise of simulacra not in relation to their weak resemblance to a model, as mere copies of copies, but rather as 'another model, a model of the Other' (Deleuze 1990: 258). Somewhat fulfilling Platonic paranoia, the proliferation of simulacra frees performance from its bondage to a representation of the same, let's say from the female's anchorage in the sado-masochism of balletic form, and opens the way to different and divergent histories of performance, each of which may share different and incompossible points of view.

It's almost as if Deleuze were describing the interface of computing and performance when he insisted that 'in order to speak of simulacra, it is necessary for the heterogeneous series to be really internalized in the system, comprised or complicated in the chaos. Their differences must be *inclusive*' (261). To be interiorised within the digital system means to perform, to be *in* difference, in the time, fantasy and heterogeneity of difference. Indeed, we can similarly appreciate the dynamics of virtual performance in terms of Deleuze's appreciation of simulation as the phantasm itself, 'that is, the effect of the functioning of the simulacrum as machinery – a Dionysian machine' (263). While the digital poetics of techne may here provide a relatively common virtual pole or electronic pulse for the experimentations of performance, it no longer sets its sights on the privileged point of view (deriving, say, from the absolutist roots of theatre or ballet) of an aesthetic object accessible to all other points of view. 'By simulacrum', Deleuze argues similarly in *Difference and Repetition*, 'we should not understand a simple imitation but rather the act by which the very idea of a model or privileged position is challenged and overturned' (Deleuze 1994: 69). Or, as Deleuze describes the event of simulation in *The Logic of Sense*, 'it establishes the world of nomadic distributions and crowned anarchies. Far from being a new foundation, it engulfs all foundations, it assures a universal breakdown [*effondrement*], but as a joyful and positive event, as an un-founding [*effondement*]' (Deleuze 1990: 263).

Prosthetic Gestures

While Deleuze's comprehension of simulation certainly prepared him philosophically for the technological revolution to follow, his writing on the theatre–cinema nexus did not foresee the extent of the digital un-foundings to come. Perhaps we can begin by questioning what it might mean within the context of digital experimentation 'to give a body' to electronic performance. In 1999, for example, the dancer Bill T. Jones literally gave his body to the digital experimentations of Shelley Eshkar and Paul Kaiser for the virtual dance piece, *Ghostcatching*. By plotting Jones' movements in the studio with sensor technology and motion capture software, Eshkar and Kaiser were able to teleport his gestures into the data field of the computer for further artistic exploration. On the screen, they then supplemented and added depth of line, animation, concept, and sound to the data stream of numbers that had become the dancing body of Jones. The virtual figures that then perform on the flat screens of *Ghostcatching* embody 'a musculator, breath, rhythm and line' (Eshkar 2004) whose agile tracings take on a form that ghosts without mirroring the performer's body. Indeed, what ends up as performance is neither the dancer's body nor an analogy of his body but the activation of a numerical archive as the thing of spectral performance. The result is not simply a screenic manifestation of the archive of dance, the dancer's body as animated line drawing, but a radical reconfiguration of gesture through which technics, the interpellation of digitality, has come full circle to ghost movement.

In its more recent incarnations, more portable systems and software permit dancers and choreographers from Jonah Bokaer of New York to Ashley Ferro-Murray of Berkeley to alter, enhance and sometimes create anew movements and choreographies via the interpellations of increasingly sophisticated motion capture systems. The process and archive of captured motion here becomes the performance event itself while disrupting traditional aesthetic assumptions about the limits and conventions of the corporeal. The digital prosthesis can lend to the performer a sense of corporeal possibilities, inscribed in technics, that the strict conventions of historical dance may have precluded. Ashley Ferro-Murray has recounted to me how her experimentations with motion capture in the practice studio, through which she plots her own movements via sensor technology, has sensitised her to the potential of unanticipated movements and motions, as seemingly insignificant as a slight finger gesture or a shifting hand vein. Indeed, I was struck during a conversation I had with her and Stelarc by how they both seemed particularly impassioned by the minute particularities of gesture that are sensed and amplified by the technological interface. Both artists then migrate the particularities and miniaturisations of gesture into broader and larger choreographic movements for their performances. Ferro-Murray not only designs specific movement patterns for her dancers based on her rehearsed patterns of personal techno-extension, but she also encourages her dancers to engage in ongoing reconfiguration of their movements and gestures in active dialogue with the techno-environment that envelopes them in performance. As medialities-in-performance, the dancers *give body* to the impromptu interface of interactive sound and visual systems on stage.

Regardless of Deleuze's quibbles with Brecht, it is crucial to acknowledge his fascination with gesture, particularly in relation to speed. Deleuze describes Bene's impromptu experimentations with gesture as musical indicators of 'speed' not simply inherent to theatre but still, he says rather paradoxically, not outside of theatre. Although his understanding of Bene's experimentation with gesture is grounded in historical analogy, today's practitioners of techno-performance will certainly recognise in his analogy the resonance of their own experiments with the variations of movement.

> Physicians of the Middle Ages spoke of deformed movements and qualities that followed the distribution of speed among the different points of a body in motion, or the distribution of intensities among the different points of a subject. It seems to me that two essential aims of the arts should be the subordination of form to speed, to the variation of speed, and the subordination of the subject to intensity or to affect, to the intense variation of affects. (Deleuze 1997: 249)

Doesn't techno-performance result in something akin to the subordination of formulaic balletic movement (form) to the variation of digitally enabled gesture (speed)? To give body to performance, in this case, means to enter into a revolutionary variation of corporeality through digitality, of action through virtualisation, of representation through event. The choreographer is no longer an author, an actor or a director. S/he works in tandem with her dancers, programmers and technicians as an operator to multiply something unexpected: like a prosthesis.

Within the field of performance, one might wonder whether the prosthetic extensions of digital dance amount to the event of 'disembodiment' or 're-embodiment' that has been subject to such a wide array of passionate discussion in new media studies, from N. Katherine Hayles and Mark B. N. Hansen to Mary Flanagan and Austin Booth. In *Bodies in Code: Interfaces with Digital Media*, Hansen embraces disembodiment with particular clarity when he describes how Rafael Lozano-Hemmer's work

> forcefully demonstrates that embodiment today can only be conceived *as collective individuation*, as an individuation that requires a certain disembodiment of embodied individuals. The reason for this is simple: Because human embodiment no longer coincides with the boundaries of the human

body, a disembodiment of the body forms the condition of possibility for a collective (re)embodiment through technics. The human today is embodied in and through technics. (Hanson 2006: 95)

Hansen is particularly engaged by artistic projects whose disembodiments articulate electronic forms of sociability which Deleuze almost could not have foreseen. Mary Flanagan and Austin Booth think similarly along the lines of a digital 're:skinning' of the body through the new media interface, while sharing Deleuze's wariness of the potential downsides of the electronic interface. 'Technology permits us not only to modify our own skins, but to cross skins, allowing us to merge with other bodies or colonize multiple bodies. The twenty-first century demands a new framework for investigating the intersection of the body, skin, and technology' (Flanagan and Austin 2006: 1). A similar framework has guided Hayles' critical contributions to the discourse of new media. In 'Flesh and Metal', her contribution to Robert Mitchell and Phillip Turtle's *Data Made Flesh: Embodying Information*, Hayles analyses robotic and installation works by Simon Penny, Victoria Vesna, and Allan Dunning and Paul Woodrow by emphasising the 'relationality' of embodiment:

> If art not only teaches us to understand our experiences in new ways but actually changes experience itself, these art works engage us in ways that make vividly real the emergence of ideas of the body and experiences of embodiment from our interactions with increasingly information-rich environments. They teach us what it means to be posthuman in the best sense, in which the mindbody is experienced as an emergent phenomenon created in dynamic interaction with the ungraspable flux from which also emerge the cognitive agents we call intelligent machines. Central to all three art works is the commitment to understanding the body and embodiment in relational terms, as processes emerging from complex recursive interactions rather than as preexisting entities. (Hayles 2004: 234)

In view of the preceding discussion, what's particularly fascinating here is Hayles' emphasis on recursivity as the ultimate form of embodiment, as constituent of any performative giving of body. Key to the performances I have discussed so far is certainly the complex recursivity of iteration, whether from the repetitive articulations of Bene that are claimed by Deleuze to render asunder the pre-existent ontologies of video and theatre or from digital tracings of rehearsal ('*la répétition*') in the dance practice studio. Also central to the artworks dear to Hayles' sensibilities is this same aleatory event of recursivity, the same repetitive motion that underlies the Deleuzian theatre of multiplicities. As if ghosting Hayles' more contemporary position, Deleuze insists in *Difference and Repetition* that repetition is actively relational in how it never means continuation, perpetuation or prolongation, nor even the discontinuous return of something which would at least be able to be prolonged in a partial cycle (an identity, an I, a Self) but, on the contrary, the reprise of pre-individual singularities which, in order that it can be grasped as repetition, presupposes the dissolution of all prior identities. (Deleuze 1994: 202)

So, if the human today is embodied in and through technics, the technological interface is particularly compelling in how it widens the performative path to the aleatory event of recursivity underlying the affirmative dissolutions inherent to the Deleuzian theatre of problems.

The Digital Cry

If Samuel Weber were to enter into this discussion of the dissolutions of the aleatory event, he would return our focus to the roots of contemporary performance practice, as it remains inscribed in *Vorstellung*. Ironically, it is something like the very techno-interface of movement that Weber has argued to underlie the same Brechtian approach to 'Gestus' which gives Deleuze such pause for not pushing the critique of representation far enough. In 'Scene and Screen: Electronic Mediality and Theatricality', Weber provides something of an interpretation counter to Deleuze by emphasising the *interruption* of representation enacted by Brechtian gesture. By reading Brecht through the eyes of Walter Benjamin, Weber interrupts the end of representation with the passing present of theatrical performance as 'placing before' (*Vor-stellung*).

> In German, *Vorstellung* – literally, 'placing-before' – signifies not just 'idea' or mental 'representation', but also theatrical performance. And it is precisely this, the production of the theatrical process in its distinctive mediality – *Vorstellung* as *representing before* rather than simply as *representation* – that Benjamin associates with the 'interruption' practiced by Brechtian theatre. When it is suspended, identity comes up short, and it does so through 'gesture'.
>
> (Weber 2004: 115)[6]

What's so fascinating about Weber's insightful linkage of gesture to *Vorstellung* is how he grounds it in the same sort of 'trembling of an irreducible alterity' that we have come to appreciate as the 'heterogeneity of variation' underlying Deleuze's admiration for Bene's 'minority consciousness'. What's more, Weber's elaborate description of such 'trembling' echoes the very procedures of techno-performance here at issue. His critical ghosting of the Deleuzian argument merits full citation:

This alterity is irreducible for two reasons. First, because it has been extrapolated and isolated from the ostensible continuity of a quasi-instinctive, habitual pattern, and second, because in this isolation and extrapolation it reveals itself to be transferable, movable, transformable –synonyms for what Benjamin designates as 'citable'. This is why the 'contours' of such a 'gesture' must be described as 'trembling': their location is always the result of a *tension* that is both in- and ex-tensive, affecting both internal composition and external situation. Both are what they are, but at the same time both are radically alterable, could be entirely different. Because these possibilities can never be reduced to or measured in terms of a single set of realizations, the medium of this theater is more akin to a 'laboratory' than to a 'work', at least in the sense of a *Gesamtkunstwerk*, a notion that marks the consummation of an aesthetic tradition that has always sought to subordinate the medium to its instantiation, precisely qua *work*. The work in this sense is held to instantiate the genre, and thus in this tradition the general always takes precedence over the singular. The interruptive gesture calls this precedence into question, even as it questions the notion of performance and of performativity, at least as teleological processes of fulfillment. (117)

Called into question by Weber's reading of Benjamin is the inscription of representation as teleology and the valorisation of the general over the singular.

In his discussion of digital performance in *Theatricality as Medium*, Weber reflects on the unique role played by the 'digit' in undermining the aesthetic weight lent to the universal as a teleological end of performance. But he doesn't begin with the digital per se. Rather, he distinguishes between the digital gestures of Balinese dancing and theatre, and the conventional movements of Western theatre, including traditional ballet. As if providing language for the analysis of the techno-performances discussed above, Weber speculates that 'the movement of the extremities, and in particular the fingers, plays a decisive role precisely to the extent that such fingers can no longer be said to be simply "in" the hand, but rather to *draw* the hand, and the body to which it is attached, to its outermost limits and beyond' (49). It is in the uncanniness of dance's inscription in the condition of what Benjamin calls *Zustand* or *stance* that Weber creates a fascinating link between the legacy of finger movement and the possibilities of the new media and their technologies, which involve 'a *standing towards* something else, a gesturing elsewhere, pulling the body after it' (49). In pointing, touching, caressing, a finger can remain as discrete as a digit thus joining with the numerical code in excluding 'the relation of part to whole from serving as a paradigm for code or discourse' (50). In pointing away from its immediate manifestation, as something other than a part to a whole, in pulling the body after it as if the interpellation of a fracture of the machinic itself, 'the "digital" signifies something', insists Weber, 'other than what it represents' (51).

In so standing towards something else, the digital signifier can be said to function similarly to Jean Laplanche's notion of the enigmatic signifier that 'signifies *to* [*signifier à*] the child without its sender(s) or addressee knowing necessarily *what* it signifies but only that it signifies without thereby losing its power to signify to' (Laplanche 1989: 45). It is the traumatic force of the signifier as the rhetorical gesture of other-than-representation that Laplanche identifies as the kernal of the performative, through which we exist *in* fantasy.[7] Deleuze evokes something similar to the structure of the enigmatic signifier in his discussion of the '*crier à*' in Francis Bacon's penchant to paint the cry without representing the source of its horror. 'This is what is expressed in the phrase, *crier à* – not to scream *before* or *about*, but to scream *at* [*crier à*] death – which suggests this coupling of forces, the perceptible force of the scream and the imperceptible force that makes one scream' (Deleuze 2003: 52). The digital, the pointer, the performative in this case disrupts representation without abandoning its gestures. The body stands *towards*, it signifies *to* while coupling forces that multiply something unexpected, perhaps something, to return to Deleuze's enigmatic phrase for critical performance, like a prosthesis.

The energetics of the interruptive gesture brings together the digital and the performative plays in the new media performance work of Sarah Drury, for whom the performance space is very much more an ongoing laboratory of forceful gesture than the spatial realm of the oeuvre. Especially relevant to the relation of gesture to performance are her new media pieces that infuse the sounds and gestures of viewing participants within the fabric of videos being screened as the horizon of performance. For *Voicebox: The Karaoke of Common Song* (2001), Drury positions the participants at the intersection of voice and image. Participants are invited to enter a voicebox situated adjacent to a screen on which plays an enigmatic video about two girls where they are invited to sing, shout, or speak into a microphone whose live sounds interact with the video never to be complete. Inside the box, participants are urged to *crier à*, not *before* or *about* the video they face, but *at* it. By initiating an uncanny response from snippets of voice recorded in the same pitch, the participants' vocal gestures directly enter the field of the video by disrupting its narrative, which shifts between the story of two girls in variation with the pitch and tone of the interactive participants. Their vocal 'tremblings' manifest an archival and performative *tension* that is both in- and ex-tensive, affecting both the internal composition of narrative and the external situation of its performance. If the participants become particularly sensational by raising their level of voice *at* the video projection, their gestures and profiles are subsequently keyed into the projection as silhouettes on the screen. Their shadows are enfolded into the field of projection, as a visual prosthesis of voice itself, in a way that calls into question the precedence of the video work and the passive legacy of its projection in performance. As I argue more thoroughly in *Digital Baroque: New Media Art and Cinematic Folds* (Murray 2008), the dynamics of new media art thus necessitate a deeply significant archeological shift from ontological systems of visual *projection* to temporal conditions of the *fold* that are here forcefully performed by the digital signifier, *crier à*.

In Drury's later piece, *Intervention Chants* (2003), participants are invited to chant into a microphone as the lyrics of the American ballad, 'Home on the Range', scroll across the screen. The participant's vocalisations catalyse an animated subtext that spins out the screenic text of 'Home on the Range', which Drury calls 'a classic articulation of the American longing for freedom and home'. The large 3D animations of blue letters and words articulate a fragmented, ironic version of the ballad that suggests the materialism, isolation and mistrust underlying the nostalgic longing of the ballad. When the participants become more energetic by raising the energy and volume of their vocal interventions, a field of red 3D letters emerges from words taken from Bob Marley's critical song, 'War', which we know to shout out *at* war and horror rather than explicate it. Here Drury's participant becomes something of the Deleuzian operator of critical theatre itself. No longer an author, actor or director, the theatre maker is an operator of the performative movement that multiplies something unexpected: like a prosthesis.

Indeed, the prosthetic literally constitutes this critical theatre not simply via the relay of digital technics but also as the linguistic bearer of prosthesis itself. It's not likely that either Drury or Deleuze consulted the OED prior to conceiving of their respective strategies of revolutionary performance, *crier à*. But, had they done so, they would have been motivated not merely by the OED's second definition of prosthesis as 'that part of surgery which consists in supplying deficiencies, as by artificial limbs or teeth', but especially by its first definition, which identifies the arbitrary deficiencies of language as constituent of prosthesis itself: 'the addition of a letter or syllable at the beginning of a word'. The OED cites Douse's *Grimm's Law* of 1876 where prosthesis 'belongs to a class of terms . . . denoting arbitrary processes, whose intrusion into the realm of language should be viewed with . . . Suspicion'. While the letters and syllables shouted by Drury's performers literally catalyse the intrusion of suspicion into the folksy calm of 'Home on the Range', the tremblings and stammerings of gesture and vocalisation constitute the very performative of minor theatricality whose interruptive gestures Deleuze values for undermining the representational passivity of the folk.

To give body to new media performance here means to voice the multiplicities of artistic form and historical sociability on the margins. Critical performance à Digital Deleuze thus embodies the theatre of problems with the virtual technics of something unexpected: like a prosthesis.

References

Deleuze, G. (1989), *Cinema 2: The Time-Image*, trans. H. Tomlinson and R. Galeta, Minneapolis: University of Minneapolis Press.

Deleuze, G. (1990), *The Logic of Sense*, trans. M. Lester with C. Stivale, edited by C. V. Boundas, New York: Columbia University Press.

Deleuze, G. (1994), *Difference and Repetition*, trans. Paul Patton, New York: Columbia University Press.

Deleuze, G. (1997), 'One Less Manifesto', trans. E. dal Molin and T. Murray, in Murray (1997b).

Deleuze, G. (2003), *Francis Bacon: The Logic of Sensation*, trans. D. W. Smith, Minneapolis: University of Minnesota Press.

Deleuze, G. and F. Guattari (1977), *Kafka: pour une littérature mineure*, Paris: Minuit.

Eshkar, S. (2004), 'Habitat: Rockefeller/NVR New Media Fellowship Proposal', Rose Goldsen Archive of New Media Art, Cornell University.

Flanagan, M. and A. Booth (eds) (2006), *Re:skin*, Cambridge, MA, and London: MIT Press.

Foster, H. (2006), *Prosthetic Gods*, Cambridge, MA, and London: MIT Press.

Grzinic, M. (ed.) (2002), *Stelarc: Political Prosthesis and Knowledge of the Body*, Ljubljana: Maska.

Hansen, M. B. N. (2006), *Bodies in Code: Interfaces with Digital Media*, New York and London: Routledge.

Hayles, N. K. (2004), 'Flesh and Metal: Reconfiguring the Mindbody in Virtual Environments', in Mitchell and Thurtle (2004).

Laplanche, J. (1989), *New Foundations for Psychoanalysis*, trans. David Macey, Oxford: Basil Blackwell.

Mitchell, R. and P. Thurtle (eds) (2004), *Data Made Flesh: Embodying Information*, New York and London: Routledge.

Murray, T. (1984), 'Theatricality of the Van-Guard: Ideology and Contemporary America Theatre', *Performing Arts Journal*, 24 (Fall): 93–9.

Murray, T. (2008), *Digital Baroque: New Media Art and Cinematic Folds*, Minneapolis and London: University of Minnesota Press.

Weber, S. (2000), 'The Virtuality of the Media', *Sites: The Journal of 20th-Century/ Contemporary French Studies*, 4 (2) (Fall): 297–317.

Weber, S. (2004), *Theatricality as Medium*, New York: Fordham University Press.

Notes

1. Stelarc, 'Obsolete Body': http://www.stelarc.va.com.au/obsolete/obsolete.html
2. In thinking Deleuze's notion of prosthetic subtraction, we need to approach it as the converse of the logics of prosthetics outlined by Hal Foster, in *Prosthetic Gods*, as constitutive of modernist aesthetic production: 'In the first decades of the twentieth century, the human body and the industrial machine were still seen as alien to one another . . . the two could only conjoin ecstatically or tortuously, and the machine could only be a "magnificent" extension of the body or a "troubled" constriction of it, as Freud suggested in a famous passage in *Civilization and Its Discontents* (1930). Even with the new machines of transportation and representation of the Second Industrial Revolution, such as automobiles, airplanes, radio, and film, technology was still often regarded as a demonic supplement, an addition to the body that threatened a subtraction from it. After Marshall McLuhan, I will call this paradoxical view of technology as both extension and constriction of the body the double logic of the prosthesis' (Foster 2006: 109).
3. See my discussion of Stelarc, 'Coda of the Paradox of Shed Skin: Stelarc "and" the Philosophical Ping', in Grzinic (2002: 81–93).
4. In 'Theatricality of the Van-Guard' (Murray 1984), I suggest an alternative theatrical model of 'van-guardism' that is in keeping with this notion of 'becoming-revolutionary'.
5. I elaborate on Deleuze's ambivalent embrace of new media in the concluding chapter of *Digital Baroque: New Media Art and Cinematic Folds* (Murray 2008).
6. Weber's readings frequently enter into critical difference with those of Deleuze. Weber is most explicit about these differences in 'The Virtuality of the Media' (Weber 2000).
7. Laplanche's notion of the enigmatic signifier significantly informs the arguments of my books *Like a Film* (1993) and *Drama Trauma* (1997a).

Chapter 12

Performance as the Distribution of Life: From Aeschylus to Chekhov to VJing via Deleuze and Guattari

Andrew Murphie

What terrifies me is just ordinary everyday routine, the thing none of us can escape. (Dmitry Silin in Chekhov's 'Terror'; quoted in Borny 2006: 21)

The task of life is to make all these repetitions coexist in a space in which difference is distributed. (Deleuze 1994: xix)

. . . the body, this crucible of energy mutations. (Gil 1998: 107)

Performance Culture

It is still perhaps possible to underestimate the importance of perform-ance to life as lived. In this chapter, performance will be understood as an important activity within life. Performance, even within the theatre, will not be taken as a repetition of life from a remove. Rather, perform-ance will be taken to fit perfectly within Gilles Deleuze's description of the task of life itself. This task is to bring repetitions together onto the same immanent plane, to make 'repetitions coexist in a space in which difference is distributed'.

Performance adds something to life's mix. A modulation of life within life is performed in order to make life liveable. Life's 'task', modulated in performance, becomes an acceptance and re-distribution, within life, of life's own ongoing distribution of differential intensity. It is in this that per-formance is close to the heart of Deleuze's philosophy as well as to life. For Deleuze's philosophy, the problematic distribution of differential intensity – always an intensity between other intensities, to infinity – is the key to 'everything'. 'Everything which happens and everything which appears is correlated with orders of difference . . . Intensity is the form of difference in so far as this is the reason of the sensible' (Deleuze 1994: 222).

Performance, then, is a series of acts employing the 'reason of the sensible' to make the intensity of life liveable. Yet performance is also like a moth to the flame of this intensity. This is why conflict is the root of dramatic action. Each performance begins with the allure of active difference, by the fact that 'every phenomenon refers to the inequality by which it is conditioned' (222). Performance's first impulse is towards active 'disparity', towards a multiplication of intensities between intensities, differences between differences. Within this disparity, performance acts involve a complex mix of the biological, social and technical. They become a balancing act as well as a distribution of intensities, a fluctuating stance traversing the high wire of the world's shifting intensities.

All performance acts fold into, fold or unfold, the world of moving intensities. At the same time, precisely because of this, performance has powers that can make things go terribly wrong. For one thing, performance can institute a seemingly transcendent 'tribunal' within life (Deleuze 1997: 126). It can also pull that tribunal apart, foregrounding immanence, but there is always a tension between these. This tension goes beyond events that are culturally marked as 'theatre and performance', to what has become a general performance culture (McKenzie 2001). The like of performance management systems are only one index of how widespread and non-trivial issues of performance have become to life or culture; as is the 'performativity' described in the work of Judith Butler (1988) and Eve Kosofsky Sedgwick (2003).

The central concern of this chapter is the way in which, from within these tensions, theatre and performance can incline themselves towards a wider distribution of difference in life. Such an inclination is found here in work as apparently disparate as that of Aeschylus, Chekhov and contemporary VJing.[1] At the same time, it is the truck and trade between all the various aspects of performance that will haunt this discussion. Indeed, this truck and trade reflects performance's immersion in life, in that which Félix Guattari described as its three dynamic and inter-related differential ecologies of the socius, self and environment (Guattari 2000).[2] In sum, if performance is not evaluated here in terms of the success or failure of its representation of life, this is because it is more important to evaluate performance's role in directly adding to, or diminishing, life as lived.

Without Critical Distance

As any performer knows, performance is nothing if not a confrontation with the world's immanence. Performance burns itself up in this confrontation, in an immanent critique of the world, as opposed to the cold-hearted critical distance founded on a point of view of transcendence.

It is precisely this question of the immanent versus that which Deleuze calls 'the doctrine of judgement' that is taken up in Deleuze's essay on Artaud, 'To Have Done with Judgement' (Deleuze 1997: 126ff).

Deleuze proposes that, like Artaud's 'theatre of cruelty', immanent critique should be relentless as regards transcendent assumptions. The entanglement in the world comes first. In this, performance is also 'not without a certain cruelty towards itself' (135). This leaves everything else – moral assumptions, philosophical systems, even the fixed arrangement of the like of the 'faculties' – up in the air. At the same time, immanent critique in performance attempts to locate the 'genetic elements that condition . . . production' (Smith in Deleuze 1997: xxiv) within a situation, not only of assumptions and systems, but of thought and action. Both thought and action become-performative. The differential intensity of the always (at least) double encounter involved is 'genetic'. Therefore, a performative engagement constitutes the 'destruction of an image of thought which presupposes itself and the genesis of the act of thinking in thought itself. Something in the world forces us to think. This something is . . . a fundamental encounter' (Deleuze 1994: 139).

Such immanent encounters reverse the assumed hierarchy of values over acts of evaluation, or of transcendent principles over everyday existence. Deleuze's philosophy insists not on an overarching philosophical or moral system but on the destruction or constant adaptation of such systems within 'our way of being or our style of life' (Deleuze 1983 :1). This style of life directs itself towards the 'power of Life as a process', within which one can 'assess the potentialities of "life"' (Smith in Deleuze 1997: xxiv). Values are folded into this performative immanence, unfolded out of it, and constantly re-evaluated. The act of evaluation becomes 'the differential element of corresponding values' (Deleuze 1983: 1). It is a kind of 'combat' (Deleuze 1997: 132) in which illusions of transcendence are brought into a kind of mud wrestling in material/ social reality.

The staging of combat explains much of the tension and potential of performance. Performance must acknowledge the simultaneously destructive and creative differential elements that emerge in the clash of antagonistic modes of becoming, or ways of living. Performance also stages a combat within particular modes of living. Can a mode of living gather the forces it needs to continue? What must be rooted out in order to continue? Thus Masha, in Chekhov's *The Seagull*, talking to Trigorin the writer about her unrequited love, tells him, 'I am courageous; I just decided I'd tear this love of mine out of my heart . . . by the roots' (Chekhov 1954: 152).

Infinite Debt and Finite Exchange

How then are the illusions of transcendence to survive, if the encounters and combats of performance are so intense? The key is the false concept of infinite debt. Nietzsche wrote that the 'condition of judgement' was '"the consciousness of being in debt to the deity"', in a manner that is of course 'infinite and thus unpayable' (Deleuze 1997: 126). Performance, especially before Naturalism, has often attempted – perhaps mistakenly, but also understandably – to fold this impossible debt into a manner of living, to make it somewhat workable. Naturalism attempted to escape this debt. However, in the work of Ibsen and other Naturalists, much of this infinite debt to the deity is merely onsold to the tribunals of science and social science ('heredity or environment'?), to which much of the social remains in 'infinite debt' to this day. The radical contribution of Chekhov's theatre within Naturalism was to rework this debt differently. Infinite debt was redistributed in immanent, social/subjective terms; for example, in the central problem of the plot in *The Cherry Orchard*, which revolves around the debt concerning the orchard itself.[3]

As in Chekhov's plays, Deleuze's rejection of critical distance does not mean that the chaosmos of the immanent finds no performative structure. In fact, like Chekhov, Deleuze's opposition to the doctrine of judgement, along with his favouring of specific justice, is precisely an opposition to generality, in favour of rigorous precision. He opposes the infinite debt that props up judgement to the more immediate and materially real debt

> that is inscribed directly on the body following the finite blocks that circu-
> late in a territory . . . the terrible signs that lacerate bodies and stain them,
> the incisions and pigments that reveal in the flesh of each person what they
> owe and are owed: an entire system of cruelty, whose echo can be heard in
> the . . . tragedy of Aeschylus. (128)

In this system of cruelty, signs arise, performatively, from blood and life. There is no transcendent realm, purely of the signifier. Deleuze writes that 'Artaud will give sublime developments to the system of cruelty, a writing of blood and life that is opposed to the writing of the book, just as justice is opposed to judgement, provoking a veritable inversion of the sign' (128). This is the performative basis for Deleuze's semiotics. For Deleuze, a sign is an immanent immersion in forces, not a distant representation of them. Signs 'always envelop heterogeneous elements and animate behaviour' (Deleuze 1994: 73). However, Deleuze also diagnoses the emergence of the disease of judgement in Greek theatre, specifically between Aeschylus' and Sophocles' tragedies. For Deleuze, this disease is then 'elaborated and developed' from 'Greek tragedy to modern philosophy' (Deleuze 1997: 126).

> What is tragic is less the action than the judgement, and what Greek tragedy instituted at the outset [with Sophocles] was the tribunal. Kant did not invent a true critique of judgement; on the contrary, what the book of this title established was a fantastic subjective tribunal. (126)

Deleuze explains the rise of the doctrine of judgement in terms of a shift in performance's ethico-aesthetics. This is a shift from the plays of Aeschylus, in which the gods 'were passive witnesses or plaintive litigants who could not judge', to the theatre of Sophocles, in which 'gods and men together raised themselves to the activity of judging – for better or for worse' (128).

Cruelty of Judgement?

The question of the constitution within performance of the relations between performance/cruelty and the doctrine of judgement underpins many other important points in Deleuze's philosophy. For example, according to the doctrine of judgement in Sophocles, there is a presumption that the gods give lots to men 'and that men, depending on their lots, are fit for some particular form, for some particular organic end' (128). Sophocles provides the beginning for so much that Deleuze will be opposed to. For a start, there is his opposition to hylomorphism: 'the doctrine that production is the result of an (architectural) imposition of a transcendent form on a chaotic and/or passive matter' (Protevi 2001: 8). In Sophoclean tragedy we also find the basis for everything to which Deleuze objects in Aristotle concerning identity, analogy, resemblance and later stratification according to form, rather than ethological relation across forms. Affective relations are also submitted to these forms and stratifications. Deleuze writes: 'this is the essential effect of judgement: existence is cut into lots, the affects are distributed into lots, and then related to higher forms' (Deleuze 1997: 129).

As far as the body is concerned, Deleuze opposes 'a body of judgement, with its organization, its segments (contiguity of offices), its differentiations (bailiffs, lawyers, judges), its hierarchies (classes of judges, of bureaucrats)' to 'a body of justice in which the segments are dissolved, the differentiations lost, and the hierarchies thrown into confusion, a body that retains nothing but intensities that make up uncertain zones, that traverse these zones at full speed and confront powers in them' (131). This is of course Artaud's body without organs.

Deleuze also gives a full description of the social world based upon the false premises of the doctrine of judgement. Far from the force of reason it proposed itself to be, judgement makes us crazy. 'Judgement bursts in on the world in the form of the false judgement leading to delirium and madness, when man is mistaken about his lot, and in the form of the judgement of God, when the form imposes another lot' (129). Eventually, the early Sophoclean form of judgement develops into a new, more extensive mode in which judgement closes in on itself. In this, 'we are no longer debtors of the gods *through forms or ends*, but have become *in our entire being* the infinite debtors of a single God' (129, my emphasis). Our lot becomes only that of judgement and 'the judgement of God . . . constitutes the infinite form'. I have begun to suggest that even the secular twentieth-century sciences and social science will feed on this judgement without end, for example in performance management. Deleuze's damning conclusion is that 'the doctrine of judgement has reversed and replaced the system of affects . . . even in the judgement of knowledge or experience' (129). This explains much of the history and performative force of the systematics of the twentieth century, from cognitivism to audit culture.[4]

However, in the system of cruelty, the combat I have mentioned replaces judgement. There is combat 'against the Other' (132), to 'repel a force' of transcendent hierarchies. There is also what Deleuze (awkwardly translated into English) calls a 'combat between'. The 'combat between' occurs as a 'combat between oneself', when one 'tries to take hold of a force in order to make it one's own' or 'through which a force enriches itself by seizing hold of other forces and joining itself to them in a new ensemble: a becoming' (132). Deleuze opposes the perhaps unfortunate term 'combat' to war, writing that the 'judgement of God is on the side of war, and not combat' (133). Combat, 'by contrast, is a powerful, non-organic vitality that supplements force with force, and enriches whatever it takes holds of' (133). It is a creative force.

If the doctrine of judgement uses performance to set up or affirm a seemingly transcendent distribution of affects and forces, or even to appear to replace affects with judgements, then combat uses performance to redistribute affective intensities, to bring them back into play. It does so transversally, across given structures. This is performance's true ethical dimension. It is founded on the question of whether forces are brought to us, or taken away in favour of the rigours of organisation (135). It involves the ongoing differential or intensive constitution of a 'we' or an 'us', or an undefined 'people to come' (Deleuze and Guattari 1994: 218). It involves a new distribution of differential intensities that passes between 'us', taking us somewhere new, redefining 'us'. It may seem that this implies a gathering of forces into an enhanced 'subjectivism', but this is not the case. Deleuze notes that 'to pose the question in terms of force, and not in other terms, already surpasses subjectivism' (Deleuze 1997: 135). This is rather an ethics of an (at least) double becoming, with an ongoing responsibility towards difference.

The Groundless Ground of Performance

New modes of existence necessarily emerge in all performance acts via performance's repetition of difference – in which 'repetitions coexist in a space in which difference is distributed'. This repetition provides the groundless ground with the potential for new modes of existence (Deleuze 1994: 67). This does not mean, as is sometimes assumed, that performance is just a matter of the superficial. It is rather that performance individuates a diagram of relations between different series of ungroundings. These series of ungroundings are not series of neat causes and effects. Rather, the series emerge from a shifting relational ecology. As Deleuze puts it: 'Everywhere, couples and polarities presuppose bundles and networks, organised oppositions presuppose radiations in all directions' (51). Chekhov was to open the theatre of his time to these relational ecologies in, for example, his move towards ensemble acting.

This opening followed the famously disastrous premiere of Chekhov's *The Seagull* in 1896, which led to the explosive re-evaluation of performance norms. Geoffrey Borny has pointed to the way in which a number of these re-evaluations are in a genetic relation to Chekhov's active, and decidedly non-tragic engagement with the world; for example, in an inflection towards ensemble acting (Borny 2006: 173), or in a radical development of a new series of intensive differences between text and subtext (77). The resolution is in a kind of immobile intensity common to many of Chekhov's play endings (in *Uncle Vanya* the tension between work and rest; in *The Three Sisters* Olga's 'If only we knew'; in *The Cherry Orchard*, the servant Feers lies motionless while we hear the famous 'sound like a string snapping' in the distance). Chekhov's structural innovation gives rise to a radically incomplete aesthetic within performance, one which only resolves things in an opening to the ecological, in Guattari's sense (Guattari 2000).

In Chekhov, a felt intensity arises between series (a character and an actor, a performer and an audience, text and subtext, everyday life and its 'mirror'; or, in *The Seagull*, a series involving lovers, relatives and friends, and another involving writing and theatre).[5] This felt intensity is neither that of a predetermined opening, nor a renewal of norms (as in romance generally); it is 'not reducible to any [of the other] terms of the series'. This felt intensity registers the descent of the virtual, in the body of the reader or audience as much as in Ryabovich in the short story 'The Kiss', for example, or in Vanya or Olga in *The Three Sisters*. Chekhov's talent was, as a VJ might say, in hacking the given configurations of performance to transform it into an ongoing series of Deleuze's 'very special and paradoxical case(s)' (Deleuze 1990: 40).

Bringing the theatre closer to the everyday only exacerbates these tensions. If Chekhov subtracts the normal dominant elements of the theatre (Deleuze 1979), he does so in favour of the proliferation of differential series within the everyday, and the production of the very idea of the singular, the intensive, within the everyday. This is at the same time a series of events that pushes everyday norms to breaking point. The most famous instance of this is, of course, the series of things literally breaking down in *The Cherry Orchard*: the breaking of Yepihodov's guitar string (Borny 2006: 86); the final chopping down of the cherry orchard; the usual broken hearts; Feers, the old servant, who at the end of the play lies forgotten and motionless in the abandoned house.

If this seems chaotic, it is. Yet it is precisely in acknowledging this chaosmos that performance immerses itself fully within life. As Chekhov wrote: 'In life there are no clear cut consequences or reasons; in it everything is mixed up together; the important and the paltry, the great and the base, the tragic and the ridiculous. . . . What are needed are new forms, new ones' (quoted in Borny 2006: 76).

The work with such inter-ecological tensions has, from Chekhov to VJing, defined the last hundred years of performance.

Deleuze and the Dramatisation of the World

Tolstoy objected that 'Chekhov's plays . . . were not dramatic or theatrical enough' (Borny 2006: 75). Yet this is precisely to miss the general claim that Chekhov's work makes for dramatisation. All the world requires a dramatic action to actualise, to attempt an impossible reconciliation between series of intensities. Or rather, the world requires dramatisation in order to break out of one set of intensities into another when this reconciliation fails, as it inevitably will, and as it does in the case of so many of Chekhov's characters.

And not only in the theatre. It is in this 'dramatisation' (Deleuze 1994: 218) that we can make a large claim for performance as essential to the world in Deleuze's philosophy. If, for Deleuze, 'the world is an egg', this is because it is full of 'dynamic processes' that actualise ideas. These 'are precisely dramas, they dramatize the Idea . . . create . . . trace a space corresponding to the differential relations and singularities to be actualised'. In short, if the 'world is an egg . . . the egg itself is a theatre: theatre of staging' (216), yet a staging that is dynamic and singular each time (Murphy 1992: 129). Dramatisation is not merely a reflection of Ideas, personalities or even motivations. It pushes towards the new in the context of an ongoing expanded engagement with the 'ecosophical' – at the junction of world/egg, differential forces and Ideas.

Bergson's work on 'intellectual effort' (Bergson 1920) perhaps describes performance's violence against intellectual organisation more simply. 'Intellectual effort' is the effort felt in attempting to reconcile mental schema and images in the world at large (here we should remember that Bergson makes a large claim for images, since matter, for him, is an 'aggregate of "images"' [Bergson 1991: 9]). Bergson gives the examples of the dramatist thinking vaguely, in 'incorporeal' terms, of characters and situation, and of a composer's first ideas for a symphony. These ideas are simple and abstract 'schemes' that must be brought into being, in process, in an actual distribution of intensities. There is more 'intellectual effort' required when the reconciliation of schema and images is more difficult, when it meets hindrances or obstacles (Bergson 1920: 214), when it is slowed down, or when it confronts its 'natural powerlessness', as Deleuze puts it, 'indistinguishable from its greatest power' (Deleuze 1994: 147). When thought is confronted by the world/images, schema are not only challenged, but sometimes even destroyed. However, the thought that emerges from the wreckage 'cannot but make a differ-ence' (McMahon, 2005: 48). The question is how much the performer/thinker can deal creatively with the sublime force that goes beyond them, beyond schema, precisely in a confrontation with a world in which some-times 'there remains nothing of the primitive scheme in the final image' (Bergson 1920: 213–14).

Performance provides a multitude of hindrances, obstacles and slowings down to schemas, to easy ideas, to lazy forms of judgement. Christophe Dejours has given a similar definition of effort/work, relevant to perform-ance, as the suffering experienced in 'bridging the gap between prescrip-tive and concrete reality', in which 'the path to be navigated between the prescriptive and the real must constantly be invented or rediscovered by the subject who is working' (Dejours 2006: 45). A general culture of 'performance' is caught between an impossible series of transcendent doc-trines of judgements, and the events of life and blood to which these may even give rise, but which will never conform to these judgements.

Chekhov himself felt the mix of tensions involved, as is registered in his medical work, his work with social reform, the theatre, his marriage, his health and even gardening. Indeed, these tensions are the generative kernel of Chekhov's work. They would open up the entire ethico-aesthetic of twentieth-century performance.

A Sensate Undoing of Sensory-motor and Other Schema

There is a literalness to these tensions. In performance, they are a felt gathering of differential intensities and their ongoing reconfiguration. A way to understand this might be in terms of what Brian Massumi has called a 'biogram' – a kind of shifting bodily memory. These are 'syn-esthetic forms . . . summoned into present perception then recombined with an experience of movement' (Massumi 2002: 186). They 'retain a privileged connection to proprioception'. Crucially, they are not clear and neat cognitive maps, or cartographic in any representational sense. They are rather topological and 'peri-personal' 'lived diagrams based on already lived experience, revived to orient further experience' (186–7). They are 'real', but not reducible to simple presence (they have a shifting virtuality as well as actuality). Where cognitive maps cannot, biograms carry the ongoing power of performance.

In particular, biograms register a sensate, performative undoing of schema as much as they register such schema's continued attempt at operation. This is so whether these schema involve the circulation of judgements, schema of the faculties, or even sensory-motor schema (those, for example, of behaviourist training or performance management, or sometimes even acting methods). This is vital to what has come to be called biopolitics. This is politics travelling precisely between: abstract circulations of judgement; new forms of retrograde perform-ance that are individual and abstractly statistical, 'preterritorialised'[6] on Capital; new potentials for life; and the pre-, post- and peri-personal movements of intensities through bodies.

Biopolitics often operates via the circulation of judgements (Rose 2007: 27), and, understandably, preferable counter-judgements. Or, biopolitics is seen to work via overarching schema and, from within these, forms of possible resistance. However, it is also important to discuss biopolitics in directly performative terms, by which I mean from the side of a sensate undoing of schema entwined with the question of what comes next.

This politics only arises in the absence of a confident set of judge-ments, or the framing of a coherent and harmonious set of faculties (or population statistics). In this absence, performance becomes 'a theatre of unbelief, of movement as Physis, already a theatre of cruelty . . . the most natural will of Nature in itself and willing itself as Physis, because Nature is by itself superior to its own kingdoms and its own laws' (Deleuze 1994: 11). Theatre and performance deal with different circulations outside these laws. They engage with the 'ecosophical problematic . . . of the production of human existence itself in new historical contexts' (Guattari 2000: 34). No longer only staged within the proscenium arch of an overwhelming Foucauldian '*dispositif*', biopolitics is also 'affirmed as the infinite tension that affects a process of constitution launched against all the strata of organisation that block becomings' (Alliez 2004). A new aesthetic paradigm becomes available at the level of the body.

This is neither a simple nor easy matter. Here, I will turn to VJing's installation of a multitude of 'inclusive disjunctions' as, perhaps, a final unravelling of the strands which I have all too briefly suggested that Chekhov began to pull apart.

VJing and the Reconfiguration of Media Performance Ecologies

> . . . he continues, between sips of lager, saying that video as a medium reminds you constantly of where you are, whereas film wants you to engage in suspension of disbelief. (Kasprzak 2008)

In 'Rebirth of a Nation', DJ Spooky remixed live the images from D. W. Griffiths' foundational film. He extracted its racism as one would extract a poison with a poultice.

In a series of interactive video artworks, often allowing interaction via bluetooth from mobile phones, and sometimes installed in nightclubs, Giselle Beiguelman subtracts even the 'VJ' from VJing.

In a small project I worked on with Anna Munster, 'Assemblage for Collective Thought' (Munster and Murphie 2007), video, sounds, text and still images gathered by a collective of about ten people were mixed in performance, with live video feeds from the 'audience' triggering events and effects in the video mix. Children danced. Technicians, bored by previous proceedings, crumpled cellophane in front of the laptop's camera.

Although brief, the above descriptions at least hint at what is a wide range of practices under the general title of VJing. VJing is everywhere now in popular culture, especially in club culture and music events, in which the 'VJ can be thought of as a filter through which the club environment is refracted' (Houston 2008). It signals a new performative distribution of intensities, new biograms and the circulation of new 'strange flows'. It is perhaps something of a new biopolitical 'process of constitution launched against all the strata of organisation that block becomings' (Alliez 2004).

VJing can be loosely defined as realtime, audiovisual performance in which visual projection plays a key role (although this is not the same as a central role). VJing usually involves the realtime mixing of video and audio samples, perhaps light sources (for example, overhead projectors and coloured liquids), and live video. Various signals can also feed into the mix – so that, for example, variations in the audio trigger might influence video signals or software operations. The technical configuration, and often creation, of hardware and software is also crucial and highly variable. In fact, VJing involves a complex series of configurations within configurations. For example, nearly every VJ will have a different collection of interconnected hardware elements, and software elements, some of these analog, some of them commercial, and many 'homemade' or 'hacked'. As Gabriel Menotti puts it: 'VJing is cinema escaping from its architectural constraints; it is audiovisual production as possibilities of the apparatus' (Menotti n.d.). Crucially, the spectators are usually able to move. Often they are dancing.

Fractalising Image/Performance Cultures

> VJing composes with intensive configuration, in a kind of 'deterritorialisation in technological glitches, samples and feedback loops'. (Agnihotri-Clark n.d.)

> Images projected by VJs are situated in what Bellour calls 'Between-Images': the space where photo, cinema and video meet and intertwine in a multiplicity of superpositions and configurations that are scarcely predictable. (Tordino 2007)

After Guattari, I would describe this as VJing's 'fractalisation' of both image events and the distributive intensities of lived image–body relations. Fractalisation describes the 'texture' (Guattari 1989: 219) of 'intermediate temporalities' (218) in life as lived, or the fractal effect of mixing temporalities – durations and syntheses – in 'becoming'. VJing is also 'synaptic' (199). For Guattari, the synaptic in general, as between neurons, is precisely the possibility of 'points of reversal' away from determination. Through fractalisation and its occupation of the synaptic within image-culture, VJing challenges foundational orders in aesthetics and in life. It does so precisely where biopolitics and the biogrammatic meet the performative – in transversal encounters across their optic, proprioceptive and synaesthetic registers.

VJing's open system of cruelty uses images against themselves, and media technologies against static media forms, in order to rigorously return the image to encounters between bodies and the immanent ecology of a particular event. This breakdown and return to immanence often produces a synaesthesia that indicates a new set of differential, intensive engagements at the level of the event itself. This 'synaesthesia . . . characterizes the shift, or move, towards increased networks and spaces where all of one's senses are tuned, activated, "on"' (Jaeger 2008). As in Chekhov's work, the synaesthesia also signals a new form of performative 'constructivism' (Alliez 2004). This 'requires a dynamic engagement where the internal parameters of the performance itself shift during the performance' (Betancourt 2008). Mark Amerika (Professor VJ) has argued that this makes the VJ something of a digital shaman, subject to the event rather than the centre of it, 'operating under the spell of what comes before consciousness'. The VJ is lost 'in the process of becoming a mesoperceptive artist-medium hyperimprovising . . . where the artist-medium is intermediating between the body, brain, and whatever digital apparatus is being used . . . a proprioceptive instrument' (Amerika 2007: 27).

There is little in this that is 'cognitive' in the sense of agency-based processing of representations. Rather, it reflects Deleuze's understanding of decision (and therefore of 'agency') in performative terms. 'A decision is not a judgement, nor is it the organic consequence of a judgement: it springs vitally from a whirlwind of forces that leads us into combat. It resolves the combat without suppressing or ending it' (Deleuze 1997: 134). Work with images is immersed in an ecological transduction or conversion of force fields. Felt performativity arises in the body via a series of 'lightning flashes' (34) within this 'whirlwind of forces'.

Gathering intensities within this whirlwind of forces that are accessible to shifting biograms, VJing first increases our power to be affected by complex image work. Perhaps this is counter-intuitive to everyone but an artist, but the power to be affected is more important than the power to affect. A sensibility that can tolerate more of the world, and be affected by that world, equals the power to exist, and only afterwards the power to engage with the world.

The increased power to be affected, and to affect, also multiplies our 'ideas of bodily transition' (Gatens and Lloyd 1999: 49). As such, VJing is an always emergent aesthetic that allows engagement with a new biogrammatic and biopolitical complexity between 'digital media [and] media such as cinema and photography . . . informatics and material strata, the organic and inorganic' (Munster 2001). If VJing culture is a distraction, it is a distraction from the illusions of infinite debt that are the glue holding standard political ecologies together; from infinite debt to the gods, to a fundamentalist God, to an infinite transcendent economy or illusorily free market.

To Have Done With the Judgement of Images

In sum, VJing, in its tight embrace of both what has been and of the unformed, attempts to have done with the judgement of images, of spectacle, and of the cultural practices spectacle often sets up via image-performance. VJing folds the transcendent references to the doctrine of judgement in images into a more immanent work. The VJing event may sometimes seem the socio-technical fulfillment of Debord's 'society of spectacle', with its overdetermined hierarchies based upon an overwhelming performative sovereignty of the image. However, like Chekhov, VJing repeats everyday experience – now the everyday experience of an image-soaked culture – in order to undo it, and to see how a 'people to come' might survive the intensities released. In this way, the VJ event is capable of bringing about the spectacle's equally techno-social demise – and a radical democratisation of the image – in the new circulations, fragmentation and realtime remixing of image fragments. It turns the unified spectacle against itself, transducing its powers into so many moving shards of affect available to the performance space.

I have suggested elsewhere that the ongoing constructivism and reconfiguraton of both the technical and the social is intrinsic to digital and networked media (Murphie 2003). These are not media in the traditional sense of film or television, with relatively fixed configurations, amenable to sub-disciplines like Film or Television Studies. They are differential or intensive media, highly variable technics, ecologically sensitive to the complexities of contingent engagement between technologies and bodies, in networks of difference, in shifting spaces and temporalities (see also Munster 2006).

Differential media are more attuned to complex, dynamic biograms than to normative configurations that stand still long enough to allow us to form a relatively stable world with them. As in VJing, these media tend to be premised on the higher levels of 'intellectual effort' that Bergson identified in the work required when schemas and images do not easily match. This drives both schemas and the production of image-relations into the creation of extremely unstable Idea-image-world-body relations. VJing, therefore, provides avenues for the sort of contemporary world equivalent to the kind of world-exhaustion found in Chekhov's work. If Chekhov 'engaged in a war of attrition with the theatre of his day' (Borny 2006: 1), VJing engages simultaneously in a 'combat' of attrition with the contemporary performativity of images. It also engages in a kind of 'combat between' of image-relation excess, multiplying the intensities between images (and ecologies) until this creates new circuits immanent to what are often temporary ecologies (for example, of dance events).

Like Chekhov, VJing suggests the possibility of entire, new, ethico-aesthetic paradigms that arise out of the failure of contemporary modes of living. Chekhov's theatre provided the most open ethico-aesthetic paradigm within the emergence of Naturalism. VJing provides the ethico-aesthetic paradigm appropriate to that which Deleuze calls the informational image, in which there is 'perpetual reorganization' and 'a new image can arise from any point whatever of the preceding image' with an image 'constantly being cut into another image' (Deleuze 1989: 265). In VJing, as in Chekhov, what at first seems obscure is made available to the everyday. In VJing, what seemed obscure in philosophy or experimental art is danced to a few decades later.

Dancing with Incipiency

VJing allows a kind of dance of total critique. To dance in a VJ'ed event is to dance with the breakdown of images, and with the breakdown of the normative configurations of image-culture. VJing, therefore, has a complex relation to the breakdown and reconstitution of the sensory-motor. It mixes the ongoing breakage of the sensory-motor schema I have mentioned into a high-level sensory-motor engagement with an environment of music and dancing in which everyone is a performer. The ongoing production of differential intensity between these two series – breakage of sensory-motor schema and high levels of sensate awareness – is very powerful. It enables the audience/performers to undergo a kind of ongoing and open reprogramming at the level of biograms. This makes possible – indeed demands – a finer degree of attention to immanence, more specifically to the incipience of intensities, the emergence of intensity as the 'form of difference', coming into the 'reason of the sensible' (Deleuze 1994: 222).

It is the response to the demand for this new kind of attention that will determine whether VJing falls back into relatively static schema or not. This response faces at least three challenges. The first challenge provided is to interface design in performance environments. Key to this is what Erin Manning calls 'preacceleration', the moment of 'incipient action' just before, and indeed continuing to pass through, any event of movement (Manning 2006). The general ecological challenge is to go beyond (or before) the constant transformation of the body in movement writ large. It is to work with the fainter transitive moments of the biogram. It is to work with the incipience of movement itself. The challenge to interface design is found in the demand for an open and mutually micro-adaptive configuration – at the level of the emergent – in concert with the multiple intensive series between technologies, bodies and general immanent ecology. This will not be helped by a setup that is only amenable to a gross 'triggering' between a stable bank of image clips, effects and sounds on the one hand, and 'pre-formed organisms' and 'gestural syntax' (Manning 2006) on the other. There must be a more receptive adaptability to the ongoing finite exchanges between incipient bodily and incipient technical actions: a mutual modulation in which the prediction of gesture-technical event-relations is impossible – in fact, irrelevant.

The second challenge is to VJing's ecological responsiveness with regard to an incipient subjectivity. Here we can turn to Massumi's understanding of the relays between the corporeal and incorporeal. The 'corporeal' side of these relays is the almost measurable clarity of sensation on sensory surfaces (the eyes and images, the ears and sound, the bones affected by deep bass, the proprioceptive body dancing, skins and kisses or the sweat of the dancefloor). The 'incorporeal' side of these relays concerns the way this clarity of sensation becomes an immeasurable quality of 'experience', in the 'conversion of surface distance into intensity'. This 'is also the conversion of the materiality of the body into an *event*'. The conversion of sensation into experience is 'not yet a subject . . . but it may well be the conditions of . . . 'an incipient subjectivity' (Massumi 2002: 14).

This is not something that can be measured. However, it can, and indeed must be reconfigured intuitively, as suggested by Mark Amerika's 'mesoperceptive artist-medium'. This might begin with the technical assemblage's own emergent 'feel for input', the way it brings effects and inputs together over time. It can surprise everyone, including the VJ herself. The inter-image production of the VJ event could be seen as a component series of a field of production of incipient subjectivity. The third challenge emerges from this, a kind of incipience in communality. Here the challenge lies in what Mat Wall-Smith has described as 'communality', meaning 'a technical incipience for realizing . . . "through-linkages"' (Wall-Smith 2007).

In sum, in the VJ event there is an entire ecology of active incipiencies: incipience of sensation, of movement, of action, of the event, of technical assemblages, of subjectivity, of communality. VJing needs to allow an intense engagement at the level of incipiency in order to survive, but it also needs to be able to survive this intensive engagement. To put this differently, VJing needs to accommodate a 'power to be affected and power to affect' at the level of incipiency. It is its lifeblood. The more it does so, the more it might take Chekhov's productive world-exhaustion, along with Aeschylus and Artaud's unremitting cruelty, in a new direction.

References

Agnihotri-Clark, D. (n.d.), 'Indeterminacy and Interface', *Avatar Body Collision*: http://www.avatarbodycollision.org/docs/dan_agnihotriclark.doc

Alliez, E. (2004), 'Anti-Oedipus – Thirty Years On', *Kein Theater*: http://theater.kein.org/node/145

Amerika, M. (2007), *META/DATA*, Cambridge, MA: MIT Press.

Bergson, H. (1920), 'Intellectual Effort', in H. Bergson, *Mind-Energy*, New York: Henry Holt.

Bergson, H. (1991), *Matter and Memory*, New York: Zone Books.

Betancourt, M. (2008), 'Wallpaper and/as Art', *Vague Terrain*, 09: http://vagueterrain.net/journal09/michael-betancourt/01

Borny, G. (2006), *Interpreting Chekhov*, Canberra: Australian National University E Press.

Butler, J. (1988), 'Performative Acts and Gender Constitution: An Essay in Phenomenology and Feminist Theory', *Theatre Journal*, 40 (4): 519–31.

Chekhov, A. (1954), *Plays*, Harmondsworth: Penguin.

Dejours, C. (2006), 'Subjectivity, Work and Action', *Critical Horizons*, 7 (1): 45–62.

Deleuze, G. (1979), 'Un Manifeste de Moins', in C. Bene and G. Deleuze, *Superpositions*, Paris: Les Editions de Minuit.

Deleuze, G. (1983), *Nietzsche and Philosophy*, trans. H. Tomlinson, London: Athlone.

Deleuze, G. (1986), *Cinema 1: The Movement-Image*, trans. H. Tomlinson and B. Habberjam, London: Athlone.

Deleuze, G. (1989), *Cinema 2: The Time-Image*, trans. H. Tomlinson and R. Galeta, London: Athlone.

Deleuze, G. (1990), *The Logic of Sense*, trans. M. Lester with C. Stivale, edited by C. V. Boundas, New York: Columbia University Press.

Deleuze, G. (1994), *Difference and Repetition*, trans. P. Patton, London: Athlone.

Deleuze, G. (1997), *Essays Critical and Clinical*, trans. D. W. Smith and M. A. Greco, Minneapolis: University of Minnesota Press.

Deleuze, G. and F. Guattari (1983), *Anti-Oedipus*, trans. R. Hurley, M. Seem and H. R. Lane, Minneapolis: University of Minnesota Press.

Deleuze, G. and F. Guattari (1987), *A Thousand Plateaus*, trans. B. Massumi, Minneapolis: University of Minnesota Press.

Deleuze, G. and F. Guattari (1994), *What is Philosophy?*, trans. H. Tomlinson and G. Burchell, New York: Columbia University Press.

Edwards, P. (1996), *Closed World: Computers and the Politics of Discourse in Cold War America*, Cambridge, MA: MIT Press.

Gatens, M. and G. Lloyd (1999), *Collective Imaginings: Spinoza, Past and Present*, London: Routledge.

Gil, J. (1998), *Metamorphoses of the Body*, Minneapolis: University of Minnesota Press.

Guattari, F. (1989), *Cartographies Schizoanalytiques*, Paris: Editions Galilee.

Guattari, F. (2000), *The Three Ecologies*, trans. I. Pindar and P. Sutton, London: Athlone.

Houston, L. (2008), 'VJing, Technology and Intelligibility: Exploring the Emergent Practices of VJing Through the Work of Gilbert Simondon', *Vague Terrain*, 09: http://vagueterrain.net/journal09/lara-houston/01

Jaeger, T. (2008), 'VJ as Hyperindividual', *Vague Terrain*, 09: http://vagueterrain.net/journal09/tim-jaeger/01

Kasprzak, M. (2008), 'An Interview with Jaygo Bloom', *Vague Terrain*, 09: http://vagueterrain.net/journal09/jaygo-bloom/01

McKenzie, J. (2001), *Perform or Else: From Discipline to Performance*, London: Routledge.

McMahon, M. (2005), 'Difference, Repetition', in C. Stivale (ed.), *Gilles Deleuze: Key Concepts*, Chesham: Acumen.

Manning, E. (2006), 'Prosthetics Making Sense: Dancing the Technogenetic Body', *Fibreculture Journal*, 9: http://journal.fibreculture.org/issue9/issue9_manning.html

Massumi, B. (2002), *Parables for the Virtual*, Durham and London: Duke University Press.

Menotti, Gabriel (n.d.), 'What is VJing and Realtime Interaction', *VJ theory.net*: http://www.vjtheory.net/what_is_it/menotti_what_is.htm

Munster, A. (2001), 'Digitality: Approximate Aesthetics', *Ctheory*: http://www.ctheory.net/articles.aspx?id=290

Munster, A. (2006), *Materializing New Media*, Hanover, NH: University Press of New England.

Munster, A. and A. Murphie (2007), 'Assembling Collective Thought': http://researchhub.cofa.unsw.edu.au/ccap/2007/08/02/assembling   collective-thought-anna-munster-and-andrew-murphie

Murphie, A. (2003), 'Electronicas: Differential Media and Proliferating, Transient Worlds', *fineart forum* 17 (8) (August): http://hypertext.rmit.edu.au/dac/papers/Murphie.pdf

Murphie, A. (2004), 'The World as Clock: The Network Society and Experimental Ecologies', *Topia: Canadian Journal of Cultural Studies*, Spring: 117–39.

Murphie, A. (2005a), 'The Mutation of "Cognition" and the Fracturing of Modernity: Cognitive Technics, Extended Mind and Cultural Crisis', *Scan* 2, 2 (September): http://scan.net.au/scan/journal/display.php?journal_id=58

Murphie, A. (2005b), 'Differential Life, Perception and the Nervous Elements: Whitehead, Bergson and Virno on the Technics of Living', *Culture Machine 7*: http://culturemachine.tees.ac.uk/Cmach/Backissues/j007/Articles/murphie.htm

Murphy, T. S. (1992), 'The Theatre (of the Philosophy) of Cruelty in Difference and Repetition', in Joan Broadhurst (ed.), *Deleuze and the Transcendental Unconscious*. Special edition of *Pli: Warwick Journal of Philosophy*, University of Warwick, 105–35.

Poxon, J. L. and C. J. Stivale (2005), 'Sense, Series', in C. J. Stivale (ed.) *Gilles Deleuze: Key Concepts*, Chesham: Acumen.

Protevi, J. (2001), *Political Physics*, London: Athlone.

Ronell, A. (2005), *The Test Drive*, Chicago: University of Illinois Press.

Rose, N. (2007), *The Politics of Life Itself*, Princeton: Princeton University Press.

Sedgwick, E. K. (2003), *Touching Feeling: Affect, Pedagogy, Performativity*, Durham: Duke University Press.

Strathern, M. (ed.) (2000), *Audit Cultures: Anthropological Studies in Accountability, Ethics and the Academy*, London: Routledge.

Tordino, D. (2007), 'Musical Language in the VJing Art', *VJ theory.net*: http://www.vjtheory.net/web_texts/text_tordino.htm.

Wall-Smith, M. (2007), 'Net Vis Links: Chris Harrison': http://researchhub.cofa.unsw.edu.au/ccap/2007/06/29/net-vis-links-chris harrison.

Notes

1. VJing is realtime audiovisual performance, usually in tandem with music performance (DJing and so on), and often, though not always, in a dance club or other venue for alternative forms of sociality.
2. See also Murphie (2004).

3. The plot of *The Cherry Orchard* concerns the fate of a family estate, with a large cherry orchard. At the beginning of the play we learn that the orchard is to be sold to pay the debts accumulated by the landowner, Liubov Andryeevna. The cherry orchard is sold at the end of the third act, and the audience hears it being chopped down at the end of the play. Of course, there is also the question of the shifts in social debt attached to the shifts in capital, and at a time when the classes in Russia were in transition. The richest character in the play, Lopakhin, who comes from one of the lower classes, is often treated with disdain by the aristocratic owners of the cherry orchard. However, it is he that buys the orchard, in order to 'save the family' (who will therefore be in his debt). Then there is the question of what is owed to the old servant Feers, a 'liberated serf' who regards this liberation as something of a catastrophe. He might be right, at least as concerns himself. He ends the play alone in the abandoned house.

4. That 'the doctrine of judgement has reversed and replaced the system of affects . . . even in the judgement of knowledge or experience' is evident in the rise of the whole set of practices in which the measurements, interventions and ongoing reviews of institutional, group and individual performance has become endemic. The rise of the social sciences has been largely premised on this, and much of this in turn on the rise of models of thinking processes in which thinking becomes 'cognition'. See Strathern (2000), Edwards (1996) and Ronell (2005), for three accounts of events related to this recent conflation of systems of judgement that impinge more and more on what counts as worthy 'knowledge or experience'. See also Murphie (2005a, 2005b) for discussions of this in the specific contexts of cognition and human–computer interaction.

5. A 'series' for Deleuze is at one level simply a chain of instances. An example might be a series of photographs. However, a series is without any necessary linear cause and effect relations. Instead it has an openness to a multiplicity of relations of difference which can constantly be reconstituted. As such the series concerns neither 'identity' nor acts of 'representation' between elements. Series are necessarily found in pairs (at least), most famously, in Deleuze's work, in series of bodies and series of events. Again the relations involved are open, not founded on linear cause and effect. For more on the series in Deleuze see Poxon and Stivale (2005).

6. This term indicates an attempt, as in performance management, to recuperate performance events within a given matrix or schema before they occur.

Chapter 13

The 'Minor' Arithmetic of Rhythm: Imagining Digital Technologies for Dance

Stamatia Portanova

Expressivity

In 1968, in his book *Changes: Notes on Choreography*, Merce Cunningham imagined a future digital technology that would allow the composition of a choreography through the representation of 3D figures on a computer screen. Ever since his first creations, Cunningham's choreographic method has always implied an exploration of movement in itself, considering it as a non-conscious, non-intentional and random process; in this sense, his use of the Life Forms (and, later, the Dance Forms) software has brought about an expansion of his analytical and creative procedures. Everything can be decided simply by chance: the selection of body parts, their number and type of movement. After taking the choreographic process on a totally de-humanised compositional plane, beyond narratives, feelings and phenomenological connotations, what kind of expressive potential is left to the technologically choreographed dancing body?

Choreography is not a practice of hylomorphic body modelling: we would be mistaken in assigning the choreographer the role of a God-artist-creator inspired by some transcendental choreographic idea. The 'odd little bodies' moving and dancing on the computer interface do not directly conform to any preconceived movement shape: ideas always leave their sediment after much experimentational and compositional practice, when enough space is left for the properties of different materials and techniques to emerge. Gilles Deleuze and Félix Guattari dismantle the Platonic hylomorphic idea of creation as a process beyond the capacities of the material substratum and only performable by some external, transcendental agency. Together with the concept of an onto-genetic, or hetero-genetic (or, in their own terminology, 'schizo-genetic') matter, the philosophers delineate the idea of creation as an autopoietic 'improvisational' event which, without being transcendentally and choreographically determined from the outside, is never purely and chaotically random but always endowed with precise order and organisation. Every 'creation' is revealed as a stratification, an immanent process coinciding with the emerging (rather than the imposition) of 'contents' and 'expressions' (or, more specifically, of 'formed ordered matters' and 'organised functional structures') 'in' matter. This stratified approach highlights the co-appearance and co-existence of contents and expressions everywhere in nature: in all physical, organic or aesthetic entities, 'as in all things, . . . lines of articulation or segmentarity, strata and territories', formal and functional organisations of all kinds, proliferate (Deleuze and Guattari 1998: 3).

Content and expression are directional forces. When adopted as a criterion of aesthetic analysis, Deleuze and Guattari's 'stratified semiotics' allows us to identify both content and expression, or bodies and their signs, as two complementary forces, each acquiring a substance and a form, a material consistency and a coded structure, in their reciprocal encounter. In a conflictual encounter of forces, the becoming expressive of something (an object, a body or a bodily movement) does not depend on an already realised form but on the selection and appearance of particular qualities (or expressive traits) which are already more defined than pure energetic intensities but not yet structured as forms or substances of expression: quality as an inchoate formed substance felt in its full expressivity. What qualitative traits express is expressive force in itself, the capacity to bend a parallel bodily content towards a functional taking form.

Every walking, running, dancing body exercises an escape force on the gravitational field, and is in its turn gravity-limited in its experiential range.[1] Expressive qualities always emerge from the modulated encounter or the counterpoint, from the parallelism and connection between at least two coded forces and two embodied territories: earth and sky, the limited range of anatomical Degrees of Freedom and the amplified motionscape of the mover. Different dance forms imply different codes, different distributions of forces and, therefore, different ways to be expressive: for example, the trained ballet dancer manages to overcome the downward heaviness of gravity and expresses a particular quality of movement in a glimpse, like a capacity to 'fly'.

Identifying the dancing body as the expressive moulded material of the choreographic creation is not enough. To escape the ontological limits of hylomorphism as an anthropocentric concept of absolute inspiration and idealistic creativity, it is necessary to understand the choreographic process as the actualisation and composition of particular forms of displacement already implicit in the dancing body's evolutions in space and time: co-choreographing with the body's infolding in a virtuality of potentials and with its unfolding of a qualitative expressivity. Anticipating a tendency (the choreographed gesture as a point of attraction) or following an event (the notation as a possibility of refinement, amplification, multiplication of gestural paths), the choreographic role can never be simply that of subjugating a bodily content by shaping it into a danced form of expression. Expressive potentialities and virtual dance forms are already immanent to the moving body's encoded capacities, techniques and preferences, and only need to be activated. In their encounter, different codes reciprocally activate incipient emerging forms, determining the appearance of qualities in between their communicating gaps: the void between an impossible choreographed step and the actual anatomical possibility is always filled by pragmatic algorithmic solutions that bring with them the sense of a qualitative shift.

The expressive qualities emerging from creative schizogenesis are often imperceptible, not limited to those capturable within the perspectival range of the human senses. This chapter questions the necessity of an exclusively human-centred perception, conception and imagination of the possibilities of dance, by postulating a series of expressive qualities potentially lurking in between the interstitial spaces and relations of the numerical, choreographic and technological codifications of the dancing body. The limited range of human sensation, thought and imagination will be confronted with the imperceptibility and ungraspability of the conceptual sensations (or sensed thoughts) generated by the experience of the relation, considering technological choreography more as a way of thinking, connecting and producing, than as an actual application of techniques. At the same time, the autonomous creativity of this form of expression can also determine a pragmatic conversion, allowing its own process to be prolonged into qualitatively different modes of operation, conceptual sensations becoming the propellers for a future experimentation yet to come.

Numberability

Expressivity does not obey a code, and yet it could not appear outside the productive rules of a codification. The codification of a dancing body always presupposes a territory delineated by the arithmetical and geometrical principles of a Cartesian oriented space and a flattened chronological time, giving shape to the illusion of a flat immobile ground on which movement unfolds along a linearly oriented chrono-metrics. The 'dimensionalisation' of space and time happens as a translation of successive points of displacement into sequenced numbers: 'magnitudes can striate space [and spatialise time] only by reference to numbers, and conversely, numbers are used to express increasingly complex relations between magnitudes, thus giving rise to ideal spaces reinforcing the striation and making it coextensive with all of matter' (Deleuze and Guattari 1998: 484).[2] Delimiting the ground and its spatio-temporal coordinates, numbers contribute the basic references and coordinates for dance, enclosing the dancer's range of movement possibilities in a well-defined grid.

Numerical cadence is key to the codification of space and time, positions and velocities, steps and directions, the shape of gestures and the lines of transition between them.[3] Deleuze and Guattari define the number considered as a counting and measuring tool as a 'numbered number', an instrument of 'major' (or institutionalised) science to inscribe, divide and measure the linearity of movement as a sequence of points and positions on the inert surface of the ground/earth (387–94). Anatomical laws constitute a parallel code, the anatomy of the senses extracting a series of unitary objects disposed on the grid of geometrical coordinates, and the musculo-skeletal system selecting a series of precoded combinatorial positions or steps from a virtual field of potential, reducing virtuality to a set of possible displacement-units with particular directions and forms, routes and paths (retroduction).[4] As a consequence, space is perceived as a 'homogenised' and 'striated' grid of coordinates and laws where the anatomical organisation of the body can easily find its right position and direction: a pre-programmed body ordering and striating space with its movements. Here, gravity is the main codifying force. Transforming every spatial displacement of the body into a predictable and programmable reproduction of the Newtonian law and of its linear, laminar model of motion and speed measurement, gravitational laws express velocity through the reduction of space and time to divisible arithmetical units (V = distance/time). Every movement is expressed as a controlled fall, or as a numerically measured attempt at flight from a gravitational centre.

Numbers are codifying operators, and yet they are also key to a more ambivalent function of de-coding. With their simultaneously unitary and multiple nature, numbers are able to divide and 'stratify' but also to 'smooth' the rigid demarcations created by them, to control and open out, to code and de-code space-time, metrically dividing them into units but also populating them with the many of which each unit (and sub-unit) is fractally composed ad infinitum. This infinite composition constitutes the complex harmonic sense of numerical codification, indicating its relation with a non-human level of perceptual and intellectual compression, like a 'minor', imperceptible mathematics of the imagination. According to Deleuze, the philosophical and mathematical concept of harmony introduced by Gottfried Leibniz precisely defines the relation between the infinitely divisible extension of space, and the compressive tendency of perception to enclose its objects into 'units' (complexity and compression). It is, for example, like hearing the noise of the sea or of a violin chord, where a multiplicity of micro-perceptions is 'non-consciously calculated' as a whole sound, the product of a numerical calculus enveloped into an affective state. The intuition of one musical note, of one gesture, as already being composed by a multiplicity of microscopic, undiscernible vibrations.

In the Leibnizian mathematics, arithmetic operations are replaced by precise but infinite calculations that intuitively project the possibility of a calculus independent of both conscience and function. As a sum or a multiplication of microscopic moments, distance (as 'covered' space) appears as an inexhaustible multiplicity of distances, each unit, however small, being different in itself. Distance, or the qualitative change from 'space' to 'covered space', is made up of a myriad of qualitative shifts (of direction, velocity, etc.).[5] Realising a philosophico-scientific connection between mathematical and perceptual codes, or between two tendencies (divisibility-compression) of the body-mind, Leibniz reveals a space potentially 'numerable' ad infinitum. Geometry and anatomy only provide the basic metric codes structuring the content and expression, the 'contained' ground and the 'expressive' body of dance; at the same time, the close range, non-human perspective of Leibnizian calculus reveals both as infinitely dissectible and compressible.

As a spatio-temporal integral, movement can be 'calculated', in Deleuze's words, as a double composite: 'on the one hand, the space traversed by the moving object, which forms an indefinitely divisible numerical multiplicity, all of whose parts – real or possible – are actual and differ only in degree; on the other hand, pure movement, which is *alteration*, a . . . qualitative multiplicity' (Deleuze 1988: 47). In other words, to the Leibnizian harmonic composition of movement in space, Deleuze adds its coincidence (and indiscernibility) with the continuity of qualitative development in time, a myriad of qualitative modifications filling the singularity of one step with multiple potential lines of spatio-temporal diversion. The illusory linearity of a jump is paradoxically made of an inextricable series of microscopic units of movement articulations without clear edges or precise beginning and end points. The intersection between the productive components of a movement simultaneously produces the expressive form of a step, but also a continuous emerging difference in between the steps; harmonic precision and subtle definition being the effect of a chaotic subterranean jittering, trembling and proliferation of movements in all directions. From this point of view, the harmony of a gesture is perceived as the product of an 'affective calculus', an approximate sum of infinitesimals tending towards limit and precise definition. The gesture is no longer able to contain the multiplicity of the moving body, because to move is to simultaneously shift, multiply, accumulate one's perceptual relations with the world in all spatial and temporal directions, towards future anticipation and past reminiscence simultaneously.

A body does not move without scattering itself in space and time as a moving multiplicity. The rhythm of the moving body is always a rhythm of qualitative distribution, rather than of quantitative pacing:

> It is well known that rhythm is not meter or cadence, even irregular meter or cadence: there is nothing less rhythmic than a military march . . . Meter, whether regular or not, assumes a coded form whose unit of measure may vary, but in a noncommunicating milieu, whereas rhythm is the Unequal or the Incommensurable that is always undergoing transcoding. Meter is dogmatic, but rhythm is critical; it ties together critical moments or ties itself up in passing from one milieu to another. It does not operate in a homogeneous space-time, but by heterogeneous blocks. It changes direction. (Deleuze and Guattari 1998: 313)

Rather than a quantifiable and determinable velocity, rhythm is the relational composition of all the deviations of the body from its (choreographic) path. As a molecular coagulation or dispersion happening behind the perceivable steps of a moving body, rhythm, or the expressivity of dance, is the qualitative alteration hidden behind linear displacement, generated by the relation between the different coded expressions of a moving body (from cellular to anatomical), or between the body and its coded outside (the body and its environment, the body and its ground).

For Deleuze and Guattari, the number is not only the correlate of the metric divisibility of space and time, but also of nonmetric, rhythmic and distributive multiplicities. In the 'minor' arithmetic of quality and rhythm, calculation is limited and general translatability almost impossible: from 'numbered', the number becomes 'numbering', i.e. acquires vagueness, irrationality, but also mobility and a potential for creation, which is revealed in its capacity to follow the microscopic mutations of a body in movement. This conceptual shift does not imply a quantitative difference between numerical values, but a qualitative difference developed by the number in its own qualitative variation.

The 'numbering' number is nomadic, ordinal, and does not divide without changing nature each time:

> The *Numbering Number*, in other words, autonomous, arithmetic organization, implies neither a superior degree of abstraction nor very large quantities . . . These numbers appear as soon as one distributes something in space, instead of dividing up space or distributing space itself. . . . The number is no longer a means of counting or measuring but of moving: it is the number itself that moves through space . . . The numbering number is rhythmic, not harmonic. It is not related to cadence or measure [but to an] *order of displacement.* (389–90)

Zeno's paradox already taught us distribution and proliferation: between the numbers/units of a code there is always another number (another micro-gesture in between two gestures, another moment in between two moments). Beyond and between codes (for example between arithmetic units), numbers reveal their limits, but also their potential level. All this can happen in extremely long or extremely short durations: between 0 and 1, 1 and 2, in the intervals of our calculations, other numbers spring. From one moment and until the next one, the number ceases to function as an exact instrument of measurement, counting and translation of movement: rather than describing or predicting movement, it follows and generates qualitative, a-subjective alterations through its potential. Without proposing any ontology of fluid processes and continuities over the metric discontinuity of the numeral, the concept of a 'numbering number' hints at the abstract potentiality to continuously split the flow of movement: the virtuality of the cut.

This conceptualisation is also at the basis of a different concept of movement in which counting is not superimposed upon but is immanent to the moving body. In its spatial occupation, or distribution of itself in space, the moving body spreads its molecular composition, drawing a kinetic and dynamic diagram of affects and speeds, forces and qualities that cannot be measured through immutable numbers but generate and multiply shifting 'ciphers', mobile segments, interconnecting strata. The body becomes a cipher, or an anonymous, collective and impersonal function: 'it' (a man, a woman, an animal, a molecule, a digital character, a number, all of them) moves, as an element of a nonsubjectified assemblage with no intrinsic but only situational and combinatorial (or connective) properties. The combinatorial nature of the body/cipher does not identify it with a numerical, statistic element (or a statistic aggregate of pre-existing units with pre-existing properties, as in the anatomical composition) but with a fractal complexity in itself, a complex of ciphers, articulated and 'assembled'. The subjective consciousness of movement as originating from one's own body and aiming at one particular point is always accompanied by the continuous motion of an infinite, uncountable number of outside–inside relational particles, a continuum virtually dissectable at any point.[6]

Through the body (rather than from it), movement becomes ephemeral and abstract, distributed and cut anywhere between its parts and relations, between its inside and outside, rather than being directed by a central point (consciousness, thought) guiding it in space according to anatomy and physical laws. This simultaneity of body/mind only appears in the distribution of thought/sensation/motion in the body, so that thought, counting and action coincide in their bodily de-localisation: a non-conscious counting immanent to the autonomic onto-genesis of matter. The same process can be imagined as being at work in classical ballet, where the displacement of gravity and its overcoming through vertical 'flight' remains the main motor of the movement, an implicit material calculation autonomically occupying the whole body consciousness as in a puppet dance with no subject-puppeteer. In his treatise 'On the Puppet Theatre', Heinrich von Kleist takes the example of puppetry to an extreme of de-subjectivation, transferring the movement of puppets and the continuous play of the puppeteer with the law of gravity (also defined as the relation of the arithmetic unit with its algorithms), into a 'spiritual' realm where the 'light' puppets overcome all gravity and do not even need to be guided by a central subject (the puppeteer) anymore (algorithms become autonomous) (Deleuze and Guattari 1998: 561, fn. 80). Drawing on Kleist's imagination, we could think choreography, or the art of imagining bodily movement, as an autopoietically algorithmic puppetry based on a non-conscious infinitesimal numerability.

Choreographability

As a procedure of aesthetic creation, choreography works in close relation with the sciences of space and body, endlessly de- and re-composing the algorithmic functions of the dancer's movements. In combination with the choreographic indication, dancers seem to move like puppets: not because of their similarity with stiff articulated performers of awkward displacements, but (or also) because of their capacity to challenge and problematise the precise ideas and accurate calculations of the puppeteer-scientist-choreographer.

Drawing on Michel Serres, Deleuze and Guattari distinguish two different 'sciences': 'a general theory of routes and paths' (science as a closed system of measurements and predictions) and 'a global theory of waves' (science as an open system of creation) (Serres in Deleuze and Guattari 1988: 371–2). Recognising the scientific character of choreography does not denote a creative limit but delineates a passage, or a conceptual/ pragmatic shift: from choreography as the act of 'ordering' the body's interactions with space and time (choreographic control being based on the fixity of the body's centre of gravity, and on the measurement and structuring of its routes and paths in space and time, the puppeteer controlling and guiding the movement), to a direct plunging into the physical complexity of movement (the centre of gravity as a shifting and easily replaceable singularity, the body as a multiplicity crossed through by waves of motion, puppets become autonomous). As stated by Merce Cunningham, in order to search for the singularities of the dancing body as a 'kinetic material' (rather than to construct its accomplished forms in advance), choreography can and should follow (rather than dictate) movement, going along with the dancer's tendency to 'escape the force of gravity' 'and enter a field of celerity'. Pointing towards a 'nomadic' notion of choreography, Cunningham's idea indicates a becoming, or a modulation of the choreographic code, along the same line of the dancer's movement. But how can choreography, whose scores are temporally disjuncted and superimposed, go along with the qualitative duration of movement?

The nomadism of choreographed dance does not have to do with the construction of a different, perhaps faster or more spontaneous form, but with a capacity to compose and play with the 'escaping', or 'flying' potential implicit in all movements. Rather than concentrating on the sequential displacements of a body going from point to point ('even if the second point is uncertain, unforeseen, or not well localized' [Deleuze and Guattari 1998: 380] as in contact improvisation), a 'nomadic' choreography takes into account the eventuality of the qualitative changes of a body, whose parts (or particles) occupy space harmonically. As a generator of qualitative transformation, rhythm (or differential energetic distribution) works through the creation of resonance between the steps of a metric organisation. To follow this resonance, choreography must cease to be a static design to become an exploration of excesses and deviations, of resonances and qualities, or of rhythms: an experimentation where points become simple relays along a trajectory of continuous creation of new forms of expression.[7] Notations and training can only intervene as anatomical potentialisations, multiplying the physical possibilities of the dancing body and bringing to the surface all sorts of motor and gestural combinations and virtuosities.

From this point of view, every choreographic system (such as Labanotation or Benesh) starts to appear as a nomadic production of meta-stable diagrams of bodily capacities based on adjustments, indecisions and uncertainty, the numerical calculations and signs always anticipating efforts and tendencies, delineating approximations rather than accomplished movements. Inducing efforts and anatomical systemic disruptions (going against one's motor habit), the choreographic notation acts like a virtual attractor, only becoming concrete in its unpredicted consequence. The tendency of the body to move is catalysed by the affective virtuality of the calculation, like an abstract form becoming active in the passage between the different codes (score, anatomy, space-time) of a mechanism of operational linkage. In this way, the dancer becomes the circumstantial agent of a future–past reciprocity (in the sense of a non-realised future, an incipient future, a tendency or effort acting back on the past of a choreographic notation). The notation works as a productive creative intermediary, determining the extraction of particular displacements, directions, lengths and sequential orders, from a number of possibilities. The possibilities do not coincide with the infinite, open virtuality of pure movement (which is always already anatomically and geometrically coded), but resonate with them. More importantly, they elicit a decision, the performance of a step. Without them, the virtuality of motion would remain stuck in the diagrammatic chaos of spontaneous articulation.

The choreographic calculation weaves a relation between pure intuition and intellectual rationality, suggesting a possibility of grounding the dance performance on a field of 'unlimited numerability'. In other words, it is through dissections, computations and combinations (of numbers, signs, bodily lines) that virtual forms are choreographically selected and actualised, producing an aesthetic consistency of content and expression without losing the aleatory vagueness of a movement's quality. The transformation of movement into a succession of points and numbers and the procedures of counting and measuring never entail a total capture and freezing of potential; rather, they compose a codified construction which allows a kinetic sequence to keep its own consistency, while containing an uncountable and non-measurable virtuality: together with affects and percepts, creation is always based on a material possibility of architectural construction which overcomes physical (or anatomical) laws and allows the most acrobatic postures to stand in equilibrium. Counting and measurement allow the dancing body to perform the most difficult and acrobatic of movements together with the simplest ones, or to fuse them, and therefore to continually re-negotiate the habit of corporeal possibilities and the novelty of movement qualities.

The conception of choreography as based on 'numbering' rather than 'numbered', allows us to speculate about a dance based more on the infinite complexity and virtuality of mathematics than on the limited fluidity of the phenomenological here and now. Realising the rhythmic connection between anatomical possibilities and choreographic notations, numbers acquire a 'numbering' quality, not only acting as the choreographer's tools of quantification (hylomorphism of cardinal numbers) but also as the non-conscious landmarks emerging from the autopoietic spatio-temporal taking place of dance as a distributive event (autopoiesis of the ordinal). A precise territorial range of movements has to be constructed through the composition of an undefinable but also rigorously precise number of gestures and steps, always on the verge of chaos but never submerged by it; without this delimitation, the dancer would be lost: 'A mistake in speed, rhythm, or harmony, would be catastrophic because it would bring back the forces of chaos, destroying both creator and creation' (Deleuze and Guattari 1998: 311).

Apart from delimiting a territory or field, numbers can also open a fissure, a crack through which chaos is let in. Since his first choreographies, a key word in Cunningham's work has been the use of numerical chance procedures (like tossing pennies) for a non-representational fragmentation of the plane of movement composition:

> As you're not referring one sequence to another you can constantly shift everything, the movement can be continuous, and numerous transformations can be imagined. You still can have people dancing the same phrase together, but they can also dance different phrases at the same time, different phrases divided in different ways, in two, three, five, eight or whatever. (Cunningham 1998: 29)

Two, three, five, eight or 'whatever': as Cunningham's own words make evident, his numerical working method implies the random creation and manipulation of different movements in different rhythms and, therefore, a multiplication of possibilities and a complexification of the whole dance performance. The classical conception of the stage/space seen through a frontal perspective is replaced by a more complex conceptualisation of all the different points of the scene as having equal value. Because the points of the stage lose their reciprocal relations of correspondence, movement can be constant and innumerable simultaneous transformations can be generated (as in Riemann's fractal space). The same goes for time: different movements can be performed with different rhythms. In order to accomplish this complexification, Cunningham's use of chance procedures (tossing coins, but also the Chinese mathematical system of the I-Ching) transforms the mobility of the dancers on stage into a sort of chaotic play with its own playground and rules.[8]

Techniques such as the I-Ching allow Cunningham to visualise what movements are to be performed and where, or the number of people performing them, easily side-stepping every subjective or emotional intervention in the composition process. But the coded possibilities of the 64 I-Ching hexagrams only become 'numbering numbers' in combination with the anatomical algorithms of the dancing body. The idiosyncratic phrases chosen by chance constitute a numerically codified set of limited movements that serve to go against the already coded and clichéd possibilities of bodily natural action and human imagination: coded transduction.[9] Rather than reflecting the acquired habits of the trained dancing body and of the choreographing mind, chance, as a vectorialising force, becomes a rigorous mathematical procedure to obtain unforeseen results, highlighting the expressivity of movement in itself. In the open methodology of numerical chance, choreographic practice becomes a qualitatively productive combinatorics of the six faces of a die, or the 64 hexagrams of the I-Ching.

Digitability

Together with the complex combinatorics of a die or the I-Ching, the two digits of binary computation, 0 and 1, already carry in their gap the potential of a multiplicity, as the result of infinite algorithmic operations. Being based on a binary codification and on precise calculations, the principle of digitisation translates the qualitative rhythmic dynamics of movement into discrete numbers, submitting the indeterminacy of matter to a new possibility of control operating through the numerical discrimination of very small differences. With the use of the Dance Forms choreographic software, movement sequences are not only imagined by the choreographer but completed by the computer through the interpolation of key positions in order to visualise the microscopic missing steps in a particular sequence. This interpolation happens through a mathematical function that calculates the missing in between value by using an average of the functional values at its disposal. Thanks to this algorithmic calculation, the Dance Forms electronic dancer can unrealistically jump at whatever height, it can fly and remain in the air; the possibilities of its muscles, articulations and ligaments are unlimited. Possible and impossible variables of movement are then composed into choreographic scores and passed to human dancers in flesh and bones who will perform them 'live'. Through this process, a new degree of control but also of bodily deformation is obtained, a tendency to 'twist' and 'gnarl' and 'fragment' the body in ways that take it increasingly far away from its habitual physical attitudes.

These new possibilities of choreographic production overcome Dance Forms' apparent aim of faithful reproduction of human movement: under a superficial level of realistic representation and resemblance, more interesting effects appear in the relation between the computer and the human body. The dancing body, as a mobile anatomical system with its own modalities and techniques, does not have to be emulated by the technical machine, because it is itself re-assembled and re-organised by its encounter with it. By modulating the intervals between information units, digital technology contributes to an imperceptible but pervasive bodily manipulation and control. In Cunningham's own words, 'With the computer, much as with a camera, you can freeze-frame something that the eye didn't' catch. But it's there. As a dance notation, it increases the possibilities – it is immediately visible' (Cunningham 1999: 5). New movements become visible and also performable, the calculation and visualisation of movements by the software having a direct effect on the biological and anatomical possibilities of the human body, implicitly leading to the discovery of new dynamics and filling the gaps between previously non-combinable positions or gestures. The body is simultaneously stimulated and guided, directed and challenged: with a combination of meter and rhythm, discipline and alteration, creation happens in parallel with an exercise of power. For example, in Cunningham's digital choreography *Change of Address* (1992), six dancers fall on the floor with their woven legs bent along strange angles: we can imagine Cunningham sitting at the keyboards, pressing some keys and coming up with some new movement sequence which suddenly leaves the dancers in a position without any legs to support them, and thus giving them the task to fill in the gap. In this case, the gap (or in between) is filled by a fall, a strange fall where the legs develop an infinitesimal deviation from the law of falling bodies and are able to trace awkward angles. The generation of physiological qualities (for example resistance) and anatomical realisations (impossible contortions and balances) is not the result of a mere formal composition of already given anatomical traits and choreographic rules, but derives from a modulation of unknown potential and virtual capacities. The expressivity of a dancing body becomes a re-combination of two parallel aspects: the constraint of habits and the potential of tendencies, choreographic code and rhythmic impulses, anatomical grids and energetic flows, through which the qualities and rhythms of a new dance emerge.

In Cunningham's computerised choreographies (such as *Trackers*, 1991; *Beach Birds for Camera*, 1992; *Ocean*, 1994; *Enter* and *CRWDSPCR*, 1996; and the motion captured performance *Biped*, 1999), the quality of the movements changes from the previous choreographic tendencies: for example, foot work becomes the main component of the performance, and the position and movement of the arms appears as an added element:

> Both arms frequently stretch up and over the head, but then curl back down towards the shoulder blades in a jagged arc. Necks often tilt upward, directing the dancer's gaze towards the ceiling. As with much of Cunningham's recent choreography, the arms now seem at least as active – and often more prominent – than the legs. But this is work that makes extreme demands on the lower body as well. For example, the dancers often execute low, rapid jumps on one foot, while the other leg is raised and tilted at a 45-degree angle. Occasionally, as both arms rise to frame the head symmetrically, both feet perform a bent-legged jump that finishes in first position. (Copeland 2004: 194)

In Roger Copeland's description of Cunningham's choreography *Biped*, the unity and wholeness of the dancer as the organised anatomical source of a motor performance appears replaced by a sort of dis-organisation of the body without 'hot spots', a decentred body that moves in a similarly decentred stage-space where no specific location prevails. This is not only expressive of a new level of formal complexity of the dance. Here, motions go beyond the usual capacities of the body, therefore preventing a centralising consciousness from directing the performance and requiring every single body part to develop its own autonomous awareness in order for the complex system to work. Apparently guided by the invisible hylomorphic hand (or mind) of the subject-choreographer, dancers are actually directed by a non-conscious power logic implicit in the relational encounter with the machine. The machine directing and controlling the performance is not simply equivalent to the technical mechanism: aiming neither at the naturalness of movement nor at the simple robotic effect of its 'mechanisation', but at its 'abstractness', Cunningham's choreographic style and use of technology could be defined as 'a-organic' and consistent with a kinetic order that rarely seems guided by a natural sense of flow, by anatomical logic or by personal conceptions (Copeland 2004: 42). Rhythmic relation and transmission (from computer algorithms to choreographic notation and dance performance) machinically emerges in between, as a creation of new potentials and new stimuli to realise apparently impossible movements and idiosyncratic phrases that go against biological and anatomical possibilities, allowing the exploration and discovery of previously unknown capacities and the overcoming of past beliefs and ideas, pushing the body towards anatomical or intellectual thresholds. The encounter or, as Deleuze and Guattari would call it, the counterpoint between two patterns, between body and computer algorithms, is what produces not only a quantitative but also a qualitative shift. Performative creativity supersedes the limits of both the human individual and of the technological application, being more clearly revealed as the effect of an assemblage, a fold in the flows, an event generated by the continuity/discontinuity of kinetic and dynamic forces, by different biological/technical machines. A machinic creation that is core to a formation of power operating on perceptions, actions and thoughts, and on their qualitative alteration.

A definite line of demarcation seems to delimit an opposition between choreographic software as an instrument of control and production able to suggest new qualities and forms of movement, and the creative failure of digital Motion Capture as a technological apparatus in which movement is simply cut and captured, limited and reduced to its simplest shape. Beyond the creation/capture dichotomy, a unique principle underlies both techniques: with digitalisation, indeterminate micro-variations (the infinitesimal differences or singularities of movement) become macroscopically coded as binary digits and re-composed (or re-shaped) by the computer's calculations. The singularity of qualitative differences is translated into a series of bits, equidistant moments of equal value and length; difference becomes repetition, 'The remarkable or singular instant remains any-instant-whatever among the others' (Deleuze 2005: 6).

Rather than implying an order of transcendental forms (or choreographed poses actualised in movement), digital technologies like Dance Forms or Motion Capture represent intermediary tools for the analysis and production of singular points immanent to movement itself (for example, in the choreographic software, the choreographer's idea is interpolated by the computer's algorithmic transitions, while the digital choreography is further interpolated by the singularities of the dancer's algorithmic solutions). The production of singularities (rhythmic qualitative shifts of movement) is not opposed but occurs through an accumulation of ordinary points (metric quantitative process of technology): with the digital (as was already the case with the older technology of cinema), the singular is extracted from a multiplication of any-instants-whatever.

In the latter half of the nineteenth century, Eadweard Muybridge used successive-exposure photography, assembling different cameras along a racetrack to measure and study the continuity of a horse's locomotion as a series of equidistant moments or points. At the same time, Étienne-Jules Marey's diagrams realised another form of visual capture of the pulses of a galloping horse. In Marey's experiments, the successive exposures and shots capturing different key points of motion were combined with the data provided by electric sensors. Around 150 years later, digital Motion

Capture systems consist of infrared colour-sensible cameras, datagloves and magnetic sensors attached to the body's joints and limbs, which do not reproduce the whole figure but only capture its motion by tracking the position-angle-orientation, velocity and pressure of the sensors or infrared markers. Motion Capture transforms the physical, anatomical and perceptual concreteness of the body into multiple series of equidistant moments, quantitatively describing the motion of segments of the musculoskeletal system.

Rather than limiting our analysis to the criticism of digital Motion Capture and its failure in actually capturing the qualitative continuity of movement and its virtually open potential, we can re-animate Deleuze's analysis of the cinematic image as a perfect example of Bergson's concept of the 'movement-image', an analysis that even goes beyond Bergson's own criticism of the limits of cinema as a technology of 'motion capture' (Deleuze 2005). Despite their obvious technical differences, the apparatuses of cinema and Motion Capture can both be considered as based on a unique conception of movement as the sum of separate points. At the same time, positioning itself in between the quantitative nature of metric displacement and the qualitative character of rhythm, the syncopated code of technology effects an expressive passage.

Marey's graphic records and Muybridge's equidistant photos of a horse's gallop represented the pre-history of cinema as a form of kinetic expression. Starting as a form of kinetic capture, cinema evolved afterwards through the addition of movement to the frames, in the same way in which digital MoCap today reconstructs movement through the juxtaposition and 'animation' of the data captured by sensors or cameras, and through the creation of a new moving image which takes movement into the field of cinematic animation again. Perception, intelligence and language are defined by Bergson as working in the same limited way as the cinematic machine, stringing instantaneous, frozen visions of an ever-flowing reality of potential affections on the continuous thread of consciousness.[10]

As pointed out by Deleuze, in 1907 Bergson defined the bad formula of the cinematographic illusion as based on two elements: instantaneous sections (images or frames) and an abstract movement contained in the machine and 'moving' them. In the same way, Motion Capture, in its old as well as in its recent versions, is based on the cutting, or breaking down, of movement in its constitutive points (the positions and displacements of the joints), and on their translation into numerical data to be re-combined, in order to give an 'illusion' of precise movement reproduction. Nevertheless, according to Deleuze, despite its illusion working through cut and re-assembled frames producing the impression of movement, what cinema shows us is an image with an intrinsic movement which is not added but belongs to it. In cinema (as in Motion Capture), the illusion is immediately adjusted at the apparition of the image, which becomes an immediate image-movement.

According to Deleuze, Bergson's philosophy totally reverses the cinematic vision, making movement correspond to a continuous change affecting the whole universe, a movement of all bodies/images continuously acting and re-acting with each other. Deleuze highlights how the Bergsonian theory is one of the moving body entering a wave, a continuously flowing matter 'in which no point of anchorage nor centre of reference would be assignable', and from which novelty continuously emerges. As a result, the idea of the human body as an original source of movement and as the conscious initiator of a series of progressive displacements aiming at a particular point, is overcome.[11] To the idea of a transcendental synthesis of movement from pre-existing poses to be realised by a conscious subject, Deleuze opposes a different theory: the instants or moments composing a movement (for example the cinematic frames) are its material immanent elements, its 'instants whatever', rather than its pre-existing positions. These instants are the singular points pertaining to movement and only successively identifiable, the moments of unpredictable qualitative change and not the moments of realisation of a transcendental script or choreography.

The way in which the technological mechanism works is explained by Deleuze through the introduction of the new kinetic concept of the 'instant whatever': rather than an intelligible synthesis of motion, techniques of motion capture (such as cinema) perform a sensible analysis of its sections or points. In other words, the technical machine takes an organised line of movement at any-point-whatever; among these points, some are critical, in the sense of being moments of qualitative shift and emerging difference (for example when Muybridge's horse has one foot on the ground, then three, two, three, one, none). Continuity is not pre-constructed, but constructed at every instant.

Merce Cunningham's choreographic creations show a break with the principle of organic composition of movement, realising a sort of choreographic Cartesianism, a mechanical composition of motion which seems very different from the Bergsonian (and Deleuzian) conception. The dance itself works like a mechanism of which the dancers are the component parts. This mechanisation is obtained in two ways. First, by transforming the dancer into a robot, a clockwork mechanism, a geometric configuration of combined, juxtaposed parts which perform their movements in a homogenised space, and according to their own relations. The use of Motion Capture technology intervenes as a further way to facilitate the mechanical composition and the translation of movement into a pure abstract line.

Cunningham's use of Motion Capture is in line with a more mechanical and also representational conception of the technology. But together with, and beyond, functions of representational or choreographic control, Motion Capture may start to express its own aesthetic potential in the very 'conceivability' of its operations. Compared to the cinematic technology, Motion Capture is characterised by a multiplicatory aspect, in the sense of a proliferation of the temporal intervals adopted as frame-variables, up to the infinitesimal bit-unit of a joint's rotation. By infinitesimally multiplying the number of instants-whatever and by opening them to infinite calculations and re-combinations, the microscopic cutting of digitalisation allows an even more detailed presentation (or micro-photography) and abstraction of a fluid line of movement in itself. This subtle capture of a multiplied number of instants-whatever can be experienced for example in the continuous trembling and 'jittering' effect due to the capture of microscopic details of a single movement by the most hyper-sensitive apparatuses. In this way, the imperfect representation of movement as a 'noisy' multiplicity to be edited and cleaned for smooth representation, reveals the very potential of the machine, giving us a sense of the illusory character of the linearity of movement, and of its composition by myriads of other tiny movements happening at the same time: rhythm, as a continuous overflowing of parallel lines of movement from a unique route, is, if not totally captured and shown, at least given a chance to be intuitively perceived.

The operation of abstracting a myriad of intervals as points where movement is frozen, re-starts, changes direction, accelerates or slows down, is what gives us its infinitesimal differentials, in the continuous attempt to abstract movement from the moving body. In video-choreographies such as *Hand-Drawn Figures*, *Biped*, *Fluid Canvas*, *Loops*, the order of displacement, or the smooth line of movement unfolding on the screen, is a superficial compressive order imposed on a multiplicity of different lines unravelling at the same time and still constituting one and the same movement. Imperfections must be edited, but what is technically imperfect in the capture suggests what we cannot grasp, giving a sense of the something 'more' in movement, of the micro-perceptions and micro-calculations, the rhythmicity exceeding the physiological and anatomical codes of the moving body and always escaping what we are able to see of it on a stage or screen. The technology works according to an exponential augmentation of possibilities of control, in which we will never be able to see everything at once; at the same time, the infinite digitability of the computer code is a force that only allows the minuscule segmentations and cuts of movement to become expressive on the wavelength of human perception and imagination.

In relation to the perceptual and rational limits of the human body, the digital cut represents only a superficial level of a myriad of further possible dissections, as if technology could not show anything but only take imagination to its limit. The sense, or idea, of a superposition of all the possible micro-dissections of a movement is what gives us its virtuality, as a continuous topological malleability drawing the concreteness and rigidity of the body with a plane of multiple, coexistent vectors or tendencies: infinite digitability paradoxically crossing with infinite malleability, imagination crossing with comprehension, mathematics crossing with art, as in a conceptual sensation of potential choreography. On the technologised dance stage, what we are left with is not a concretely accomplished application or effect, an actual substance or a form of expression, but the possibility of technologically elevating calculus beyond its empirical condition, in a sort of minor 'choreographic algebra' pointing towards the imagination of a future dance.

References

Ansell-Pearson, K. (2001), 'Thinking Immanence: On the Event of Deleuze's Bergsonism', in G. Genosko, *Deleuze and Guattari: Critical Assessments of Leading Philosophers*, London: Routledge.

Copeland, R. (2004), *Merce Cunningham: The Modernizing of Modern Dance*, New York: Routledge.

Cunningham, M. (1968), *Changes: Notes on Choreography*, New York: Something Else Press.

Cunningham, M. (1990), *Il Danzatore e la Danza. Colloqui con Jacqueline Lesschaeve*, Torino: EDT.

Cunningham, M. (1998), 'Torse: There are no Fixed Points of Space', in A. Carter (ed.), *The Routledge Dance Studies Reader*, London: Routledge.

Cunningham, M. (1999), 'I Like to Make Steps. Interview by Cynthia Joyce': http://www.salon.com/weekly/interview960722.html

Deleuze, G. (1988), *Bergsonism*, trans. H. Tomlinson and B. Habberjam, New York: Zone Books.

Deleuze, G. (2003), *The Fold: Leibniz and the Baroque*, trans. T. Conley, London: Continuum.

Deleuze, G. (2005), *Cinema 1: The Movement Image*, trans. H. Tomlinson and B. Habberjam, London: Continuum.

Deleuze, G. and F. Guattari (1998), *A Thousand Plateaus: Capitalism and Schizophrenia*, trans. B. Massumi, London: Athlone.

Gough, M. (2004), 'Notation Reloaded: eXtensible Dance Scripting Notation': http://people.brunel.ac.uk/bst/bst7/papers/MattGough/MattGough.htm

Kleist, H. von (1982), 'On the Puppet Theater': http://www-class.unl.edu/ahis498b/parts/week9/puppet.html. From *An Abyss Deep Enough: Letters of Heinrich von*

Kleist with a Selection of Essays and Anecdotes, edited by Philip B. Miller, Boston: E. P. Dutton.

Le Boulch (1991), *Verso una Scienza del Movimento Umano. Introduzione alla Psicocinetica*, Rome: Armando.

Massumi, B. (1992), *A User's Guide to Capitalism and Schizophrenia: Deviations from Deleuze and Guattari*, Cambridge, MA: MIT Press.

Notes

1. 'Content and expression are indeed reversible, but the "perspective" according to which one becomes the other is not fundamentally the point of view of an outside observer. It is the angle of application of an actual force. Content and expression are reversible only in action. A power relation determines which is which. Since each power relation is in turn a complex of power relations, since each thing is taken up in a web of forces, the distinction may seem untenable. Complicated it is, but not untenable. The strands of the web can be unwound. We can follow the trajectory of a force across its entanglements with other forces . . . and we can follow the trajectory of a thing as it passes from one knot of forces to the next' (Massumi 1992: 15).

2. According to the most 'Pythagorean' of Plato's writings (such as the *Timaeus*), the world is comprehensible through reason because it has a numerical structure. And it has such a structure because it is an artwork created by God, a mathematician. Or, more abstractly, the structure of the world consists in the thoughts of God, which are mathematical. The real is therefore constructed on the basis of the eternal mathematical truth. Through the centuries, the same ideas can be found, mutatis mutandis, in Spinoza and Leibniz, and in the research of most contemporary physicians and mathematicians, up to the latest extreme theories according to which the whole universe is the product of a deterministic computer program.

3. More specifically, in the composition of the dance script, numbers can be used for example to calculate, measure and describe the orientation of the limbs' movement in three-dimensional (Euclidean) space according to the Euler angles (Pitch, Roll, Yaw) with an axis rotation, assigning to these parameters sets of three digit numbers from 000 to 360 (a full circle being 360 degrees) in negative and positive numbers, with clockwise and upward movement direction for positive numbers, anti-clockwise and downward direction for the negative ones. Numerical values can also be used to describe the path a movement takes and its direction (line, angle, rectangle, curve, circle, spiral, twist, zigzag, release, arbitrary, translation), or the effort related to movement dynamics (direct/indirect, strong/light, sudden/sustained, bound/free), measuring all these properties with numerical values, for example varying from -10 to +10. These numerical sets give identified values to what is technically defined as the body's 'Degrees of Freedom' (DOFs), the limited rotational and kinetic possibilities delineated by anatomy. In the articulated anatomy of the human body, DOFs work at every joint, generating local movements in a coordinated (or un-coordinated) system of disparate independent points connected by the limited frame of the body and by the limitations of physical laws (gravity, mass, etc.). See Gough (2004).

4. On the functional and structural approach to the psychological analysis of movement in psycho-kinetics, see Le Boulch (1991: 43–7).

5. On differential and integral calculus, see Deleuze (2003), and Deleuze and Guattari (1998).

6. This definition corresponds to the irrational number, or differential quotient. See Deleuze (2003).

7. Choreographic probing by 'legwork' is a definition given by Merce Cunningham of his methodology. See Copeland (2004).

8. An example of this choreographic method is represented by *Torse*, a composition in which everything is decided by chance, by the 64 hexagrams of the I-Ching. The performance is composed of 64 movement phrases, each one conceived as a number (for example phrase one implying the performance of one movement, phrase two of two movements, etc.), and each shift defined by weight changes: standing on one foot counts as one, but bending a knee is two because the body weight shifts once, so that in the phrase number 64 there are 64 weight shifts. In the same way, space is divided in 64 squares. By tossing coins, the choreographer decides how many dancers will perform a particular phrase in a particular square. See Cunningham (1990).

9. In Cunningham's dance performances, the sound/movement relation was also numerically realised in the form of two distinctive, autonomous and parallel series indirectly connected and without any perceivable linear stimulus-cause link. The sudden appearance of the chance-guided sound score became noise for the dancers, a flow striking their perceptual apparatus and affecting performative linearity. John Cage's sonic compositions accompanying Cunningham's performances were often very rarefied, almost silent, but they could also become suddenly loud and aggressive, making it extremely difficult for the dancers to execute complicated rhythmic counts without having their concentration interrupted by random eruptions of sound (often introduced into the performance only during the last rehearsal, and therefore totally unexpected and unknown). In these conditions, counting had to be replaced by a different, more 'trance-like' kinetic practice, leaving numbers outside consciousness. See Copeland (2004).

10. See Deleuze (2005). On this model, time is either reduced to an image of eternity or to a linear progression, and therefore deprived of any productive reality.

11. 'Movement . . . cannot be made reducible to the positing and positioning of a phenomenological or psychological consciousness' (Ansell-Pearson 2001: 413).

Notes on Contributors

Herbert Blau is Byron W. and Alice L. Lockwood Professor of the Humanities at the University of Washington. He has also had a distinguished career in the theatre, as co-founder and co-director of *The Actor's Workshop* of San Francisco, then co-director of the Repertory Theater of Lincoln Center in New York, and as artistic director of the experimental group *KRAKEN*, the groundwork for which was prepared at California Institute of the Arts, of which he was founding Provost, and Dean of the School of Theater and Dance. Among his books are *Take Up the Bodies: Theater at the Vanishing Point* (1982), *The Audience* (1990), *To All Appearances: Ideology and Performance* (1992) and, more recently, *Sails of the Herring Fleet: Essays on Beckett* (2000). He has also published a recent book on fashion, *Nothing in Itself: Complexions of Fashion* (1999), and a new collection of essays, *The Dubious Spectacle: Extremities of Theater, 1976–2000* (2002). He is currently working on *As If: An Autobiography and Reality Principles: From the Absurd to the Virtual*.

Maaike Bleeker is a Professor and Chair of Theatre Studies at Utrecht University. Previously, she lectured at the School for New Dance Development and on the Piet Zwart postgraduate programme in fine arts, performed in several lecture performances, ran her own theatre company and translated five plays that were performed by major Dutch theatre companies. She is the author of *Visuality in the Theatre: The Locus of Looking* (2008) and editor of (among others) *Anatomy Live: Performance and the Operating Theatre* (2008).

Lorenzo Chiesa is Lecturer in Critical Theory at the School of European Culture and Languages, University of Kent, and a Visiting Research Fellow at the Institute of Philosophy ZRC SAZU, University of Ljubljana. He has published widely on contemporary French and Italian philosophy.

Laura Cull is part-time Lecturer in Performance at Northumbria University and a PhD candidate in Drama at the University of Exeter, where she is a member of the research team of the major AHRC-funded project, *Performing Presence: From the Live to the Simulated* (http://presence.stanford.edu). Her publications include 'A dialogue on becoming', co-authored with Matthew Goulish, in the volume *Theatres of Thought: Theatre, Performance and Philosophy* (2007); 'How Do You Make Yourself A Theatre-Without-Organs', in the journal *Theatre Research International* (forthcoming 2009); and an essay on Deleuze, Carmelo Bene and Georges Lavaudant in the edited collection *Contemporary French Theatre* (forthcoming 2009). She is founder and chair of the Performance and Philosophy working group in Performance Studies International, and co-chair of the PSi Graduate Student Committee. She is also a practising artist, working primarily with performance. She has presented her individual practice at Tate Britain (2003) and Studio Voltaire (2005), and most recently at the Serpentine Gallery's *Manifesto Marathon* (2008) as a member of the collective, SpRoUt.

Matthew Goulish is Adjunct Full Professor of Liberal Arts and Writing at the School of the Art Institute of Chicago. He was a founder member of the Chicago-based performance group, Goat Island, who have presented their work at countless international venues and events including the Venice Biennale, the Eurokaz Festival in Croatia and the ICA in London. He is author of *39 microlectures: in proximity of performance* (2000) and co-editor, with Stephen Bottoms, of *Small Acts of Repair: Performance, Ecology and Goat Island* (2007). He is currently developing new performance work with Every House has a Door, the company he co-founded with Lin Hixson.

Anna Hickey-Moody is Lecturer in Education at Monash University, where she teaches subjects pertaining to the sociology of education. She is co-author of *Masculinity Beyond the Metropolis* (2006) and co-editor of *Deleuzian Encounters: Studies in Contemporary Social Issues* (2007). Her forthcoming monograph, *Unimaginable Bodies: Intellectual Disability, Performance and Becomings*, will be published by Sense (Netherlands).

Barbara Kennedy is Reader in Film and Cultural Studies at the University of Staffordshire. She is author of *Deleuze and Cinema: The Aesthetics of Sensation* (2000) and co-editor with David Bell of *The Cybercultures Reader* (2000; 2007). She has published articles on film and post-feminist theory, on Deleuze and cinema, and presented work at international venues. In September 2001 she convened and coordinated the Tate Symposium 'Immanent Choreographies' at The Tate Modern, London. More recently, she co-convened and organised, with Dr. Anna Powell, the symposium 'Re-Mapping Deleuze' at MMU in September 2005. She is currently working on dance/choreography (both practice and theory) and Deleuzian/Bergsonian ideas on creativity, the creative act and the mind/body relational in performativity.

Andrew Murphie is at the School of English, Media and Performing Arts, University of New South Wales, Australia. Recent online publications include 'Differential Life, Perception and the Nervous Elements: Whitehead, Bergson and Virno on the Technics of Living' in *Culture Machine* and 'The Mutation of "Cognition" and the Fracturing of Modernity' in *Scan*. He very occasionally pretends to be an amateur VJ, as VJ Comfy. (http://www.andrewmurphie.org)

Timothy Murray is Professor of Comparative Literature and English and Director of Graduate Studies in Film and Video at Cornell University. His areas of research include new media, film and video, and visual studies, as well as seventeenth-century studies and literary theory, with strong interests in philosophy and psychoanalysis. He is the founding Curator of The Rose Goldsen Archive of New Media Art in the Cornell Library, the Co-Curator of CTHEORY Multimedia, and curator of the travelling exhibition, 'Contact Zones: The Art of CD-Rom'. He is the author of *Zonas de Contacto: el arte en CD-Rom* (1999); *Drama Trauma: Specters of Race and Sexuality in Performance, Video, Art* (1997); *Like a Film: Ideological Fantasy on Screen, Camera, and Canvas* (1993); *Theatrical Legitimation: Allegories of Genius in XVIIth-Century England and France* (1987). He is editor of *Mimesis, Masochism and Mime: The Politics of Theatricality in Contemporary French Thought* (1997) and, with Alan Smith, *Repossessions: Psychoanalysis and the Phantasms of Early-Modern Culture* (1997). He is currently completing an edited collection, *Digitality and the Memory of Cinema*, and a monograph, *Digital Intensities: Electronic Art, Baroque Vision, and Cultural Memory*.

Stamatia Portanova received her PhD from the University of East London, School of Social Sciences, Media and Cultural Studies. She has just started a post-doctoral project at the Concordia University, for the preparation of a monograph dedicated to the relationship between choreography, technology and science. She is also a member of The Sense Lab and of the editorial board of *Inflexions: A journal for research-creation*. Her articles have been published in various peer-reviewed journals and online magazines.

Edward Scheer is Associate Professor in the School of Theatre, Performance and Cultural Policy Studies at the University of Warwick and President of PSi, Performance Studies international. He is a founding editor of the journal *Performance Paradigm* and has completed a monograph on Mike Parr's performance art (forthcoming from Schwartz Press 2009). He has edited two books on Antonin Artaud and aesthetics: *100 Years of Cruelty: Essays on Artaud* (2000) and *Antonin Artaud: A Critical Reader* (2004). He is co-editor with Peter Eckersall of *The Ends of the 60s: Performance, Media and Contemporary Culture* (2006), and with John Potts of *Technologies of Magic: A Cultural Study of Ghosts, Machines and the Uncanny* (2006). He served as chairman of the board of directors of the Performance Space in Sydney from 2005 to 2007. His current Australia Research Council funded research project is a study of time and performance in nineteenth-century experiments in art and science.

Anthony Uhlmann is Associate Professor in the School of Humanities and Languages at the University of Western Sydney, Australia. He has published extensively on Deleuze and Beckett and his translation of Deleuze's essay on Beckett, 'The Exhausted', appears in Deleuze's *Essays Critical and Clinical*. He is the author of two books on Beckett, the most recent being *Samuel Beckett and the Philosophical Image* (2006).

Daniel Watt is a Lecturer in English and Drama at Loughborough University. His research interests include fragmentary writing, ethics and literature and philosophical and literary influences on theatre and performance in the twentieth century. He is author of *Fragmentary Futures: Blanchot, Beckett, Coetzee* (2007) and has co-edited *A Performance Cosmology* (2006) and *Theatres of Thought: Theatre, Performance and Philosophy* (2008). His work includes chapters on Edmond Jabès, Jacques Derrida, Puppets and Glossolalia, and articles in *Performance Research*, *RIDE*, *Journal for Cultural Research* and *Wormwood*.

Julian Wolfreys is Professor of Modern Literature and Culture in the Department of English and Drama at Loughborough University. He has published extensively on nineteenth- and twentieth-century literature and literary theory. His most recent publications include *Transgression: Space, Identity, Time* (2008) and *Souvenirs d'amour: Love and the*

Mnemotechnic of Alterity (2007). He is currently completing a study of Thomas Hardy. Other projects include a concordance of the works of Jacques Derrida.

Stephen Zepke is a freelance researcher living in Vienna. He has published numerous essays exploring the intersection of art, philosophy and politics. He is the author of *Art as Abstract Machine: Ontology and Aesthetics in Deleuze and Guattari* (2005), and co-editor, with Simon O'Sullivan, of both *Deleuze, Guattari and the Production of the New* (2008), and *Deleuze and Contemporary Art* (forthcoming in this series in 2009).

Index